NEW QUEER CINEMA

NEW QUEER CINEMA

A Critical Reader

Edited by
Michele Aaron

RUTGERS UNIVERSITY PRESS
New Brunswick, New Jersey

First published in the United States 2004
by Rutgers University Press, New Brunswick, New Jersey

First published in Great Britain, 2004
by Edinburgh University Press
22 George Square, Edinburgh

Library of Congress and British Library Cataloging-in-Publication
records for this book are available upon request.

ISBN 0-8135-3485-2 (cloth)
      0-8135-3486-0 (paper)

CONTENTS

ACKNOWLEDGEMENTS

I would like to thank the contributors for their patience and the pleasure of working with them. I am grateful to Alexander Doty, Richard Dyer, Richard Fung, Jackie Stacey and Julianne Pidduck for recommending potential contributors, and to the latter, especially, for her general support and co-conspiracy. This one's for Vita Aaron Pearl, for delaying the project (and so much else) so delightfully.

B. Ruby Rich's article, 'New Queer Cinema', *Sight and Sound* 2:5 (September 1992) reprinted with permission from *Sight and Sound*.
Anneke Smelik's chapter is a different version of 'Bodies That Kill. Art Cinema And Its Murderous Girls In Love' in *Textus. English Studies in Italy*, XIII, 2000, pp. 449–68.
Michele Aaron's discussion of *Boys Don't Cry* was first published as 'Pass/Fail' in *Screen* 42.1 (Spring 2001): 92–6, reprinted with permission from Oxford University Press.

LIST OF ILLUSTRATIONS

NOTES ON THE CONTRIBUTORS

Michele Aaron (Brunel University) is editor of *The Body's Perilous Pleasures: Dangerous Desires and Contemporary Culture* (Edinburgh University Press, 1999) and author of *Spectatorship: The Power of Looking On* (Wallflower, 2004). She has published articles on New Queer Cinema, spectatorship, and the 'queer Jew', and is currently working on a book on Death and the Moving Image.

Harry M. Benshoff (University of North Texas) is the author of *Monsters in the Closet: Homosexuality and the Horror Film,* and co-author (with Sean Griffin) of *America on Film: Representing Race, Class, Gender, and Sexuality at the Movies* (Blackwell Publishers, 2003). With Sean Griffin, he also co-edited *Queer Cinema: The Film Reader* for Routledge, 2004.

Daniel T. Contreras is Assistant Professor of English and American Studies at Colby College in Maine. His book, *What Have You Done to My Heart: Unrequited Love and Utopian Longings* will be published this Spring by St. Martin's Press.

Glyn Davis is a lecturer in screen history and theory at Edinburgh College of Art. He is the co-editor, with Kay Dickinson, of *Teen TV: Genre, Consumption and Identity* (BFI, forthcoming) and is currently writing about Dirk Bogarde.

Michael DeAngelis is Assistant Professor at DePaul University's School for New Learning, where he teaches in the areas of media and cultural studies. He is the author of *Gay Fandom and Crossover Stardom: James Dean, Mel Gibson, and Keanu Reeves* (Duke University Press, 2001), along with articles in such journals as *Cultural Critique and Film Criticism*. He is currently writing a book-length study of the distribution and exhibition of art cinema in the United States during the 1960s and 1970s.

Ros Jennings has taught film and television studies in both Britain and Australia and is currently Research Director for Arts and Humanities and also Principal Lecturer in Film Studies at the University of Gloucestershire. She is the author of a forthcoming cultural history of Australian television in Britain.

Helen Hok-Sze Leung is Assistant Professor of Women's Studies at Simon Fraser University where she teaches queer theory, film and cultural studies. She is working on a book manuscript on queer issues in Hong Kong culture. Her articles on Hong Kong cinema and queer politics have appeared in numerous journals and anthologies.

Loykie (Loïc) Lominé is a lecturer in tourism management at King Alfred's College, Winchester. He has a PhD in Sociology from the University of Essex which is based on empirical work related to gay tourism in Australia. He is currently working on various teaching and learning focused topics in the subject area of tourism management.

Monica B. Pearl lectures in twentieth-century American literature in the English and American Studies Department at the University of Manchester. She has published work on AIDS and representation, and is currently working on self-representation in literature and visual media.

Anat Pick received her PhD from the University of Oxford in 2001. She taught English literature at Tel Aviv University and Film Studies at Brunel University and is currently a Postdoctoral Fellow at the Rothermere American Institute, University of Oxford. She works on nineteenth- and twentieth-century American literature and culture.

Julianne Pidduck lectures at Lancaster University in the Institute for Cultural Research. She is author of *The Woman at the Window: Contemporary Costume Drama* and writes widely on gender, sexuality and the moving image.

B. Ruby Rich is Adjunct Professor of Film Studies at the University of California, Berkeley. She lives in San Francisco, writes for numerous publications, works frequently as an independent curator, and is completing her forthcoming volume, *The Rise and Fall of the New Queer Cinema*.

Anneke Smelik is Professor in Visual Culture at the University of Nijmegen, the Netherlands. She is author of *And the Mirror Cracked. Feminist Cinema and Film Theory* (Palgrave, 1998) and co-editor of *Women's Studies and Culture: A Feminist Introduction* (Zed Books, 1995).

Louise Wallenberg recently completed a PhD on Gender Theory and Queer Cinema at Stockholm University, where she lectures in the department of Cinema Studies and at The Swedish Program. She is currently working on the representation of queer male ideals within certain male film star personae in 1930s' Swedish films.

PART I

NEW QUEER CINEMA IN CONTEXT

1. NEW QUEER CINEMA:
AN INTRODUCTION

Michele Aaron

New Queer Cinema is the name given to a wave of queer films that gained critical acclaim on the festival circuit in the early 1990s. Coined, and largely chronicled, by film theorist B. Ruby Rich, New Queer Cinema, or NQC as I will refer to it, represented the exciting prospect that lesbian and gay images and filmmakers had turned a corner. No longer burdened by the approval-seeking sackcloth of positive imagery, or the relative obscurity of marginal production, films could be both radical and popular, stylish and economically viable.

The wave, or movement, consisted of the surprise hits of Sundance 1991 and 1992 – *Paris is Burning* (Jennie Livingston, 1990), *Poison* (Todd Haynes, 1991), and *Swoon* (Tom Kalin, 1992) – and many other films. The larger crop is generally noted to include *Tongues Untied* (Marlon Riggs, 1990), *My Own Private Idaho* (Gus Van Sant, 1991), *Young Soul Rebels* (Isaac Julien, 1991), *R.S.V.P* (Laurie Lynd, 1991), *Edward II* (Derek Jarman, 1991), *Khush* (Pratibha Parmar, 1991), *The Hours and Times* (Christopher Münch, 1991) and *The Living End* (Gregg Araki, 1992) as well as work by filmmakers Sadie Benning, Cecilia Dougherty, Su Friedrich, John Greyson and Monica Treut. The films, as Rich pointed out, had few aesthetic or narrative strategies in common, but what they seemed to share was an attitude. She found them 'irreverent' and 'energetic', and, according to J. Hoberman, their protagonists were 'proudly assertive'.[1] Indeed, what binds the group together is, I feel, best described as defiance. This defiance can be thought of as operating on several levels, all of which serve to illuminate the characteristics of NQC.

First, despite the fast rules of acceptable subjects dictated by western popular culture, these films give voice to the marginalised not simply in terms of focusing on the lesbian and gay community, but on the sub-groups contained within it. For example, both *Tongues Untied* and *Young Soul Rebels* explore black gay male experience (the latter also offering the rarity of the interracial couple). *My Own Private Idaho* has male prostitutes for protagonists. The documentary *Paris is Burning* attends to the gay and transsexual Hispanic and Latino youth of the New York drag ball scene.

Second, the films are unapologetic about their characters' faults or, rather, crimes: they eschew positive imagery. *Swoon*, *Poison* and *The Living End* beautify the criminal and (homo)eroticise violence. The gay male couples at the centre of *Swoon* and *The Living End* revel in their murderous relationships. Kalin's highly stylised cinematography and use of black and white in *Swoon* turn the film's unseemly events into an exquisite period piece. In a central scene, a high angle tableau of the courtroom is cross-cut with footage from the original trial, upon which the film is based. As an 'alienist' describes the pair's pathology from the stand, a bed upon which they frolic, floppy-haired and embraced, fills the space in front. Araki, on the other hand, poses his main characters as West coast-cool, well-groomed despite being on the road, 'hot' but preoccupied. Meanwhile, Haynes borrows heavily from Jean Genet's *Un Chant d'Amour* (1950), especially its aesthetic and erotic charge, in imparting one inmate's sexual obsession for another in the dark vaults and unshaven terrain of a men's prison.

Third, the films defy the sanctity of the past, especially the homophobic past. *Edward II*, *The Hours and Times* and *Swoon* all revisit historical relationships and firmly instate the overlooked homosexual content. *Edward II* tells of King Edward's homosexual relationship with Gaveston. *The Hours and Times* develops the erotic dynamic between John Lennon and Brian Epstein. *Swoon* retells the Leopold and Loeb murder case, and, most importantly, Hitchcock's rendition of it in *Rope* (1948), but with the homosexuality of the murderers fully present.

Fourth, the films frequently defy cinematic convention in terms of form, content and genre. The shorts of Sadie Benning, shot on a Fisher Price Pixel Vision, employ all manner of textual innovation to provide ragged, experimental but no less confident pieces. John Greyson's *Zero Patience* (1993) offers the unlikely pairing of AIDS and the Musical. (A combination which later would find remarkable international success in the Broadway hit *Rent*.) Indeed, Greyson has been distinguished for his dislocation of traditional film practices. Julianne Pidduck sees him as 'reappropriating mainstream media' through his use 'of split screens and embedded images'.[2] Like other new queer artists he also reappropriates mainstream genres and formats (feature length rather than just shorts), and, ultimately, distribution/exhibition channels. NQC also incorporates a defiance of the sanctity of mainstream cinema history. Just in case one misses Kalin's swipe at Hitchcock, *Swoon* restages a scene right out of *Rear Window* with Jeff and Lisa's romantic dialogue now taking place between the male lovers. Haynes, in firmly identifying with the outlaw filmmaking of Genet, grounds New Queer Cinema in, well, Old Queer Cinema – the uncompromising work of Genet, Fassbinder, Warhol, Sayles – rather than in the mainstream gains in gay representation. The lack of respect for the governing codes of form or content, linearity or coherence, indeed, for Hollywood itself, has much in common with postmodernism. In fact, it was in terms of postmodernism, as 'Homo Pomo', that Rich first described NQC.[3] Although there is much to link postmodernism to the advent and progression of queer theory and practice, and to the aesthetic strategies employed by the NQC films (as its frequent appearance in this book will illustrate), in its apolitical foundations postmodernism provides a relevant but often distracting context for the discussion of NQC (and as such will not be dwelt upon in this Introduction).

Finally, the films in many ways defy death. The joyful murderers of *Swoon* and *The Living End* resist its sobering effect. But the key way in which death is defied is in terms of AIDS. Death is defied as the life-sentence passed by the disease: the HIV+ leads of *The Living End* instead find the 'time-bomb' to be 'totally' liberating. It is even defied as final: in *Zero Patience* the first victim of AIDS comes back to life.

It is not simply that a sense of defiance characterises these films, but that it marks them as queer. Indeed, 'queer' and its critical and cultural ascendancy are the crucial context for understanding the emergence and evolution of NQC, and it is to this that I now turn.

QUEERLY THERE

Queer, a derogatory term levelled at the non-hetero-seeming, was reappropriated in the late 1980s, early 1990s by its victims as a defiant means of empowerment echoing black activists' use of 'nigger' in the 1960s. Relieving the burden of the titular expansion of L-G-B-T- (lesbian, gay, bisexual and transgender), queer's most basic function is as an umbrella term or catch-all for uniting various forms of non-straight sexual identity. But it means much more than this. Queer represents the resistance to, primarily, the normative codes of gender and sexual expression – that masculine men sleep with feminine women – but also to the restrictive potential of gay and lesbian sexuality – that only men sleep with men, and women sleep with women. In this way, queer, as a critical concept, encompasses the non-fixity of gender expression and the non-fixity of both straight and gay sexuality. As Richard Dyer rightly reminds us, the contemporary formulation of queer functions in sharp contrast to its past, it signifies a fluidity of identity where, historically, queer represented an 'exclusive and fixed sexuality'.[4] To be queer now, then, means to be untethered from 'conventional' codes of behaviour. At its most expansive and utopian, queer contests (hetero- and homo-) normality.

As a theoretically lucrative 'oppositional stance',[5] and the latest trajectory of gender theory, queer gained in academic currency throughout the 1990s, fuelled by the cultural marketplace. Indeed, *Paris is Burning* was a prime example in Judith Butler's *Bodies That Matter* (a work central to the academic ascendancy of queer).[6] As a cultural trend – coming to characterise the so-called queer nineties – queerness represents the flirtation with non-fixity embodied in the mainstream by 'lesbian chic' and films like *The Object of my Affection* (Nicholas Hytner 1998) and, alternatively, by 'dykes-fuck-fellas' storylines found in lesbian erotica and staged in the NQC film *Go Fish* (Rose Troche 1994).[7] The queer figure *par excellence* was the transsexual, and the decade saw the publication of work on the subject by the 'community's' quasi leaders, Kate Bornstein and Leslie Feinberg.[8] It would also see the use of Del la Grace Volcano's transgendered images in an episode of *Sex in the City* and climax in the major success of Kimberley Peirce's *Boys Don't Cry*, which told Brandon Teena/Teena Brandon's short-life-story, in 1999.[9]

In order to understand NQC fully, one must understand 'queer' as critical intervention, cultural product and political strategy – and NQC as an art-full manifestation of the overlap between the three. Queer represented the re-appropriation of the power of the antagonistic, homophobic society, through reclaiming the term of abuse but also through a new approach to 'gay' politics: a taking on of the institution, rather than a fearful, assimilated, complicity. Direct action, as practised by Queer Nation, ACT UP and Outrage, was the key strategy of queer politics in the late 1980s early 1990s, with AIDS accelerating its urgency. The sense of defiance characterising NQC is the obvious product of this political exigency and practice.

> For many members of a generation coming to political consciousness haunted by AIDS but collectively strengthened by AIDS activism, *queer* has become an attractive and oppositional self-label that acknowledges a new cultural context for politics, criticism, reception-consumption, and production.[10]

Many of NQC's practitioners, Tom Kalin and John Greyson most obviously, are firmly located within this activist background.[11] In fact, NQC cannot be removed from the context of the AIDS epidemic. While *Paris is Burning* is, ostensibly, about the issues of race, queerness and poverty in the late 1980s, AIDS nevertheless lurks in the background. José Arroyo has claimed that AIDS is the absent centre of two of the foundational new queer films, *Edward II* and *My Own Private Idaho*.[12] Monica Pearl identified it as the subtext of two mainstream genres of contemporary cinema: the sex thriller and the 'reincarnation film'.[13] Both Kalin and Haynes have concluded that AIDS is, actually, what their films were all about.[14] Pearl, in Chapter 3 in this collection, will pursue the ongoing marriage between the two.

Douglas Crimp, using AIDS activist history to comprehend queerness, sees ACT UP members as the archetypal queers for they were characterised by 'identification *across* identities': a straight woman fought for a gay male friend's treatment, a white lesbian pursued health access for black HIV-infected mothers.[15] This is what made AIDS activism necessarily queer. Of course, 'identification across identities' is, fundamentally, what happens in cinema, as the spectator aligns him or herself with someone else on-screen. NQC, then, marks the emphasis upon and success of this 'cross-identification', as, say, the gay or, more significantly, the straight spectator's identification with the queer villain who is so unlike 'him'self. Cross-identification is, also, as I will suggest below, central to popular cinema's altered stake in queer spectatorship.

It must be remembered that queer's defiance is levelled at mainstream homophobic society *but also* at the 'tasteful and tolerated' gay culture that cohabits with it.[16] In fact, the new queer artists or 'queercore' of the early 1990s, as Dennis Cooper refers to them, were defined as much, if not more, by their opposition to gay culture as to straight.[17] It is no surprise then that NQC would have a particularly fraught relationship with the mainstream – after all, popular success undermines oppositionality – and would find many of its strongest critics within the gay community. Indeed, my exposition of the films' commonalities glosses over several of the charges levelled at the categorisation and celebration of NQC. Most immediate is the issue of the movement's roll-call. As was often pointed out, NQC, in its earliest formulation, was a boys' own story. The female delegates and those of colour were added in haste and retrospectively.[18] The narrowness of queer's application has been an ongoing issue among its proponents (and opponents, of course) and Part III of this collection (in particular, chapters by Anat Pick, Daniel Contreras and Louise Wallenberg) elucidates NQC's limitations even as the section broadens its influence. Queer is not just about gender and sexuality, but the restrictiveness of the rules governing them and their intersection with other aspects of identity. To be really queerly there is to apprehend 'the complexity of what actually happens "between" the contingent spaces where each variable [race, class, gender] intersects with the others'.[19] Second, the embracing of negative stereotypes and, in particular, the enduring centrality of the queer villain continue to torment. While, as Michael Sanders points out, such characters embody queer defiance and anti-assimilationism, for many, their radical status is always to be tempered if not upstaged by their overwhelming ability to confirm and perpetuate the homophobic stereotypes of the majority.[20] That said, the argument is not so simply polarised within the films themselves. Indeed, one must evaluate the difference between the more apparent politics of *Swoon* and the seeming gratuity of *The Living End* . . . or just resist the call to judge them altogether. As Ellis Hansen notes,

> [e]very film with a queer theme, no matter what the sexuality of its director or the origin of its funding, is still embattled in a highly moralistic debate over the correctness of its politics, as though art were to be valued only as sexual propaganda.[21]

NQC is, of course, a contested category. It is contested for its exclusivity (and tokenistic inclusivity). It is contested for its unwarranted optimism: in heralding a minor revolution when a few films do not a movement make; in promoting queer villainy while homophobic violence rages; and in suggesting a queer-friendliness of mass culture when the majority of the audience, as Harry Benshoff argues in this book, remain unaltered.[22] The category is contested also for the US-centricity of its films and theory. Perhaps the most irreparable of charges against NQC is that the promise indicated by the films of the early 1990s was never fully realised. Despite that initial furore on the Indie scene, and the dramatic increase in the production of, and audience for, queer films during the 1990s, a new *and enduring* sector of popular radical work failed to materialise.[23] In many ways this is hardly surprising, for how can a marriage between the popular and the radical be sustained when such an association erodes the very meaning of each? By the end of the decade, NQC had, as Rich argued, journeyed from 'radical impulse to niche market' with its range of fairly innocuous and often unremarkable films targetting a narrow, rather than all-inclusive, new queer audience.[24] These films included *Clare of the Moon* (Nicole Conn, 1992), *Bar Girls* (Marita Giovanni, 1994), *Jeffrey* (Christopher Ashley, 1995), *The Incredibly True Adventures of Two Girls in Love* (Maria Maggenti, 1995), *Gazon Maudit* (Josephine Balasko, 1995), *Thin Ice* (Fiona Cunningham-Reid, 1995), *When Night is Falling* (Patricia Rozema, 1995), *Hollow Reed* (Angela Pope, 1997), *Losing Chase* (Kevin Bacon, 1996), *The Watermelon Woman* (Cheryl Dunye, 1996); *Kiss Me Guido* (Tony Vitale, 1997), *Everything Relative* (Sharon Pollack, 1997), *All Over Me* (Alex Sichel, 1997), *High Art* (Lisa Cholodenko, 1998), *Fucking Amal/Show Me Love* (Lukas Moodysson, 1998) and *But I'm a Cheerleader* (Jamie Babbit, 2000). *Swoon* and *Poison* stand almost alone in terms of critical attention garnered by the New Queer films. Indeed, it is not until *Boys Don't Cry* that queerness could claim such a spotlight again, but for some the Academy's praise, if not the film itself, reeked of mainstream recuperation.[25] Cynically put, NQC kick-started Hollywood's awareness of a queerer audience (a combination of the 'pink profit' zone and the general public's current delectation) and its appropriation and dilution of queer matters. Albeit 'gaysploitation', queer work and queer themes found financial support, and the careers of Haynes and Araki were launched.[26] (These two key players of New Queer cinema are the subjects of Michael DeAngelis' and Glyn Davis' discussions in this book.) Ultimately, however, there was little more than superficial change.

That said, there is evidence to suggest that NQC triggered significant cultural and critical (and small-p political) gains. Its real impact, and value, are not to be measured by the quantity or quirkiness of potential members, but by the queerer culture it ushered in. As Rich asked of NQC ten years on: 'Did it disappear, or is it everywhere?'[27]

QUEERLY CULTURED

The upside of Hollywood's appropriation of the new queer potential, was the acceptability of queer themes and queer characters in the mainstream. (Mainstream in terms of exhibition and distribution, if not production: for this was also a period when the polarity of the Independent and Hollywood sectors was fraying.) No longer consigned to the sole role of gay neighbour (who meets untimely death), 1990s' Hollywood's homosexuals lived varied and accomplished lives. Not sad young men but sane, sexy stars (as in, for example, *My Best Friend's Wedding* and *In and Out*): not merely manly but hot and feisty women (as in, for example, *Basic Instinct* and *Bound*). Stereotypes were revised rather than rejected. *As Good as it Gets* (James L Brooks, 1997), for example, offers the 'gay man next door', but the character is soon shown to be far more stable than the film's protagonist whose homophobia becomes one of his and the narrative's learning curves. According to *In and Out* (Frank Oz, 1997), the shorthand signs for male homosexuality – a love of show tunes and over-gesticulation – are alive and well in Kevin Kline's gay man but accompanied by macho-incarnate 'Magnum' (Tom Sellick). There were, what might be called, 'queer experiment' films, those where characters explore their sexuality, such as *Chasing Amy* (Kevin Smith, 1997), *The Object of My Affection*, and *The Next Best Thing* (John Schlesinger, 2000). All of these, however, offer the explorations of a gay character and it is not until *Kissing Jessica Stein* (Charles Herman-Wurmfeld, 2002) that we receive 'straight' protagonists (or, rather, a 'straight' audience) secure enough in themselves to enjoy a short spell of sexual re-orientation.

The legacy of NQC is evident also in the surge of non-Hollywood films in 1994/5 about lesbian couples who kill. This art-house group clearly testifies to the currency and exploitation of the queerer text, and is explored by Anneke Smelik in Chapter 6 in this collection. *Fun* (Rafael Zelinski, US/Canada, 1994), *Sister my Sister* (Nancy Meckler, UK, 1994), *La Cérémonie* (Claude Chabrol, Fr./Ger., 1995), *Butterfly Kiss* (Michael Winterbottom, UK, 1994) and *Heavenly Creatures* (Peter Jackson, NZ, 1994) raised the same kinds of questions as NQC (primarily the rejection of positive images) and offered similarly innovative, stylish narratives and compelling, if corrupt, characters. Although embraced, and lambasted, by queer critics (as is the norm), the group confirms that queer films are not the sole provenance of queer filmmakers. And hopefully, by return, this suggests that 'straight' films are not the sole provenance of 'straight' filmmakers. This erosion of the essentialism of the creative process has been noted by Rich who, looking beyond the directors, attributes the triumphs of straight actors playing gay to the 'runaway success of the New Queer Cinema works'.[28] Likewise, in Rupert Everett's recent successes, *An Ideal Husband* and *The Importance of Being Earnest* (Oliver Parker I, 1999 and 2002), we find the out, queer, actor enjoying 'straight' roles (although how straight comedic and Wildean characters can be is questionable to say the least).

The queering of contemporary western culture is not about the products alone, but about their theorisation. Dovetailing with the emergence and evolution of NQC was the proliferation of queer film theory. This can be thought of as operating on three, not unrelated, levels. First, as the critical exploration of queer imagery and directors: in other words, the wave of films provided a focus for those cinema scholars among the expanding audience. Second, as a rereading and reclaiming of classical texts: a retrospective queering of film history. Third, as a discussion of queer spectatorship: what these queer texts reveal about the spectator's experience of cinema.

Alongside the ever-increasing body of critical work on the films of NQC and on the queerer mainstream that followed, theorists have pursued the movement's impact upon non-Anglo-American and non-narrative filmmaking. Broadening the category and challenging our understanding of NQC, attention has turned to queer film within, for example, European, antipodean, Third and experimental contexts, as Ros Jennings and Loykie Lominé, Helen Hok-Sze Leung and Julianne Pidduck exemplify later in this collection.[29] Perhaps the most noted scholarly contributions exist, not surprisingly, within the realm of revising cinema history. For example, Patricia White's (1999) book *Uninvited* and Alexander Doty's *Flaming Classics* in 2000 both queered classical Hollywood, by which I mean they revealed queer themes and characters within a range of conventional texts. Indebted to lesbian and gay film history (of Richard Dyer, Vito Russo, etc.), these studies are, instead, queer. While they similarly uncover gay or lesbian encodings or decodings (that is, the intervention of the films' creators or audiences), they question narrative cinema's normative rather than heterosexual economy. Such studies are, inevitably, about spectatorship, about how the general spectator is 'invited to make lesbian inferences',[30] or to adopt 'reception positions that can be considered "queer" in some way, regardless of a person's declared sexual and gender allegiances'.[31] But this queer spectatorship is not the sole domain of the classical period or the subtext-rich narrative.

Founded upon the spectator's alignment or identification with or gravitation towards a 'character-not-you', narrative cinema itself depends upon establishing empathy, alliances and desire along lines not restricted to normative patterns of attraction. Cinema, as I implied above, is rooted in queer processes. Not only has NQC helped generate this kind of thinking, it has encouraged mainstream culture to harness cinema's queer potential. This is not just another way of describing Hollywood's flirtation with queer imagery but, instead, represents a shift from the disavowal to the avowal, the open affirmation, of queer implications, as I will illustrate in the final chapter of this book. No longer does popular culture have to seem to render queer configurations safe – through, for example, humour, homophobia (or other memos of heterosexuality) and, especially, closure. In the remarkably popular *Boys*

Don't Cry, the queerness of Brandon's girlfriend (and the spectator by implication) is indulged rather than repressed, as time and time again the narrative constructs her complicity in Brandon's disguise as a man. Popular culture no longer *has to* disavow queerness, but, of course, it still does – for to keep queerness at bay, safely restricted in its influence, ensures the impact of its interventions and, more than this, sustains the status quo. And, after all, such things underline mainstream entertainment. What is crucial to remember is that disavowal is a defensive mechanism; queerness must only appear to be quelled. This, perhaps, is the lesson of NQC: it must be contested that it can endure, it must remain marginal that it can flirt effectively with the centre. While the films and the directors stopped 'stealing' the show at Sundance a long time ago, edgy, inspiring, acclaimed but still defiant films – like *By Hook or By Crook* (Silas Howard and Harry Dodge, 2001), or *L.I.E.* (Michael Cuesta, 2001) – just keep on coming.

Siding against complete cynicism, *New Queer Cinema: A Critical Reader* does see the categorisation and study of this wave of films as productive: as provoking and intervening within important discussions on the evolution of lesbian and gay representation, but also on the nature of cinema and spectatorship itself. At the same time, however, all the chapters collected here are, with varying degrees of explicitness, embroiled in questioning the value, that is the aesthetic, critical and cultural implications, of NQC: its characteristics, its location, its impact. Indeed, it is along these lines that the book has been divided, with the following sections responding to these three issues.

Part I sets the scene for a study of NQC. My introduction has outlined the various qualities and key issues surrounding the movement that will be taken up in the chapters that follow. B. Ruby Rich's initial article on NQC, reprinted here, offers the primal scene for the development of the debate and underlies many of the subsequent discussions. But it is AIDS that provided the key site for the development of queer practices and productions. Its impression will shape many of the arguments within this book (by Pidduck, by Contreras) but, in Part I, Monica Pearl maps the relationship between NQC and AIDS.

Part II explores the characteristics of NQC in terms of its key filmmakers and its related filmmaking practices. An air of defiance will continue to describe the movement, but the chapters are about much more than this. Through a study of Todd Haynes, Michael DeAngelis isolates a rejection of the linearity of time as central to the queer project (something that Pearl saw as distinctly AIDS-related). For Glyn Davis it is the prominence of camp, and in particular the irreverence of Gregg Araki's work, that characterises the films. Anneke Smelik confronts the repetition of the queer criminal in the art-house hits of the mid-1990s, and champions their rejection of positive imagery. Through an investigation of the work of certain avant-garde practitioners, Pidduck considers how such marginal and even anarchic texts challenge definitions of NQC. As well as isolating the thematic and visual preoccupations of the movement's films and assorted filmmakers, this part initiates the book's ongoing scrutiny of the meaning of queer as it becomes associated with these often divergent directors and creative impulses.

Leading on from Pidduck, the question of the limitations of NQC determines the next section of the book, which responds to its problematic homogeneity. Part III attempts to locate NQC, and progress its theorisation, in terms of its gendered, geographic, and racial coordinates. Pick examines the complicated relationship between NQC and lesbian film resulting from the seeming male-dominance of the movement, while chapters by Wallenberg and Contreras reconsider NQC in relation to race. Wallenberg looks at the work of key black filmmakers, Isaac Julien and Marlon Riggs, and Contreras at the pivotal film of the movement, *Paris is Burning*. Both authors stress the significance of these films to NQC's development, even as they lament their marginality within appreciations of the movement. Ros Jennings and Loykie Lominé use Australian cinema to undermine the US-centricity of NQC, and explore the dynamic between cinematic queerness and national or cultural identity. Helen Hok-Sze Leung investigates the relationship between NQC and Third cinema, through a consideration of Chinese film. Like Jennings and Lominé, she identifies NQC, or its influence, well beyond the Anglo-American location.

Part IV responds to the question of NQC's impact upon contemporary western society. The two chapters offer very different takes on the queering of spectatorship, one text-based (Michele Aaron) and one audience-based (Benshoff), one almost optimistic, one less so. Yet all the chapters in the book are, in many ways, wrestling with the question of the positive impact, the political or cultural worth, of NQC, with what is meaningful, troublesome, exquisite or fun about these films. The purpose of this *Reader* is to both map out and develop the key issues surrounding the emergence and evolution, the naming and shaming, of NQC. As such, its many arguments chart the stormy relationship between NQC and the mainstream, and the influence of NQC upon other cinemas and cinema practices, and upon film studies itself. One of the resounding concerns of the collection is to evaluate how useful the distinction of New Queer Cinema has been for our understanding of contemporary, primarily western, culture and the impact of queerness upon it. Another is to interrogate the value and meaning of 'queer' as it becomes attached to all kinds of filmmaking – and all kinds of critical thinking – located at both the fringes and centre(s) of cultural production.

NOTES

1. B. Ruby Rich, 'New Queer Cinema', *Sight and Sound*, 2:5 (September 1992): 32, reprinted in this book; J. Hoberman, 'Out and Inner Mongolia', *Premiere* (October 1992): 31.
2. Julianne Pidduck, 'After 1980: Margins and Mainstreams', in Richard Dyer, *Now You See It*, 2nd edition (London: Routledge, 2002), p. 270.
3. Rich, 'New', p. 32.

4 Richard Dyer, *The Culture of Queers* (London: Routledge, 2002), p. 4.

5 Moe Meyer, 'Introduction: Reclaiming the Discourse of Camp', in M. Meyer (ed.), *The Politics and Poetics of Camp* (London: Routledge, 1994), p. 3.

6 See Judith Butler, *Bodies That Matter: On the Discursive Limits of 'Sex'* (New York: Routledge, 1993), pp. 121–40.

7 For discussions of lesbian chic see Belinda Budge and Diane Hamer (eds), *The Good, the Bad, and the Gorgeous: Popular Culture's Romance with Lesbianism* (London: Pandora, 1994). For examples of 'queerer' gay/lesbian sexual scenarios, or 'dykes-fuck-fellas' stories, see collections of erotic short fiction by Pat Califia, and, more specifically, Trish Thomas, 'Me and the Boys', in Susie Bright (ed.), *The Best American Erotica 1993* (New York: Macmillan, 1993), pp. 91–104.

8 See Kate Bornstein, *Gender Outlaw: On Men, Women and the Rest of Us* (New York and London: Routledge, 1994), and Leslie Feinberg, *Transgender Warriors: Making History from Joan of Arc to Ru Paul* (Boston: Beacon Press, 1996).

9 See Series One of HBO's *Sex in the City*.

10 Corey K. Creekmur and Alexander Doty, 'Introduction' to *Out in Culture: Gay, Lesbian, and Queer Essays on Popular Culture* (London: Cassell, 1995), p. 6.

11 AIDS activist Jean Carlomusto, although working with video only, should also be noted here.

12 See José Arroyo, 'Death, Desire and Identity: The Political Unconscious of "New Queer Cinema" ', in Joseph Bristow and Angelia R. Wilson (eds), *Activating Theory: Lesbian, Gay, Bisexual Politics* (London: Lawrence & Wishart, 1993), pp. 70–96.

13 See Monica Pearl, 'Symptoms of AIDS in Contemporary Film: Mortal Anxiety in an Age of Sexual Panic', in Michele Aaron (ed.), *The Body's Perilous Pleasures: Dangerous Desires and Contemporary Culture* (Edinburgh: Edinburgh University Press, 1999), pp. 210–25.

14 See Todd Haynes, interviewed in Michael William Saunders, *Imps of the Perverse: Gay Monsters in Film* (Westport, CT: Praeger, 1998), p. 134, and Tom Kalin in Dennis Lim, 'The Reckless Moment: Two Pioneers of the New Queer Cinema Look Back on a Short-Lived Sensation', *Village Voice* (26 March 2002): 43.

15 Douglas Crimp, 'Right On, Girlfriend!', in Michael Warner (ed.), *Fear of a Queer Planet: Queer Politics and Social Theory* (Minneapolis: University of Minnesota, 1993), p. 315.

16 Cherry Smyth, *Lesbians Talk Queer Notions* (London: Scarlet Press, 1992), p. 48.

17 See Dennis Cooper, 'Queercore', *Village Voice*, 30 June 1992, in Donald Morton (ed.), *The Material Queer: A LesBiGay Cultural Studies Reader* (Boulder, CO: Westview Press, 1996), p. 296; and Smyth *Lesbians*.

18 See Pratibha Parmar, 'Queer Questions', *Sight and Sound*, 2:5 (September 1992): 35, and Amy Taubin, 'Beyond the Sons of Scorsese', *Sight and Sound*, 2:5 (September 1992): 37.

19 Kobena Mercer, 'Skin Head Sex Thing', in Bad Object Choices (eds), *How Do I Look?* (Seattle: Bay Press, 1991), p. 193.

20 For discussions of the charms of the 'monsters', see Saunders, *Imps*, p. 19, and Harry Benshoff, *Monsters in the Closet: Homosexuality and the Horror Film* (Manchester: Manchester University Press, 1997). For the debate on homophobia and lesbian villains, see Julianne Pidduck, 'The Hollywood Fatal Femme: (Dis)Figuring Feminism, Family, Irony, Violence', *Cineaction*, 38 (1995): 64–72; Cathy Griggers, 'Phantom and Reel Projections: Lesbians and the (Serial) Killing-Machine', in Judith Halberstam and Ira Livingston (eds), *Posthuman Bodies* (Bloomington, IN: Indiana University Press, 1995), pp. 162–76; Christine Holmlund, 'A Decade of Deadly Dolls: Hollywood and the Woman Killer', in Helen Birch (ed.), *Moving Targets: Women, Murder and Representation* (Berkeley, CA: University of California Press, 1994), pp. 127–51; Michele Aaron, ''Til Death Us Do Part: Cinema's Queer Couples Who Kill' M. in Aaron (ed.), *The Body's Perilous Pleasures*, pp. 67–84. See also Anneke Smelik's chapter in this book.

21 Ellis Hansen (ed.), *Out Takes: Essays on Queer Theory and Film* (Durham, NC: Duke University Press, 1999), p. 11.

22 The 1990s saw the brutal murders of, for example, Matthew Shepard and Brandon Teena.

23 Submissions had increased by 50 per cent, and the audience had doubled at the 1992 San Francisco Film Festival see B. Ruby Rich, 'Reflections on a Queer Screen', *GLQ*, 1:1 (1993): 85.

24 B. Ruby Rich, 'Queer and Present Danger', *Sight and Sound*, 10:3 (March 2000): 23.

25 See the debate on *Boys Don't Cry* in *Screen*, 42:1, 42:2, 42:3 (Spring/Summer/Autumn 2001).

26 Lim, 'Reckless', p. 39.

27 B. Ruby Rich, 'Vision Quest: Searching for Diamonds in the Rough', *Village Voice* (26 March 2002): 43.

28 Rich, 'Queer and Present', p. 24.

29 See also forthcoming books on British (Routledge) and European (Intellect Press) queer cinema edited by Robin Griffiths.

30 See Patricia White, *Uninvited: Classical Hollywood Cinema and Lesbian Representability* (Bloomington, IN: Indiana University Press, 1999) and Alexander Doty, *Flaming Classics: Queering the Film Canon* (London: Routledge, 2000).

31 Alexander Doty, *Making Things Perfectly Queer: Interpreting Mass Culture* (Minneapolis: University of Minnesota Press, 1993), p. xi.

2. NEW QUEER CINEMA

B. Ruby Rich

Anyone who has been following the news at film festivals over the past few months knows, by now, that 1992 has become a watershed year for independent gay and lesbian film and video. Early last spring, on the very same day, Paul Verhoeven's *Basic Instinct* (1992) and Derek Jarman's *Edward II* (1991) opened in New York City. Within days, the prestigious New Directors/New Films Festival had premiered four new 'queer' films: Christopher Münch's *The Hours and Times* (1991). Tom Kalin's *Swoon* (1992), Gregg Araki's *The Living End* (1992) and Laurie Lynd's *R.S.V.P.* (1991). Had so much ink ever been spilled in the mainstream press for such a cause? *Basic Instinct* was picketed by the self-righteous wing of the queer community (until dykes began to discover how much fun it was), while mainstream critics were busily impressed by the 'queer new wave' and set to work making stars of the new boys on the block. Not that the moment isn't contradictory: this summer's San Francisco Gay and Lesbian Film Festival had its most successful year in its sixteen-year history, doubling attendance from 1991, but the National Endowment for the Arts pulled its funding anyway.

The queer film phenomenon was introduced a year ago at Toronto's Festival of Festivals, the best spot in North America for tracking new cinematic trends. There, suddenly, was a flock of films that were doing something new, renegotiating subjectivities, annexing whole genres, revising histories in their image. All through the winter, spring, summer, and now autumn, the message has been loud and clear: queer is hot. Check out the international circuit, from Park City to Berlin to London. Awards have been won, parties held. At Sundance, in the heart of Mormon country, there was even a panel dedicated to the queer subject, hosted by yours truly.

The Barbed Wire Kisses panel put eight panellists on stage, with so many queer film-makers in the audience that a roll call had to be read. Film-makers stood, one by one, to applause from the matinee crowd. 'Sundance is where you see what the industry can bear', said panellist Todd Haynes, there to talk about *Poison*'s year on the firing-line. He stayed to be impressed by earnest eighteen-year-old Wunderkind Sadie Benning, whose bargain-basement videos, shot with a Fisher-Price Pixelvision and produced for less than $20 apiece, have already received a retrospective at MoMA.

Isaac Julien was suddenly cast in the role of the older generation. Summarising the dilemmas of marketing queer product to general audiences, he described a Miramax Prestige advertising campaign for his *Young Soul Rebels* (1991) that used a bland image of guys and gals hanging out, like a Newport ad gone Benetton. Julien got them to change to an image of the black and white boyfriends, Caz and Billibud, kissing on a bed. The box office improved.

Tom Kalin struggled to reconcile his support for the disruptions of *Basic Instinct*'s shoot last spring with his film *Swoon*'s choice of queer murderers as subjects. Australian film-makers Stephen Cummins and Simon Hunt related the censorship of an episode of *The Simpsons* down under, where a scene of Homer kissing a swish fellow at the plant was cut. The panel turned surprisingly participatory. One Disney executive excoriated the industry. A film-maker called for a campaign to demand that Oliver Stone not direct his announced biopic of Harvey Milk (now being directed by Gus Van Sant, with Stone as co-producer). Meanwhile, Derek Jarman, the grand old man in his fourth decade of queer activity, beamed. He'd never been on a panel of queers at a mainstream festival.

Try to imagine the scene in Park City. Robert Redford holds a press conference and is asked, on camera, why there are all these gay films at his festival. Redford finesses: it is all part of the spectrum of independent film that Sundance is meant to serve. He even allows that the awards last year to *Poison* (1991) and Jennie Livingston's *Paris Is Burning* (1990) might have made the festival seem more welcoming to gays and lesbians. He could just as easily have said: these are simply the best films being made.

Of course, the new queer films and videos aren't all the same, and don't share a single aesthetic vocabulary or strategy or concern. Yet they are nonetheless united by a common style. Call it 'Homo Pomo': there are traces in all of them of appropriation and pastiche, irony, as well as a reworking of history with social constructionism very much in mind. Definitively breaking with older humanist approaches and the films and tapes that accompanied identity politics, these works are irreverent, energetic, alternately minimalist and excessive. Above all, they're full of pleasure. They're here, they're queer, get hip to them.

All the same, success breeds discontent, and 1992 is no different from any other year. When the ghetto goes mainstream, malaise and paranoia set in. It can be ideological, or generational, or genderational. Consider the issues that might disturb the peace. What will happen to the lesbian and gay film-makers who have been making independent films, often in avant-garde traditions, for decades already? Surprise, all the new movies being snatched up by distributors, shown in mainstream festivals, booked into theatres, are by the boys. Surprise, the amazing new lesbian videos that are redefining the whole dyke relationship to popular culture remain hard to find.

Amsterdam's Gay and Lesbian Film Festival made these discrepancies plain as day. The festival was staged last November, wedged between Toronto and Sundance. It should have been the most exciting place to be, but wasn't, not at all. And yet, that's where the girls were. Where the videos were. Where the films by people of colour and ex-Iron Curtain denizens were. But the power brokers were missing.

Christine Vachon, co-producer of *Swoon* and *Poison*, is sure that the heat this year has been produced by money: 'Suddenly there's a spotlight that says these films can be commercially viable'. Still, everyone tries to guess how long this moment of fascination will last. After all, none of this is taking place in a vacuum: celebrated in the festivals, despised in the streets. Review the statistics on gay-bashing. Glance at would-be presidential candidate Pat Buchanan's demonising of Marlon Riggs' *Tongues United*. Check out US immigration policy. Add the usual quota of internecine battles: girls against boys, narrative versus experimental work, white boys versus everyone else, elitism against populism, expansion of sights versus patrolling of borders. There's bound to be trouble in paradise, even when the party's just getting going.

DATELINE: TORONTO

Music was in the air in Toronto in September 1991, where the reputation of queer film and video started to build up. Or maybe I just loved Laurie Lynd's *R.S.V.P.* because it made my elevator ride with Jessye Norman possible. Lynd's film uses Norman's aria from Berlioz's *Les Nuits d'été* as its madeleine – supposedly Lynd sent Norman the finished film as a belated form of asking permission, and she loved it so much she agreed to attend the world premiere at Toronto (with red carpet in place and a packed house going wild, she sat through the screening holding Lynd's hand). *R.S.V.P.* suggests that the tragedy and trauma of AIDS have led to a new kind of film and video practice, one which takes up the aesthetic strategies that directors have already learned and applies them to a greater need than art for its own sake. This time, it's art for our sake, and it's powerful: no one can stay dry-eyed through this witty elegy.

Lynd was there as a producer, too, having worked on fellow-Canadian John Greyson's *The Making of 'Monsters'*. In it, George Lukács comes out of retirement to produce a television movie and hires Bertolt Brecht to direct it. Along with the comedy and boys in briefs, there's a restaging of the central aesthetic argument of the Frankfurt School as it might apply to the crises of representation engendered by today's anti-gay backlash, violence, and television treatments of the AIDS era.

Both low-budget and high-end film-making showed up in Toronto. Not surprisingly, the guys were high end, the gals low. Not that I'd begrudge Gus Van Sant one penny or remove a single frame from *My Own Private Idaho* – a film that securely positions him as heir-apparent to Fassbinder. So what if it didn't get a single Oscar nomination? At the other end of the spectrum was veteran avant-gardist Su Friedrich, whose latest film, *First Comes Love*, provoked catcalls from its largely queer audience. Was it because its subject was marriage, a topic on which the film is healthily ambivalent, mingling resentment with envy, anger with yearning? Or was it an aesthetic reaction, since Friedrich returns to a quasi-structuralist mode for her indictment of institutionalised heterosexuality and thus possibly alienates audiences accustomed to an easier queer fix? Was it because the director was a woman, since the only other lesbian on hand was Monika Treut, who by now should probably be classified as post-queer? Whatever the reason, Friedrich's elegant short stuck out, a barometer in a pack of audience-pleasers.

The epiphanic moment, if there was one, was the screening of Jarman's *Edward II*, which reinscribed the homosexuality so integral to its sixteenth-century source via a syncretic style that mixed past and present in a manner so arch that the film easily fits its tag, the 'QE2'. Think pastiche, as OutRage demos and gay-boy calisthenics mix with minimalist period drama. Homophobia is stripped bare as a timeless occupation, tracked across centuries but never lacking in historical specificity. Obsessive love, meanwhile, is enlarged to include queer desire as a legitimate source of tragedy.

For women, *Edward II* is a bit complicated. Since the heroes are men and the main villain is a woman, some critics have condemned it as misogynist. Indeed, Tilda Swinton's brilliance as an actor – and full co-creator of her role – invests her character with more weight, and thus more evil, than anyone else on screen. But the film is also a critique of heterosexuality and of a world ruled by royals and Tories, and Isabella seems more inspired by Thatcher than woman-hating. Annie Lennox is clearly meant to be on the side of girls and angels. Her solo 'Every Time We Say Goodbye' accompanies Edward and Gaveston's last dance, bringing grandeur, modernity, even post-modernity, to their tragedy. The song comes from the AIDS-benefit album, *Red Hot and Blue*, in which video Lennox inscribed images of Jarman's childhood in a tribute to his activism and HIV status. Thus does Jarman's time travel insist on carrying the court into today's gay world.

DATELINE: AMSTERDAM

The official car showed up at the airport with the festival's own steamy poster of girls in heat and boys in lust plastered all over it. Amsterdam, city of lights for faggots and dykes, offered the promise of an event purely one's own in the city celebrated for queerness. Expectations were running high, but in fact the festival showed all the precious advantages and irritating problems that life in the ghetto entails. It was a crucible for queer work, all right, but some got burned. How does this event fit into the big picture set by the 'big' festivals? Well, it doesn't. The identity that elsewhere becomes a badge of honour here became a straitjacket. But would 'elsewhere' exist without the 'here'?

Amsterdam was an exercise in dialectics in action, with both pleasures and dangers. Film-maker Nick Deocampo from the Philippines was planning his country's first gay festival and hoping that the 'war of the widows' wouldn't forestall it. Race, status, romance, gender, even the necessity of the festival came up for attack and negotiation, on those few occasions when the public got to talk back. Pratibha Parmar affirmed the importance of a queer circuit – 'my lifeline' – sure that it's key to the work. Jarman disagreed: 'Perhaps their time is up' maybe life in the ghetto now offers diminished returns. So though Jarman and Ulrike Ottinger got awards here, and though Jarman used the opening night to call for the decriminilisation of Oscar Wilde, the meaning of such an event remained contested.

Not that there weren't good films at Amsterdam. But the best work seemed to come from long ago or far away, like the great shows of German cross-dressing movies or the Mary Wings tribute to 'Greta Garbo's lesbian past' or the extraordinary 60s fantasy from Japan, *Funeral of Roses*. There were even two terrific new lesbian films, both deserving of instant cult status. Cleo Uebelmann's *Mano Destra* brought bondage and domination straight to the viewer, serving up knot fetishism and the thrills of specular anticipation with an uncanny understanding of cinema's own powers. From a trio of Viennese film-makers (Angela Hans Scheirl, Dietmar Schipek, Ursula Puerrer) came *Flaming Ears*, a surreal fable that draws on comics and sci-fi traditions for a near-human love story visualised in an atmosphere of cabaret, rubble and revenge. Its fresh 'cyberdyke' style reflects Austrian sources as diverse as Valie Export and Otto Muehle, but shot through with Super-8 visual rawness and a script that could have been written by J. G. Ballard himself.

It was a shame that the Dutch press marginalised the festival, because the kind of 'scoop' that the *New York Times* and *Newsweek* would later find in Utah could have been theirs right at home. A new kind of lesbian video surfaced here, and with it emerged a contemporary lesbian sensibility. Like the gay male films now in the limelight, this video has everything to do with a new historiography. But where the boys are archaeologists, the girls have to be alchemists. Their style is unlike almost anything that's come before. I would call it lesbian camp, but the species is, after all, better known for camping. And historical revisionism is not a catchy term. So just borrow from Hollywood, and think of it as the Great Dyke Rewrite.

Here's a taste of the new genre. In Cecilia Dougherty's *Grapefruit*, white San Francisco dykes unapologetically impersonate John, Yoko and the Beatles – proving that appropriation and gender-fuck make a great combination. Cecilia Barriga's *The Meeting of Two Queens* re-edits Dietrich and Garbo movies to construct the dyke fan's dream narrative: get the girls together, help them get it on. It's a form of idolatry that takes the feminist lit-crit practice of 'reading against the grain' into new image territory, blasting the results on to the screen (or monitor, to be exact). In one episode of Kaucylia Brooke and Jane Cottis' *Dry Kisses Only*, Anne Baxter's back-stage meeting with Bette Davis in *All About Eve* is altered, inserting instead of Baxter a dyke who speaks in direct address to the camera about her tragic life, her life working in a San Francisco lesbian bar, her love lost to Second World War combat. She's cross-cut with Bette's reaction shots, culminating with Davis taking her arm (and taking her home).

Apart from the videos, festival lesbians pinned all voyeuristic hopes on the 'Wet' Party, where they would finally get to the baths. Well, sort of. Everyone certainly tried. Outfits ranged from the campiness of childhood-at-the-beach to show-your-leather seriousness. Women bobbed in the pool, playing with rubber rafts and inflated black and white fuck-me dolls. (Parmar would later note that there were more inflatables of colour in attendance than actual women of colour.) San Francisco sex-stars Shelly Mars and Susie Bright both performed, though the grand moment in which Bright seemed to be lecturing us on "Oedipal underwear" turned out to be a cruel acoustical joke: she was actually extolling the virtue of *edible* underwear. But the back rooms were used for heart-to-hearts, not action. Caught between the states of dress-up and undress, everyone waited for someone else to do something.

Other parties offered other pleasures. At one, Jimmy Somerville, unscheduled, did a Sylvester homage. At another, Marilyn Monroe appeared, frosted on to a giant cake, clutching her skirt, only to be carved up by a gaggle of male chefs. In the end, somehow, Amsterdam was the festival you loved to hate, the place where everyone wanted the world and wouldn't settle for less, where dirty laundry could be washed in public and anyone in authority taken to task, where audiences were resistant to experimental and non-narrative work, and where criticisms were bestowed more bountifully than praise. Still, while the market place might be seductive, it's not yet democratic. Amsterdam was the place where a 'Wet' Party could at least be staged, where new works by women and people of colour were accorded pride of place, where video was fully integrated into the programming. Amsterdam was a ritual gathering of the tribe and, like a class reunion, filled with ambivalence.

PARK CITY, UTAH

Everything came together at the Sundance Film Festival in Park City. Christopher Münch's *The Hours and Times* is a good example. Audiences fell in love with this imaginary chronicle of Brian Epstein and John Lennon's last tango in Barcelona. Münch's camera style and script are a reprise of *cinéma vérité*, as though some dusty reels had been found in a closet in Liverpool and expertly edited, as though Leacock or Pennebaker had turned gay-positive retroactively. Epstein tries to get Lennon into bed, using old-world angst, homo-alienation, Jewish charm. Lennon tries to sort out his life, balancing wife Cynthia against groupie against Epstein, trying to have it all and to figure out whatever will come next. Just a simple view of history with the veil of homophobia pulled back. It's rumoured that the dramatic jury at Sundance loved it so much, they wanted to give it the Grand Prize – but since it wasn't feature length they settled on a special jury award.

"Puts the Homo back in Homicide" is the teaser for Tom Kalin's first feature, *Swoon*, but it could easily apply to Gregg Araki's newest, *The Living End*, as well. Where Kalin's film is an interrogation of the past, Araki's is set resolutely in the present. Or is it? Cinematically, it restages the celluloid of the 60s and 70s: early Godard, *Bonnie and Clyde*, *Badlands*, *Butch Cassidy and the Sundance Kid*, every pair-on-the-run movie that ever penetrated Araki's consciousness. Here, though, the guys are HIV positive, one bored and one full of rage, both of them with nothing to lose. They could be characters out of a porn flick, the stud and the john, in a renegotiated terrain. Early Araki films are often too garage-hand, too boychick, too far into visual noise, but this one is different. Camera style and palette update the New Wave. Araki's stylistic end runs have paid off, and this time he's got a queers-on-the-lam portrait that deserves a place in movie history – an existential film for a post-porn age, one that puts queers on the map as legitimate genre subjects. It's quintessentially a film of its time.

And so is *Swoon*, though it might seem otherwise, what with the mock-period settings, the footage purloined from the 20s, and the courtroom-accurate script, based on the 1924 Chicago trial of Leopold and Loeb, the pair of rich Jewish boys who bonded, planned capers, and finally killed a boy. In the wake of the Dahmer case, it would be easy to think of this as a film about horrific acts. *Swoon*, however, deals in different stakes: it's the history of discourses that's under Kalin's microscope, as he demonstrates how easily mainstream society of the 20s could unite discrete communities of outsiders (Jews, queers, blacks, murderers) into a commonality of perversion. The whole look of the film – director of photography Ellen Kuras won the prize for cinematography in dramatic film in Park City – emphasises this view with the graphic quality of its anti-realism, showing how much Kalin, Kuras and co-producer Vachon tailored its look.

As part of a new generation of directors, Kalin isn't satisfied to live in the past, even a post-modern past. No, *Swoon* takes on the whole enterprise of 'positive images', definitively rejecting any such project and turning the thing on its head. I doubt that anyone who damned *The Silence of the Lambs* for toxic homophobia will swallow *Swoon* easily, but hopefully the film will force a rethinking of positions. Claim the heroes, claim the villains, and don't mistake any of it for realness.

Throughout Sundance, a comment Richard Dyer made in Amsterdam echoed in my memory. There are two ways to dismiss gay film: one is to say, 'Oh, it's just a gay film'; the other, to proclaim, 'Oh, it's a great film, it just happens to be gay'. Neither applied to the films in Park City, since they were great precisely because of the ways in which they were gay. Their queerness was no more arbitrary than their aesthetics, no more than their individual preoccupations with interrogating history. The queer present negotiates with the past, knowing full well that the future is at stake.

Like film, video is a harbinger of that future, even more so. Yet Sundance, like most film festivals, showed none. To make a point about the dearth of lesbian work in feature film and to confront the industry with its own exclusions, the Barbed Wire Kisses panel opened with a projected screening of Sadie Benning's video-tape *Jollies* – and brought down the house. With an absolute economy of means, Benning constructed a *Portrait of the Artist as a Young Dyke* such as we've never seen before. 'I had a crush. It was 1978, and I was in kindergarten'. The lines are spoken facefront to the camera, black-and-white images floating into the frame alongside the words enlisted to spell out her emotions on screen, associative edits calling settled assumptions into question.

The festival ended, of course. Isaac Julien returned to London to finish *Black and White in Colour*, his documentary on the history of blacks in British television. High-school dropout Sadie Benning left to show her tapes at Princeton, and to make another one, *It Wasn't Love*, that proves she's no fluke. Derek Jarman and Jimmy Somerville were arrested for demonstrating outside parliament. Christopher Münch and Tom Kalin picked up prizes in Berlin. Gregg Araki found himself a distributor. New work kept getting produced: the San Francisco festival found its submissions up by 50 per cent in June. The Queer New Wave has come full circle: the boys and their movies have arrived.

But will lesbians ever get the attention for their work that men get for theirs? Will queers of colour ever get equal time? Or video achieve the status reserved for film? Take, for example, Cheryl Dunye, a young video-maker whose *She Don't Fade* and *Vanilla Sex* put a sharp, satiric spin on black romance and cross-race illusions. Or keep an eye out for Jean Carlomusto's *L is For the Way You Look*, to catch a definitive portrait of dyke fandom and its importance for, uh, subject position.

For one magical Saturday afternoon in Park City, there was a panel that traced a history: Derek Jarman at one end on the eve of his fiftieth birthday, and Sadie Benning at the other, just joining the age of consent. The world had changed enough that both of them could be there, with a host of cohorts in between. All engaged in the beginnings of a new queer historiography, capable of transforming this decade, if only the door stays open long enough. For him, for her, for all of us.

3. AIDS AND NEW QUEER CINEMA

Monica B. Pearl

New Queer Cinema is gay independent cinema, made in the midst of the AIDS crisis, that defies cinematic convention. This defiance can take the form of being fragmented, non-narrative, and ahistorical. I follow, roughly, José Arroyo's pronouncement (who follows, roughly, B. Ruby Rich's), in his formative article on AIDS and New Queer Cinema, 'Death, Desire and Identity', that films that constitute new queer cinema 'utilize irony and pastiche, represent fragmented subjectivities, depict a compression of time with sometimes dehistoric results, and . . . are dystopic'.[1] In his analysis of the status and origins of Queer Cinema, he asserts that AIDS gave rise to what we call New Queer Cinema. If, as Arroyo argued, 'AIDS has affected what amounts to an epistemic shift in gay culture', then New Queer Cinema is the result of that shift.[2] Arroyo makes the claim that as gay men '[w]e know different things about ourselves and we know ourselves differently (and part of this change is a questioning of who is "we" and what is the self)'.[3] From this he concludes that 'AIDS is why there is New Queer Cinema and it is what New Queer Cinema is about'.[4]

Arroyo's article concentrates on the films of Gus Van Sant and Derek Jarman. B. Ruby Rich, in a follow-up article to her original pronouncement of New Queer Cinema as a movement, refers to Jarman as 'the godfather of the movement'.[5] I too will focus on a film of Jarman's, a film of his that emerged the same year as Arroyo's essay: *Blue* (Derek Jarman, 1993). It is my contention that New Queer Cinema *is* AIDS cinema: not only because the films, as I will argue, emerge out of the time of and the preoccupations with AIDS, but because their narratives and also their formal discontinuities and disruptions, are AIDS-related. Like Arroyo in 1993, I want to account for the connection between AIDS and New Queer Cinema, but, now, using an expanded grouping of films, and with particular consideration to the role of AIDS activism. So how did AIDS make movies?

Although New Queer Cinema is not always about the subject of AIDS – indeed, often the films that are included in the designation are not at all overtly about AIDS – it is a form and expression that emerges from the cataclysm of AIDS in the Western world. It is not only in film that AIDS inspired new forms of expression: this was true also in literature, in music, and in other visual arts besides cinema. AIDS disrupted individuals, communities, and the ways that things could be thought of or said or expressed. It was disruptive partly because it caused illness and death, and therefore aggravated loss among small groups of individuals in particular communities, but it was disruptive also because of the kind of illness it was – or, rather, the kind of virus that caused the illness and the way it took hold on the human body. The films that constitute New Queer Cinema represent these many levels of disruption.

The virus – that is, the illness – also, then, disrupted identity, the ways that people could think about themselves. HIV is a retrovirus, which compromises the body's immune system by becoming part of the body that it infects. In this way, when the immune system attempts to fight the foreign infection, it ends up battling the body that harbours it. The body's attempt to save itself is what kills it. In this way, the boundaries of the body in the realm of illness, *this* illness, are no longer so clearly demarcated as they have been in the past – partly because the metaphors for what the immune system does are no longer applicable.[6] That narrative no longer works: the story of self versus foreign object does not apply. The self as whole, sacrosanct, inviolable, and definable became, even for those who were not ill, an illusion of self and subjectivity that could not be sustained.

Much of AIDS representation follows the course of the virus itself – or what the virus is perceived to be doing, according to scientific narratives and metaphors.[7] A retrovirus does not follow the 'traditional' trajectory of infection, whereby a foreign substance infects the body and is 'conquered' by an army of antibodies,[8] rather it insidiously convinces the body that its very being is the foreign substance, and so the body fights itself. HIV, as a retrovirus, is a postmodern virus. It makes the body unable to differentiate between itself and what is external, or foreign, to itself. It takes the virus in like a friend, and then battles with itself. The lack of coherent narrative, or genre recognition, or familiarly fulfilled cinematic expectations in New Queer Cinema, is partly a representational, or 'artistic', reaction to the nature of retroviral behaviour. In other words, representation mimics the 'narrative' of the virus.

But AIDS was disruptive in a far less narrative, more material, way. It disrupted communities because people became very ill; people died. But even here the 'normal' narrative of illness was disrupted. Although every illness is different, we have come to expect a certain storyline to illness, a progression: one becomes ill, one's health declines, sometimes there is a period of recovery, and finally there follows either death or a triumphant overcoming of the illness.[9] AIDS does not permit of this normative narrative progression.

New Queer Cinema is a reflection and a recapitulation of these disruptions, and most particularly the disruption of identity. The self could no longer be expressed or thought of in the same way, so the visual media that reflected and constructed that identity had to change too, and had to recapitulate the sense of disorder and chaos that was the experience of people, and communities, living with, and dying from, AIDS. Although the virus associated with AIDS has been thought of as resisting visual representation, it has been represented over and over, but obliquely, at an angle, from perspectives that suggest just how disruptive the virus has been.

It could be said that New Queer Cinema emerged from the AIDS crisis through AIDS activism. The direct action group, ACT UP (the AIDS Coalition to Unleash Power), mobilised against government and pharmaceutical forces to stem the spread of illness and save the lives of people infected with HIV.[10] ACT UP was committed to the disruption of business as usual in order to end the AIDS crisis. This end to 'business as usual' took many forms. Life was different, and life therefore for everyone had to be different. For life to go on as usual only represented a kind of complacency in the face of the loss and suffering experienced by others. Through such machinery as peaceful protest resulting in arrest, demanding and winning meetings with powerful government and industry officials, lowering the prices of much needed antiviral medication, bringing to a standstill (for the first time in history) the New York Stock Exchange (in protest at Burroughs Wellcome's exorbitant prices for AZT), staging kiss-ins and die-ins, challenging laws that spread the incidence of HIV (such as those prohibiting the distribution of sterile hypodermic equipment to injecting drug users), ACT UP itself mimicked the disruption and unrest brought about by the retroviral HIV. ACT UP was motivated by visual attention: the more media, the more publicity, the better. It was this tool that forced organisations and institutions to change their policies, lower their prices, and open their doors to people living with AIDS. 'Publicity,' writes Stanley Aronowitz, 'is the movement's crucial strategic weapon, embarrassment its major tactic'.[11] As Arroyo writes: 'The context of the pandemic has created a demand for representation, both political and artistic at a time when representation in the media increasingly becomes a precondition for political representation'.[12]

One of the many important things that ACT UP, and its subgroups and offshoots, did was to disrupt and challenge the representation of AIDS, and of people living with AIDS, in the mainstream media. It did this by protesting erroneous and misleading and incomplete stories and reports on television news, but it did this also by making its own videos – videos that showed another side to living with AIDS, that aimed to correct the misreportage in the mainstream media, and that provided representation that felt more authentic and accurate to the experience of living with HIV than anything that was theretofore available. A subcommittee of ACT UP/New York, DIVA TV (Damned Interfering Video Activist Television) was dedicated to documenting

ACT UP demonstrations and making alternative AIDS media.[13] AIDS video was first used to document AIDS demonstrations, partly because the police could not be trusted not to fabricate infringements upon the law, when indeed it was more often the law enforcement officials who were breaching acceptable conduct procedures for arrest and crowd containment: videotape was used to record what had actually occurred. This coincided with the formation of other AIDS video collectives, namely the Testing the Limits collective that produced the 1987 video documentary *Testing the Limits*, and then, in 1992, a video that focused specifically on ACT UP, *Voices from the Front*.

AIDS and AIDS activism coincided with new video technology, and the production of alternative AIDS media was made possible by the availability of relatively affordable video equipment. Alexandra Juhasz, in her book, *AIDS TV*, writes that the 'lining up of the new video technologies (the camcorder, satellite, VCR, and relatively low-cost computer editing) with the AIDS crisis, and with theories of postmodern identity politics and multiculturalism is the founding condition upon which alternative AIDS media is built'.[14] She goes on to suggest why the possibility of alternative visual representations of AIDS was so crucial:

> The potential of media production for those individuals and communities who never before could afford it or master it occurred just as a social crisis of massive proportions and multiple dimensions begged to be represented in a manner available to the most and the least economically privileged. The politics of AIDS – the demands for better quality of life for the people affected by this epidemic – are well matched by the potentials and politics of video.[15]

Early AIDS video was also meant to fill in the gaps of what government health education authorities might have been consigned to do: educate the 'general population' that the government imagined most needed to know about how to protect themselves and others from HIV infection. These videos also gave a voice, and a public image, to otherwise silenced communities in the AIDS crisis – often the communities at risk that needed the most intervention. These tapes also did more than educate about transmission, but about how to obtain healthcare and other benefits, and how to stand up for one's rights when disenfranchised – through illness or other marginal status.

When Juhasz asks, '[w]hy this form of response instead of or in addition to marching, lobbying, or leafleting?',[16] she affirms the link between video production and activism, indeed, pointing to an early coined amalgam: 'video activism'. Two key New Queer filmmakers, Tom Kalin and John Greyson, started out making activist videos. Kalin was an early member of ACT UP/ New York and the activist arts group Gran Fury, and in 1988 produced the video *they are lost to vision altogether*, a video 'heavily inflected by an "ACT UP vocabulary"'.[17]

John Greyson's feature film *Zero Patience* offers an interesting amalgam of AIDS activism, AIDS alternative video documentary, and New Queer Cinema. It is the story of 'Patient Zero', the alleged first person with AIDS who, according to Randy Shilts' book *And the Band Played On*, was responsible for the spread of AIDS in North American and probably beyond.[18] A Canadian flight attendant, Gaetan Dugas, is portrayed in Greyson's film as a ghost who has come back to life to correct this misrepresentation, in this way fictionalising the very tactics of ACT UP: to correct misinformation. Meanwhile, AIDS activism is itself represented in the film when the local AIDS activist group intervene, literally – by breaking into a museum at night – to correct the erroneous assumptions about how AIDS is spread. That *Zero Patience* is a musical only further subverts the ways we might expect to be 'entertained' by such serious matters as AIDS, history, media representation, and the legacy of moralism and sexuality.

AIDS was disruptive as a virus, as an illness. It was sudden and quick, decimating communities. It also disrupted – and, indeed, also coalesced – identities, particularly gay identity. It coalesced identity by making people 'gay' who might not have, or might not needed to have, thought of themselves in that way before. By contracting HIV through sex with another man, or by being interpellated as someone who might require safe sex information based on a history of, or desire for, sexual relations with another man, some men 'became gay' with the advent of the AIDS crisis. AIDS caused shifts in identity.

But most pertinent to this discussion, is the way that what was experienced, since at least the Stonewall riots of 1969, as a fairly known and stable gay identity, was disrupted with the advent of the AIDS crisis. Part of that disruption has to do with the nature of the illness: the chaotic and non-narrative and non-progressive nature of AIDS. Films were needed that represented this disrupted chronology, as it were.

As Sarah Schulman puts it, what appears to be 'experimental' cinema, for a lesbian and gay audience contains 'a far more visceral and accurate presentation of how we really live than the commercial films prepared for a straight audience'.[19] Schulman suggests that 'as gay people have had to interrogate and invent themselves, films that re-imagine the world resonate for us with deep and familiar emotions'.[20]

But it is more complicated than this. AIDS needed representation, partly because it was considered unrepresentable. So, although there are 'AIDS movies', that is, films that deal directly with the difficulties with living with HIV and AIDS, and more generally, loss from AIDS, even independent films that are *about* AIDS, are often about AIDS only indirectly. Take the film *Grief* (Richard Glatzer, 1994), for example. The underlying premise and plot of the film is that Mark's lover Kenny died from AIDS a year earlier, and Mark doesn't know his own HIV status. But the film itself is about daily life at work on the set of a torrid daytime television programme: romance and sex and jealousy. But of course the details in this film are a distraction from, and an absorption in, grief. The film is about grief – Mark's grief and perhaps also a more widespread grief among *Grief*'s viewers – but also about daily losses and mourning: job insecurity, romance and desire and inter-office tensions, promotions. But it is precisely the narrative coherence and dailiness of this film that make it not New Queer Cinema.

Although I contend that New Queer Cinema emerges from and is more often than not *about* AIDS, not all New Queer Cinema is overtly about AIDS. And even some of the films that are about AIDS seem sometimes to deflect it rather than to focus on it. *The Living End* (Gregg Araki, 1992) is a good example of a film that is, in many ways, an AIDS film, but what makes it New Queer Cinema is not the ways that it is overtly about AIDS, but the ways that it is preoccupied with death and time and history. There is a character in *The Living End*, Jon, who discovers he is HIV infected, but this is information gained and put aside early in the film. This is a premise of the film, we are told, but not the underpinning of it. There are films that are 'about' AIDS, that are gay, contain gay themes and gay characters – are independently produced – but are not New Queer Cinema. Like *Grief*.

The Living End is a film that incorporates HIV into its plotline. Both main characters, Jon and Luke, are HIV positive. But that is only the most obvious way that it betrays a concern with AIDS. The film's preoccupation with death, and control over death, is the less obvious, but more pervasive, 'AIDS-related' theme of the film. The film opens with a piece of graffito, 'fuck the world', that suggests the film's irreverent pursuit of such questions as to what extent AIDS might – very radically – be freeing. This film boldly suggests that for those marginalised by the world – by sexual identity, but not only by that – the spectre of death makes one more empowered, more free, than one was before one was haunted by that spectre. Jon tells Luke before they have sex for the first time that he has HIV; Luke replies, 'It's no big deal'. The next morning he changes his mind; it is a big deal: but liberating; because as HIV positive they can do 'whatever the fuck we want'. They can embrace life, they can take risks. The film is precisely about the liberation of AIDS.

Derek Jarman's film *Blue* is another example of New Queer Cinema that is about AIDS. It is New Queer Cinema because it is formally 'fragmented' and challenging. *Blue* has no 'body', no cinematic image. *Blue* is asking the viewer to contend with the disorientation of watching a film that has no variation in the visual image. All one watches, for seventy-five minutes, is a blue screen. Jarman made the film when he was going blind from cytomegalovirus, an AIDS-related infection. 'I have to come to terms with sightlessness', he narrates. But in this film he has done away with the image, with the body, the thing that betrays. There is nothing to see; no need for eyes, for vision. Gabriele Griffin writes that

> [i]n *Blue* looking and seeing acquire new meanings because the gaze is denied, or rather the desire for the gaze to be met by a visual object is

unexpectedly re-directed. For it is, in fact, not exactly the case that there is nothing to see – what we have is an immense, screen-filling blueness.[21]

Blue disrupts visual and narrative expectations. Like *The Living End* (though it is in all other respects *unlike The Living End*), *Blue* is a film that is obviously about AIDS, but what makes it an AIDS film is not this overt 'plot line'.

RESPONSIBILITY

New Queer Cinema is trying to interrogate, rewrite, and reassign responsibility, much like the original activist AIDS videos that aimed to 'correct, augment, or politicize the paltry, timid, and incorrect representations found on broadcast television'.[22] This is not to say that the films are pedantic or pedagogic or didactic. But their narrative trajectory and conclusion – unlike the heterosexual romance that concludes most conventional Hollywood films – often are a reassignment of blame and responsibility.

John Greyson's film *Lilies* (1996) is a film about taking responsibility for death – or, more accurately, about not being irresponsible about where one casts blame. The film's story is about a man, Simon, who serves a life sentence for a murder for which he was not responsible, indeed for the death of the man he loved. It is not hard to read this as an AIDS story, the story of blame wrongly assigned: as gay men are accused of recklessness, of spreading infection. In 1952 Canada, a bishop is called to prison to hear the confession of a dying prisoner. But it turns out that this prisoner, Simon, with the help of his fellow inmates, has prepared to lock the bishop, Bilodeau, in his own confessional, and forced him to watch the reenactment of the 'murder' and the events leading up to it, the crime for which Simon was held responsible and incarcerated. Forty years earlier, as late adolescent boys, Bilodeau looked on jealously as Simon declared his love for Vallier, and it was he who set the fire that led to Vallier's death. It was not Simon who was responsible for the death of his lover. If we want to take Greyson's symbolism specifically, he not only removes blame from the gay lover, but assigns blame to the Catholic Church, for which the bishop can easily be read as the synechdochal stand-in.

What *Lilies* does extraordinarily is convince us that the prisoners are the figures from Simon's past, that they are Simon and Vallier and the Bishop, and that Vallier's mad mother, and Simon's elegant mistress, all played by the male prisoners, are from that past too. It helps a little that cinematically Greyson elides the 'play' within the prison into a film, but we are not convinced by the fact that it is film; we are convinced by the acting. *Lilies* depends on artifice and fantasy. That the men play both the male and female characters, and that the reenactment switches from play within the prison to cinematic flashback, both blur and reinstate the boundaries of what is artifice, what is cinematic, what is 'real'. Narrative and cinematic form is convincing but not reliable. One can see this as well in Christopher Münch's film *The Hours and Times*

(1991). It is a convincing set piece about John Lennon and Brian Epstein on holiday in Spain, but it is hardly historically reliable. Nevertheless, it encourages a reimagination of the past, the creative manipulation of history.

TIME

New Queer Cinema attempts not only to reassign responsibility but is trying to counter the devastation of AIDS, often by a narrative effort to control death. The most important feature that marks New Queer Cinema as AIDS related is its films' ahistoric, non-chronological, and even sometimes anachronistic sense of time. Arroyo points to this when he writes that films within the designation New Queer Cinema 'depict a compression of time with sometimes dehistoric results'.[23] This being out of time takes different forms in different films, but what it echoes is the way that AIDS, as a retroviral, chronic, and recurring illness, disrupts the story and progression of illness narrative, whereby one gets ill and dies, or ill and triumphs over death, and also disrupts, quite simply, the progression of life.

Blue, with its lack of visual image, is all voiceover, but no story. There is no narrative that unfolds, only endless blue with voices describing or incanting, or music or sound effects playing. The film opens with the sound of bells, as a clock chiming, and returns to these sounds, incorporating near the end a ticking clock. It also includes, in the voiceover, a preoccupation with time, as the narrating figure (who could be taken to be Jarman himself, and which is sometimes actually the voice of Jarman, but is also sometimes the voices of John Quentin, Nigel Terry, and Tilda Swinton), attached to his DHPG drip (the medication meant to stabilise his eyesight), muses, 'the drip ticks out seconds, the source of a stream along which the minutes flow, to join the river of hours and the sea of years in a timeless ocean'. 'The years', the disembodied voice tells us near the end of the film, 'slip off the calendar'.

Set in the past – the mid-twentieth century, and also the turn of the century – *Lilies* is in no obvious way an AIDS film. But *Lilies* is not unlike Greyson's earlier film, *Zero Patience*, in that it plays with time and filmic convention and genre. *Zero Patience* – an AIDS musical and fictitious documentary – resurrects the dead Patient Zero to clear his name. *Lilies* is most like *Zero Patience* in that it rewrites a story – it corrects history, and reassigns responsibility. The bishop in *Lilies* – the man really responsible for Vallier's death forty years earlier – cannot remain blameless; indeed, as the film closes it seems that he might kill himself with the knife Simon has supplied to him.

Lilies also plays with filmic convention when it incorporates what we are accustomed to thinking of as a 'flashback', but because the prisoners are acting out the past in 'real time', it is not the past but the filmic present that is on display. It is why (besides the marvellous acting) we are meant to suspend our disbelief about the gender of the roles played. Because it is *not* flashback but asks us to imagine the past, it incorporates past and present into the same moment – into synchronous time. There is no (filmic) past and present in this film, only one moment, the present.

Looking for Langston (Isaac Julien, 1989), another primary example of New Queer Cinema, dehistoricises its narrative. Though it is meant to be the reappraisal of Langston Hughes, African American poet of the Harlem Renaissance, it is a film that, while very stylised and aestheticised, is out of time. The mise en scène displays photographs of Hughes himself and of James Baldwin, non-contemporaries but both important (gay) African American writers. The scene at the end of the film devolves musically into a contemporary dance club, as the music in this refined 1920s' setting, turns to disco. The voiceover blends the poetry of Hughes with that of out gay black poet Essex Hemphill (now deceased, but alive at the time the film was made), and contains versions of Hughes' poetry – a dream deferred – set to music. Finally, as in the case of *Blue*, *Looking for Langston* has no obvious narrative.

Münch's *The Hours and Times* reimagines a four-day holiday in Barcelona taken by John Lennon and Brian Epstein in 1963. Issued in 1991, this black-and-white film invents an anguished homoerotic relationship between the laconic Beatle and his devoted manager. The convincing mise en scène makes the film historically plausible, but still, like Tom Kalin's film *Swoon*, *The Hours and Times* imaginatively narrativises a past as one needs it to have been. It is a way of controlling – not death, as I have asserted among the aims of New Queer Cinema – but history. It is a way of claiming control over time and events, as one might like to given the catastrophic outcome of the AIDS crisis.

DEATH

Swoon is narratively and historically appropriate, within its terms, and unfolds in 1924, making it not an obvious contender for an AIDS film. However, the film is focused on death, and control over death. Further, it focuses on death as the point around which a gay relationship turns. The film is a retelling of the oft-told story of Leopold and Loeb, two men who in 1924 murdered a young boy for what seemed to be the mere pleasure of it. In Kalin's film, their 'crimes' are meant to glue them together (they exchange rings at the beginning of the film; when Richard Loeb dies, Nathan Leopold slips the band off Loeb's finger and pushes it into Loeb's mouth), they are the pivot, it seems, of their (sexual) relationship, which the murder itself seals: Nathan remarks in a voiceover, a 'diary entry', that 'killing Bobby Franks together would join Richard and I for life'.

Swoon also, incidentally, tries to make a narrative out of, and make beautiful, what is thought of as senseless: the historical motiveless murder of a small boy. It tries to make sense of, and aestheticise, senseless death. An AIDS film indeed. While I have said that *Swoon* is historically 'appropriate' to its time, there is the matter of the anachronistic walkmans and pushbutton phones. It has been suggested that this is a way to make the film more obviously a film of our time. [24] This is right, I think; but it does more than this: it is another way to make the film 'not fit' a timeline. It makes the film unreliable. Like *Lilies* and *The Hours and Times*, *Swoon* is a film that points to the artifice of film, even while it luxuriates in a recognisably noir aesthetic, making it seem known even while it contravenes the convention.

Like *Lilies*, *Swoon* is also a meditation on responsibility. The end of *Swoon* is taken up with the trials and imprisonment of Leopold and Loeb, and while they do not protest their innocence, the two men are throughout unashamed and unapologetic for what they have done. What might seem senseless to the viewer, seems to make sense to them. What does not seem immediately obvious as an AIDS film, becomes more so when the plot suggests the way gay men have had to defend or explain their lives.

Todd Haynes' film *Safe* (1995) is least obviously New Queer Cinema. It has no announced gay characters and focuses on the disaffection of a rich bored California housewife. However, as the housewife, Carol, is increasingly afflicted with environmental illness and menaced by the world around her, it is not difficult to read the film as an AIDS allegory. It is a film about an individual who is vulnerable to infection, who, as the title nearly mocks, cannot be made safe, either sexually or otherwise, and who is shunned by her community.[25] *Safe* is not noticeably unconventional in its narrative unfolding, but it is eccentric in its acceleration of Carol's dis-ease in the world, making it seem normal in the end for her to live in the smallest possible enclosure, safe from the world's ills.[26]

Finally, I would like to comment on a recent film, *The Hours* (Stephen Daldry, 2002). *The Hours* is not New Queer Cinema. Chiefly because it was produced outside of the general timeframe of what has been designated New Queer Cinema; but it carries significant traits of the movement (its title a monomial modified by a gerund). For one thing, its preoccupation – announced in the title – with time. Although the title is the restoration of Virginia Woolf's discarded title for *Mrs Dalloway*, 'The Hours' points most poignantly to the idea of postmodern time – the way that time present emerges out of, but absorbs and carries within it, time past. The narrative of *The Hours* incorporates three separate historical timeframes, showing not a chronological progression, but shifts in the meaning of time, of the hours of a day. AIDS is only one theme among many in this film – and that the 'hero' is dying of AIDS is not exactly incidental, but not the *point* of the film's present-day episodes – but it underwrites the preciousness of time for the characters. Time, in the parallel episodes in the other timeframes, is speeded up through editing and pacing to emphasise the rush of life. It is the present-day Clarissa who has, in the end, the most to gain – because she *does* live in the present day – from utilising time, rather than succumbing to it.

CONCLUSION

In *The Living End*, Luke cuts his wrist, and slumped, shirtless, against Jon's car, he peers into his wound and says, 'I know it's inside me, but I can't see it. Can you?' Gabriele Griffin has called AIDS a 'visually under-determined illness'.[27] Juhasz suggests that AIDS is '*only* manageable in representation'.[28] It seems that AIDS – invisible, ungraspable, and, as Judith Williamson has pronounced, 'meaningless' – requires visual representation to make it known, or understood, or manageable. Williamson writes that 'nothing could be more meaningless than a virus. It has no point, no purpose, no plan; it is part of no scheme, carries no inherent significance'.[29] Visual representation can provide a story to a virus that has no natural narrative. This is precisely what John Greyson does with his film *Zero Patience*, the premise of which is the search for a story that will make sense of contagion and death ('tell the story of a virus,' one character sings[30]).

However, New Queer Cinema is less interested in the story – in something that renders the virus coherent – than in something that authentically represents the experience of living with the virus. New Queer Cinema provides another way of making sense out of the virus, that does not placate and does not provide easy answers – that reflects rather than corrects the experience of fragmentation, disruption, unboundaried identity, incoherent narrative, and inconclusive endings. It is a way of providing meaning that does not change or sanitise the experience.

In many ways the 'opposite' of New Queer Cinema is mainstream cinema: mainstream film is generally not challenging, not defiant, and not reflective of the shifts in personal identity wrought by AIDS. *Philadelphia* (Jonathan Demme, 1993) is the obvious example. But another 'opposite' of New Queer Cinema is a kind of 'realist' gay AIDS independent cinema, epitomised by the documentary *Silverlake Life: The View from Here* (Peter Friedman, Tom Joslin, Jane Weiner, and Doug Block, 1993). *Silverlake Life*, contemporaneous with many examples of New Queer Cinema, is not New Queer Cinema, even though it also emerges out of the AIDS crisis and the need for authentic visual representation.

Although the film *Silverlake Life* does not employ deliberate techniques of innovative idiosyncratic filmmaking, but records from life, 'life' can be idiosyncratic indeed. *Silverlake Life* has much in common with grassroots AIDS activist video production, in that it is low budget and records what it sees in real time. As a 'video diary', *Silverlake Life* records the lives and deaths of Tom Joslin and Mark Massi. It is quotidian in the extreme, as we are subjected to holiday visits home to family, hospital visits, shopping mall visits, meals being prepared and eaten, medication swallowed. What makes the film 'dramatic', is that in the course of this dailiness, Tom, and then Mark, deteriorate and die. Peggy Phelan calls the film a 'thanatography, a study in dying'.[31]

There are gaps in the video diary when Tom is too ill or dejected to film. The camera shakes when Mark is crying, filming Tom moments after Tom has died. The chronology is out of order when Tom is referred to at the beginning of the video in the past tense and then depicted alive and narrating. All these techniques might be associated with what I have argued is AIDS-inspired New Queer Cinema. Perhaps this opposition is what best proves the point of what New Queer Cinema is doing, and how it emerges out of the disruptions caused by AIDS. *Silverlake Life* is edited and pasted together: two hours of film from forty hours of footage; we are not, obviously, seeing the events in real time, but nevertheless it is as 'real' as film gets. That this video diary and New Queer Cinema have more in common than either does, for example, with mainstream cinema suggests the success of the project of New Queer Cinema, that the techniques of New Queer Cinema, though perhaps seemingly random or stylised for their own sake, are what manage best to capture the exigency and urgency and dailiness and drama of AIDS and its catastrophic disruptions – disruptions to narrative and to life as we have known them.

NOTES

1 José Arroyo, 'Death, Desire and Identity: The Political Unconscious of "New Queer Cinema"', in Joseph Bristow and Angelia R. Wilson (eds), *Activating Theory: Lesbian, Gay, Bisexual Politics* (London: Lawrence and Wishart, 1993), p. 90.
2 Ibid., p. 92.
3 Ibid., p. 92.
4 Ibid., p. 92.
5 B. Ruby Rich, 'Queer and Present Danger', *Sight and Sound*, March 2000, as visited at http://www.bfi.org.uk/sightandsound/2000_03/queer.html, accessed 23 June 2003.
6 For a discussion of these metaphors see Emily Martin, *Flexible Bodies: The Role of Immunity in American Culture from the Days of Polio to the Age of AIDS* (Boston: Beacon Press, 1994).
7 For a scientific explanation of how HIV acts in the body see, for example, Edward King, Peter Scott, and Peter Aggleton, 'HIV and AIDS', in Peter Aggleton, Kim Rivers, Ian Warwick, and Geoff Whitty (eds), *Learning About AIDS: Scientific and Social Issues*, 2nd edition (London: Churchill Livingstone, 1994), pp. 21–3.
8 See Martin, *Flexible*.
9 See Jackie Stacey, *Teratologies: A Cultural Study of Cancer* (London and New York: Routledge, 1997) for an interrogation of narrative expectations of illness.
10 ACT UP was formed in 1987 when Larry Kramer, addressing a group attending a monthly speaker's series at the New York Lesbian and Gay Community Services Center incited the group to fury and fear.
11 Stanley Aronowitz, 'Against the Liberal State: ACT-UP and the Emergence of Postmodern Politics', in Linda Nicholson and Steven Seidman (eds), *Social Postmodernism: Beyond Identity Politics* (Cambridge: Cambridge University Press, 1995), p. 364.
12 Arroyo, 'Death', p. 92.
13 ACT UP's visual imagery was not limited to the moving image; the demographics of the ACT UP subgroup Gran Fury, which included the now iconic Silence=Death image, featuring a bright pink inverted triangle against a black background, became the key images by which AIDS activism was recognized (see Douglas Crimp with

Adam Rolston, *AIDS Demo/Graphics* (Seattle, WA: Bay Press, 1990) for an account of this image and many others that originated with ACT-UP). However, it was 'guerrilla video' that provides the trail from AIDS and AIDS activism to New Queer Cinema.

14 Alexandra Juhasz, *AIDS TV: Identity, Community, and Alternative Video* (Durham, NC, and London: Duke University Press, 1995), p. 2.

15 Ibid., p. 2.

16 Ibid., p. 2.

17 Ibid., p. 59. See Juhasz for more on the early activist work of Kalin and Greyson.

18 Randy Shilts, *And the Band Played On: Politics, People, and the AIDS Epidemic* (New York: St. Martin's, 1987).

19 Sarah Schulman, 'Fame, Shame, and Kaposi's Sarcoma: New Themes in Lesbian and Gay Film', *My American History: Lesbian and Gay Life During the Reagan/Bush Years* (New York: Routledge, 1994), p. 228.

20 Ibid., p. 228.

21 Gabriele Griffin, *Representations of HIV and AIDS: Visibility Blue/s* (Manchester and New York: Manchester University Press, 2000), p. 14.

22 Juhasz, *AIDS TV*, p. 31.

23 Arroyo, 'Death', p. 90.

24 For example, see the review at www.tvguide.com/movies/database/showmovie.asp?MI=35364, accessed 30 June 2003.

25 One is struck by the monomial titles of much New Queer Cinema: *Lilies*, *Swoon*, *Safe*, *Blue*, even *Poison* and *Grief*. None of them is called *AIDS*, but I think the persistent monomial manifestly suggests, and avoids, that very title.

26 Haynes comments that it is exactly how closely *Safe* approximates but doesn't achieve filmic convention that makes it so disturbing: 'the film creates expectations for a more linear, accessible type of film that it doesn't fulfill', quoted in an interview with Larry Gross in *Filmmaker* 3:4 (Summer 1995) as found at http://home.comcast.net/~rogerdeforest/haynes/text/haynint1.htm, accessed 30 June 2003.

27 Griffin, *Representations*, p. 17.

28 Juhasz, *AIDS TV*, p. 3, emphasis in original.

29 Judith Williamson, 'Every Virus Tells a Story: The Meanings of HIV and AIDS', in Erica Carter and Simon Watney (eds), *Taking Liberties: AIDS and Cultural Politics* (London: Serpent's Tail, 1989), p. 69.

30 See Monica B. Pearl, '*Zero Patience*: AIDS, Music, and Reincarnation Films', in Bill Marshall and Robyn Stilwell (eds), *Musicals: Hollywood and Beyond* (Exeter: Intellect Press, 1999) for more on John Greyson's film.

31 Peggy Phelan, *Mourning Sex: Performing Public Memories* (London and New York: Routledge, 1997), p. 154.

PART II
NEW QUEER FILMMAKING

OVERVIEW

What is New Queer filmmaking, and where is it taking place? What makes a director or a film queer, or 'new queer'? What unites the NQC directors: thematic or visual preoccupations, political provocation, media, budget? How are these films distinct from the gay works of the past (and present)? How is queer distinct from camp? How is it detached from homophobia? How might it maintain its radical edge? The following chapters address the various forms and forums of queer cinema in the wake of NQC. They encompass out queer directors' crossover success, Art cinema's exploitation of queerness, and the alternative frames of avant-garde practitioners.

The first two chapters in this part celebrate the work of two of NQC's key directors: Todd Haynes and Gregg Araki. Both chapters isolate the negotiation of past and present as a key characteristic of their films, and label it as distinctly queer. For Michael DeAngelis in Chapter 4, this negotiation, and its very queerness, are enacted through Haynes' temporal and spatial dislocation of psychic and social realities. For Glyn Davis in Chapter 5, it is the persistence of camp in Araki's work that represents the junction between the past and the present, in terms of gay representation but also in terms of cultural attitudes to sexual identity. For both DeAngelis and Davis, the filmmakers offer uncompromisingly queer fare despite their increasingly popular status. Haynes' work is found to consistently oppose, or queer, mainstream 'straight' narrative by 'making whatever might be familiar or normal about it strange'. Araki, on the other hand, queers gay culture through a politicisation of camp, which is found to be 'serious *and* silly, political *and* irreverent, contemporary *and* historically informed, elitist *and* open'.

While the queerness of the works of Haynes and Araki is presented as unequivocal, and unequivocally 'positive', the same cannot be said of the films that Anneke Smelik focuses upon in Chapter 6. Indeed, the remaining two pieces in this part are more sober in their celebration of NQC, as they leave the exclusive fold of American Independent cinema and look to clearly queer characteristics elsewhere in mid-1990s' film culture (and later). Smelik's study of the art-house fascination with lesbian killer couples in 1994/5 is a meditation on the longevity of the negative image but also on the more radical potentiality of these films. Smelik finds that the films do not just replicate vicious stereotypes but intervene into them. In so doing, she sees the films as affording some profound propositions: that queer is not just what is defiant, that defiance is not always healthy, that queer need not be 'positive' to be welcome. These films, then, 'may not only point to a deconstruction of the stereotype of the murderous lesbian, but more importantly, may also help to understand the confusion and grief involved in processes of queer subjectivity and sexuality'. Like Smelik, Julianne Pidduck in Chapter 7 focuses upon texts that explore and privilege what is painful in queer life. Unfashionable and even uncomfortable, these avant-garde videos 'unravel pat discourses of identity, politics and relationality'. As such, and in contrast to the ever-glossier products of their feature-making peers, Pidduck finds that they are able to sustain queer's radical potential and critique NQC itself.

4. THE CHARACTERISTICS OF NEW QUEER FILMMAKING: CASE STUDY – TODD HAYNES

Michael DeAngelis

In her seminal 1992 article, B. Ruby Rich describes the shared characteristics of the evolving 'New Queer Cinema' in terms of a 'Homo Pomo' style involving 'appropriation and pastiche, irony, as well as a reworking of history with social constructionism very much in mind', and an associated break from the identity politics of an earlier era.[1] By the time of a follow-up piece in 2000, however, Rich reflects upon the decade-old New Queer Cinema as a product of a specific historical and now lost moment – a cinema that has since devolved into 'just another niche market, another product line pitched at one particular type of discerning consumer'.[2] As Rich intimates, the directions of New Queer Cinema are shaped by the ways in which a subculture constructs and imagines its own history – relations of past, present, and future certainly, but also, and more specifically, relations of remembering and forgetting. Many gay and lesbian filmmakers in the early 1990s confronted historical dynamics by attempting to 'rework' them; disconnected from their cinematic antecedents as well as formative social and political movements, the recent films which qualify as New Queer Cinema appear to disavow historical relations altogether. Certainly, New Queer Cinema has changed partly because, from the perception of mainstream, popular film industries, things 'queer' have attained a renewed popularity and qualified public acceptance. If the 'product line' to which Rich refers comprises those films identified as 'queer' solely on the basis of themes and characterisations, the recent 'niche market' is certainly prominent and well established through the subgenre of queer coming-of-age and 'coming out' narratives, with recent examples including *Edge of Seventeen* (David Moreton, 1998), *The Journey of Jared Price* (Dustin Lance Black, 2000), and *The Broken Hearts Club* (Greg Berlanti, 2000). Alongside these more conventional narratives the experiments of filmmakers such as Gregg Araki continue to maintain a closer relation to the more dynamic 'PoMo' style that originally inspired Rich to classify New Queer Cinema as a movement in the first place.

And then there's Todd Haynes, the director who became notorious even before the New Queer Cinema was ever labelled as such, with his now-suppressed version of the Karen Carpenter story enacted by Barbie dolls (*Superstar*, 1987), and the subsequent National Endowment for the Humanities funding controversy surrounding his first full-length feature *Poison* in 1990. At first glance, Haynes might appear to be firmly grounded in the PoMo/social constructionist tradition with a body of films that renounces the realist aesthetic while highlighting pastiche, irony, and the blending of seemingly discordant genres, as well as his open rejection of the notion of an 'essential gay sensibility'.[3] Especially (though not exclusively) in some of his post-*Poison* films, however, Haynes has developed narrative strategies that steer New Queer Cinema towards a version of social constructionism that strives to express something integral to a uniquely queer perspective on human experience. In a 1993 interview with Justin Wyatt, Haynes explains that:

> I have a lot of frustration with the insistence on content when people are talking about homosexuality. People define gay cinema solely by content: if there are gay characters in it, it's a gay film. It fits into the gay sensibility, we got it, it's gay. It's such a failure of the imagination, let alone the ability to look beyond content. I think that's really simplistic. Heterosexuality to me is a structure as much as it is a content. It is an imposed structure that goes along with the patriarchal, dominant structure that constrains and defines society. If homosexuality is the opposite or the counter-sexual activity to that, then what kind of a structure would it be?[4]

What would it be? Vehemently rejecting any notion of essence in identity, Haynes' discoveries in the exploration of this question comprise his unique contributions to the New Queer Cinema. Using a variety of cinematic forms, Haynes 'queers' heterosexual, mainstream narrative cinema by making whatever might be familiar or normal about it strange, and in the process hypothesising alternatives that disrupt its integrity and ideological cohesiveness. He accomplishes this by arranging an intricate juxtaposition and dialectic of 'realities' and restructuring the spatial and temporal relations that order them. What emerges from this dialectic is the imagination of new times and spaces that exist apart from, and in opposition to, dominant, patriarchal culture.

The resonances of Haynes' dialectic extend, however, far beyond this ideological intervention, ultimately engaging in a dynamic historical confrontation that extends Rich's original prescription for an oppositional New Queer Cinema. This confrontation situates gay culture within a set of historical relations that includes the social, personal, and psychological, and that also emphasises gay culture's political responsibilities of remembering its own past, as well as the associated implications of forgetting and disavowing. The vehicle of this dialectic 'imagining' is fantasy, and Haynes engages his central male protagonists in fantasy scenarios that succeed in both momentarily stabilising time and ultimately re-ordering relationships between past, present and future. The result of Haynes' use of fantasy and his interrogation of history is a politically engaged version of New Queer Cinema whose power and momentum stem from relationships of identification and desire, the dynamics of which implicate protagonists and viewers alike. Through a close examination of formal and representational matters affecting the historical relationship between past and present 'realities' in two films steeped in networks of history and heavily invested in the workings of fantasy – the short video narrative *Dottie Gets Spanked* (1993) and his feature *Velvet Goldmine* (1998) – I will illuminate the workings of Haynes' queer aesthetic as well as the sexual and political confrontations that it enables.

Although it is anything but didactic, the 27-minute *Dottie Gets Spanked* could readily serve as a textbook illustration of the workings of identification in Freudian psychoanalysis; indeed, the first of the two fantasy sequences is conspicuously interrupted with the intertitle 'A Child Is Being Beaten', referring to the case study of the same name that Freud himself used to describe identification within the fantasy network.[5] The film begins by revealing the daily, suburban, early 1960s' life of eight-year-old Stevie (Evan Bonifant) as sharply divided between two realities. The first to be introduced is his close relationship with Dottie Frank (Julie Halston), the protagonist of a *Lucy-Show*-like sitcom who inspires Stevie to produce vibrant artistic sketches as he sits silent and transfixed before the television screen; as a contest winner later in the film, Steve earns the honour of visiting the set of the show, meeting the actress who inspires him, and witnessing the rehearsal of an episode. The second reality comprises Stevie's not-so-inspiring, wholly isolated, routinised, extra-Dottie existence, made bearable only by a doting mother (Harriet Harris) who intervenes when her husband (Robert Pall), glued to the TV screen watching a football game, rudely dismisses Stevie's fandom. Stevie's life outside the home extends the domestic tensions, as he yearns to participate in his female schoolmates' heated conversations about Dottie, instead earning only their ridicule since, like Stevie's father, they find his devotion to the screen star a pursuit unsuitable for a male ('My sister says you're a feminino', a younger girl jeers).

This second daily reality positions Stevie as a rather helpless subject, at the mercy of divisive gender politics that monitor his identity within and outside the home. His relationship with the Dottie character initially seems to provide momentary release from social restrictions, as well as a creative outlet in which to interpret experience on his own terms, especially through the illustrated narrative that Stevie prepares as a gift for Dottie in anticipation of their meeting. Soon enough, however, his drawings belie this 'escapist' function when the TV taping that Stevie witnesses begins to replay the gender relations that surround the young boy in his everyday life: as punishment for a lie told to her husband (Adam Arkin), Dottie is forced to endure a carefully staged, brutal spanking which Stevie struggles furiously to recapture in a vivid colour drawing.

The inseparability of the two realities is driven home by Stevie's two dream-nightmares, both of which centre upon beating and the exercise of power. In waking life, Stevie maintains the role of observer and acted-upon subject at home and with Dottie Frank, but the polymorphously perverse nightmares compel the boy to move among a number of positions in relationships of identification. In the first dream, Stevie initially assumes the role of a ruthless king who humiliates Dottie in the same ways that her husband does on the TV show. The scene then shifts to a male adult beating a male child who appears to be Stevie (the lighting conditions and camera distance obscure the child's identity). The beaten child is transformed into a young girl who exists in Stevie's daily reality as a schoolmate who ignores him, and who undergoes frequent spankings at her father's hand. With this transformation, Stevie switches to the role of observer, cheering on her beating as he looks on smiling. Occurring after Stevie's visit to the Dottie set, the second nightmare finds King Stevie himself punished for the murder of a woman, and sentenced to be beaten by 'the strongest man in the kingdom'; with a forceful hand raised to inflict the punishment, the aggressor's face becomes a mustachioed Dottie's. As the final beating is carried out, the scene juxtaposes all of the positions and participants from the first nightmare, to which confusion is added the beating of another son by his father – a beating that Stevie and the schoolgirls witnessed earlier that day in the playground. With the frenzy of this accelerated and out-of-control spanking, a startled Stevie soon awakens in a panic, meticulously folds up his latest drawing of Dottie, secures the artwork in Reynolds Wrap, and buries it under a rock in his backyard.

Do Stevie's fantasies constitute an unconscious attempt to liberate himself from oppressive social restrictions, or are they instead a symptom of something inherently 'wrong' with the young boy? Psychoanalytic frameworks provide a useful starting point here. While Freud asserts that dreams and fantasies constitute a desire for the fulfilment of a wish, Elizabeth Cowie explains that representation in fantasy is altered and transformed by defensive mechanisms.[6] Freud's essay 'A Child Is Being Beaten' concerns a fantasy of the child's attempt to seduce his own father, and the child's movement among various positions of identification is less an act of liberation than a result of repressive processes that guard the child from bringing the wish to the surface.

This fantasy is also a primal fantasy, an investigation requiring a movement backward in time to help the boy in his search for answers about his own origin as a subject in the world. According to Freudian logic, Stevie's nightmare fantasies constitute an investigation of the past – in this case, a psychic past – that informs the way he lives each moment of his life in the present. Thinking about the protagonist's conflict as an (ultimately, and perhaps necessarily, failed) attempt to negotiate the boundaries between 'then' and 'now' brings us closer to an understanding of Haynes' narrative strategies in the structuring of queer sexual desire. Working from concepts originally theorised by Laplanche and Pontalis, Elisabeth Cowie explains that fantasy 'involves . . . not the achievement of desired objects, but the arranging of, a setting out of, desire; a veritable mise en scène of desire'.[7] Stevie's own story comprises a series of settings and scenes, from those staged on the set of a television show, to those played out in his uneasy dreams. His burial of the product of his emotions and fantasies once and for all demonstrates a rather naïve belief that these scenes could ever remain separate in the first place, and an equally naïve (as it could only be, for a young boy) conviction that the scenes could be ordered such that fantasies would ever become the exclusive realm of the 'past'. The uneasy juxtaposition of past and present enacted by both Stevie's story and the film itself comments upon the inescapability of desire (the inevitable return of the repressed) and the inability to do anything else but to continue to repress it, in a culture that offers its subjects no other options. Considering how fantasy is kept alive throughout most of *Dottie Gets Spanked*, the final burial quite self-consciously plays like a conclusion imposed upon the narrative by the demands of the normative version of sexuality circulated at the time the story takes place. Or is it Stevie who gets the last laugh, and his formal burial of the artwork only a means of keeping desire 'safe' for some unrevealed future moment?

A 'gay' film less in its overt representation of homosexuality than in what its narrative both actively and self-consciously represses, *Dottie Gets Spanked* speaks of a desire that is not, or not yet, accessible to its central protagonist. It articulates a structure of repression imposed upon its subject because of his own youth and the constraints of a society that demands that deviant youngsters grow out of their bad habits and assimilate with heterosexual normalcy. Whether or not Stevie will achieve this desired result is never revealed, but for journalist Arthur Stuart (Christian Bale), the central protagonist of *Velvet Goldmine*, the matter of assimilation is self-admittedly a given as the narrative begins in present-day 1984 New York. After his superiors at the *Herald* commission Arthur to investigate what happened to Brian Slade (Jonathan Rhys-Meyers), a 1970s' glam rocker who faked his own assassination in a failed publicity ploy, Arthur reflects in voiceover narrative that 'suddenly I was being paid to remember all the things that money, future, and the serious life made so certain I'd forget'. *Velvet Goldmine* continues and responds to Stevie's final act in *Dottie Gets Spanked*, extending Haynes' queer version of everyday life by articulating the ultimate effects of any attempt at 'burying the past' of fantasy and desire. As a narrative much more overtly concerned with the workings of both the personal/psychic and social/political history, *Velvet Goldmine* also situates the past as a field of resistance that induces an inevitable confrontation with present realities, providing an opportunity for Haynes to 'queer' the present by reconstituting the notion of 'reality' itself through multiple juxtapositions of histories remembered, forgotten, and repressed.

The film announces its temporal confrontation of repression in the first words of its voiceover narrative, juxtaposed against a visual field of twinkling stars: 'Histories, like ancient ruins, are the fictions of empires, while everything forgotten hangs in dark dreams of the past, ever threatening to return'. Initiating a historical trace spanning over 130 years, the artifact that survives the ruins of time is a jewel pinned to the blanket of the newborn and abandoned Oscar Wilde, who is discovered on the doorstep of a family in the 1850s on a dark, Dublin street. Over the course of the narrative, the jewel is recovered from a gutter in the 1950s by the soon-to-be glam rocker Jack Fairy (Osheen Jones) after he is beaten by schoolmates, stolen by Brian Slade twenty years later after the men's New Year's Eve sexual encounter, and offered to Brian's lover Kurt Wilde (Ewan McGregor) as a gift, before it is ultimately coughed up from Arthur Stuart's throat during his final meeting with Kurt in a tavern, at which time Kurt reveals the legend of the jewel's origin. Against the progression of this historical narrative of the survival of a form of sexual rebellion and resistance, are counterposed active processes of disavowal, forgetting, and 'burial' by both investigative subject and object. The reasons motivating the feigned, onstage assassination of Brian (and his adopted onstage persona, Maxwell Demon) are never explained, though the narrative does suggest connections between the act and Brian and Kurt's recent break-up. It also offers an indirect comparison to the fate of Dorian Gray (quoted and referenced in the first part of the film), who elected an aging self-portrait over an aging body; in *Velvet Goldmine*, however, the 'deceased' rock star himself ages into the portrait of the more famous yet less glamorous persona of another musical performer, Tommy Stone, who has effectively disguised the identity and sexual ambiguity of his former incarnation as Brian/Maxwell until Arthur discovers the secret.

While Haynes does not assign clear motives and cause/effect relationships in human experience, Arthur's own conflict with the past is more fully elaborated than Brian's, because of the narrative's investment in Arthur as the film's primary perspective and central protagonist.[8] The investigation of another's disappearance sets the stage for Arthur's self-examination, initially occurring not out of his innate desire to know, but specifically because he has been professionally commissioned to do so. Arthur is the ideal vehicle for the type of remembering that this search requires: even before he is given his press assignment – and before the narrative has situated the 1970s as 'the past' – the film reveals scenes of his teenage days as a glam fan, running through the streets of Manchester with his friends, one of whom accidently bumps into Jack Fairy (played as an adult by Micko Westmoreland). Arthur is also 'present' at the concert where Brian is 'assassinated', and an eyewitness to a later interaction between Brian's by-then-ex-wife Mandy (Toni Colette) and Kurt Wilde after a 'Death of Glitter' concert.

Unlike Brian, who has summarily excluded his 1970s' glam-rocker incarnation, Arthur acknowledges the source of his conflict between past and present, and between remembering and forgetting, quite early in the film. After receiving his investigative charge, he admits in voiceover that 'clearly, there was something, something from the past, spooking me back. I didn't realise at the time that it was you'. Instead of providing any sort of explanation, however, his admission sets forth a deeper temporal paradox. Although the narrative never specifically identifies the 'you', Arthur appears to be referring to Kurt Wilde, foreshadowing the interview with Kurt in the tavern at the end of the film – a meeting intercut with scenes of the two men before, during, and after a sexual encounter on a rooftop in the 'past' of the 1970s. The voiceover of the early scene is thus presented at a double remove from the incident(s) to which it refers, from the perspective of the most recent version of Arthur, reflecting back to the start of his journalistic search, to incidents occurring some ten years earlier.

The voiceover also establishes a plot trajectory that is both motivated and undermined by repressive processes. According to Haynes, the film 'had to be about a lost time from the start, about something repressed – and great fears had risen up around whatever this was, which had changed completely and buried it. That's why for Arthur it's an ambivalent search back'.[9] His ambivalence clearly does not stem from any perfect or idealised present moment in Arthur's life that memories of the past might disrupt; the search engages him in a subjectively rendered re-vision of experience in space and time, such that the familiar present is rendered queer and strange. Arthur's version of the 1984 New York that he inhabits is rather gruesome, sterile, and alienating: sunless exteriors; cold, dark and colorless spaces stripped of ornament; crowds of workers with blank and worn-out expressions; muffled voices over loudspeakers announcing the clichéd platform of an unseen President Reynolds, who urges citizens to join the 'Committee to Prosper'. Arthur is depicted in work settings where he remains apart from his co-workers; more often, he is entirely alone, the narrative providing neither an indication of social ties or connections, nor any domestic spaces or situations that are not related to his work.

In sharp contrast, the spaces of Arthur's memories of 1970s in the streets and clubs of Manchester are immersed in light, colour, ambient movement, and the crisp and seductive sounds of glam rock music, signalling the sexual awakenings of a past that is more real to him than the present. The pleasant memories are, however, those confined to Arthur's life outside of the domestic sphere, within which he is depicted as alienated from his parents on the rare occasions when they happen to inhabit the same space. At home, Arthur finds respite only when he retires to his room filled with posters of rock stars, perusing album covers and music magazines with the same devoted attention that Stevie invests in Dottie. In fact, the similarities between the fans of the two films are most prominent when the males inhabit the only tentatively private spaces of their respective bedrooms. As Stevie draws his latest sketch of the spanking he witnessed on the TV set, his father enters the room unannounced, insisting that an embarrassed Stevie show him the portrait. Arthur's confrontation with his parents is more traumatic: as the teenager masturbates over a magazine picture of Brian and Kurt kissing, both of his parents barge into his room, his father decrying the boy's actions as disgraceful while Arthur retreats in shame from their view.

The colours, sounds, and rhythms of the glam rock scene that Arthur later embraces (at first through his fandom and subsequently by sexual encounters with two rock performers) are thus chronologically situated between two more uninviting realities – the bleakness of the journalist's life in the present, and the memories of his equally constraining upbringing decades earlier. Accordingly, for Arthur, the glam scene signals a most uneasy intersection of time trajectories, initiating both a willing movement forward and a reluctant movement backward. If the planned death of Brian/Maxwell becomes the impetus for investigating what appears to be the much more gradual and less conspicuous death of Arthur's past life, the identity of the 'you' that spooks Arthur back is not only Kurt Wilde, but also a 'self' that demands to be reclaimed – a self once but no longer elated by its own identifications and desires. No wonder, then, that Arthur is so bitter when his ultimate revelation of Brian's new 'Tommy Stone' incarnation is almost stifled by what appears to be an elaborate, political hush manoeuvre, and a premature curtailment of his commissioned investigation; his conviction to 'out' Brian as Tommy has become the result of a rigorous struggle with his own demons.

If the glam rock past is the setting upon which repressive operations converge in the story of *Velvet Goldmine*, the workings of identification and desire in fantasy effect a parallel convergence in the space of queer desire, at the level of the film's structure. Through the contrast between the visual splendour of the glam rock scenes and the starkness of both present and childhood realities, the film appears to offer no present at all except for its immersion in the continuous present of fantasy. While Stevie's nightmare fantasies in *Dottie Gets Spanked* ultimately signal a most frightening relinquishing of control of his own repressive operations – as well as his own compulsion to bury his desires – the fantasies of *Velvet Goldmine* are structured as scenes of a much more carefully orchestrated and idealised desire, rendered so that it can be remembered as perfect, unchangeable, and insusceptible to the workings of time.

As *Dottie Gets Spanked* illustrates, fantasy scenarios carry and rework the residues of daily realities that the fantasy subject has experienced, and the stagings and scenes of any individual fantasy clearly require a subject who imagines and who orchestrates. Part of the queer pleasure that *Velvet Goldmine* offers is in the plethora of fantasy perspectives that the film intermingles in scenes of identification and desire. As does its structural model *Citizen Kane, Velvet Goldmine* 'hands off' its narration to other characters as the film progresses: both Brian's first agent Cecil (Michael Feast) and Mandy Slade assume the role of central storyteller at different points in the film. Unlike its predecessor, however, the investigator in Haynes' film is also a witness to several of the scenes narrated by these other storytellers (even, at some points, encountering the narrators themselves), resulting in an instability and fluidity in the act of remembering, even though the extended flashback to the 1970s is rendered chronologically. In the same way that this investigative journalist motivates the progression of the narrative from the time that his present-day character is introduced, Arthur Stuart also functions as the orchestrator of fantasy – what induces pleasure in the film emerges from his own memories of past events that situate him as an emerging queer subject steeped in his own identifications and desires, even when these memories are triggered by the narration of others. Arthur's function within the narrative and fantasy of the film parallels the 'lesson' from Oscar Wilde that Arthur's schoolteacher directly addresses to Arthur in an early scene:

> There were times when it appeared to Dorian Gray that the whole of history was merely a record of his own life – not as he had lived it in acts and circumstance, but as his imagination had created it for him, as it had been in his brain, and in his passions. He felt that he'd known them all, those strange, terrible figures that had passed along the stage of life, and made sin so marvelous and evil so full of subtlety. It seemed that in some mysterious way, their lives had been his own.

Echoing and reiterating the responsibilities of resuscitating history that B. Ruby Rich identifies as integral to the vitality of a New Queer Cinema, the 'lesson' that Arthur is about to learn through his investigation is that the history of an era that the journalist is commissioned to investigate objectively is also his own history, and one which cannot be relegated to the past – precisely the lesson that Stevie is denied the opportunity to learn in *Dottie Gets Spanked*. The fact that fantasy provides the vehicle by which the past is made 'real' to the investigative subject helps us to come to terms with the ways in which the fantasy scene – real and imagined – becomes the only setting of reality for Arthur.

'The genealogy of desire is always a history of the subject's identifications', Leo Bersani proposes, and the untroubled move from identification to desire is inherent in the fantasy scenarios that Arthur constructs and orchestrates, evidencing his self-constitution as a queer subject in these very 'real' scenes of his own historical past.[10] This movement is apparent in Arthur's masturbation scene, part of an elaborately orchestrated segment that begins with press photographers capturing a kiss between Brian and Kurt – a kiss then reproduced in the pages of a newspaper that Arthur peruses in his bedroom. Brian and Kurt's onstage performance of Brian Eno's 'Baby's on Fire' provides the musical orchestration, as extreme close-ups of Arthur are intercut with shots of the two stage performers enacting a slow, graceful, and balletic seduction scene – one which eventually finds Brian on his knees, licking the strings of Kurt's electric guitar in erotic frenzy. As tongue touches wire, the scene shifts to Arthur turning the newspaper pages to witness a photo of the encounter. The music bridges to a third scene, of an orgy taking place after the night's performance, as Kurt and Brian reciprocate beckoning glances before they surreptitiously retreat to a private room. Before Arthur can bring himself to a climax, the fantasy scenario is disrupted, and the music is softened as his parents barge into the room. 'Stand up!' the father exclaims, but as the terrified and ashamed Arthur rises to view his image in a mirror, the scene shifts to Brian himself standing up in the orgy room, moving away to meet Kurt. This vivid remembering of the imaginations of fantasy is at the same time both firmly grounded in space and time (a specific room, a specific moment in Arthur's past), and entirely liberated from spatial or temporal groundings: the three separate spaces intercut in the sequence build upon and extend one another, with Brian continuing movements initiated by Arthur, and the 'real' space of both the kiss and the musical fellatio magically transported via print media to the fantasy space that Arthur imagines at home. The musical continuity that unites the three spaces also effects a sense of simultaneous action and 'continuous present', emphasised by the slow pace of action and movement in each of the spaces.[11]

Here and elsewhere, however, the fantasies of the film – whether comprising past memories or wholly imagined scenes – are enacted as settings for the playing out of desire rather than scenes in which desire itself yields to climax or ultimate fulfilment. The emphasis upon settings adds to the feeling that fantasy suspends time in the film. From the frozen images of Brian constructed for media circulation, to the stagings of musical numbers with either real or implied audiences, to the more private stagings of sexual attractions now lost or past, the film presents desire as an intersection of knowing glances, an immanent possibility of queer desire always in the process of being fulfilled. 'Come closer', a voice on a rooftop beckons, 'Don't be frightened'. As Arthur ultimately yields to the signals sent by Kurt, this man 'who ended my life . . . in waves', the scene plays out as a ballet of gradual approaching bodies, a hand caressing the flesh of another, all magically lit by a shooting star and spaceship above, as the camera slowly retreats from the connected couple, a snowy shower of stars obscuring them from view.

The erotic charge of these hypnotically orchestrated scenarios appears to have been lost on several of the film's critics. 'Haynes doesn't want to show us the dirty parts, that ecstasy, excess, and eroticism have no place in his portrayals of gay sexuality', Christopher Kelly suggests, adding that 'the emotions and experiences [the film] relates are hardly ones that connect to real gay people'.[12] Craig Seligman argues that in the second half of the film the love scenes aren't charged, and the characters are underdeveloped: 'The sex feels like a gay artist's statement: obligatory and earnest'.[13] Such criticisms, however, arise from the presumption that eroticism is limited to those art-works that engage a realist aesthetic – a presumption that Todd Haynes' reliance upon fantasy networks challenges at every juncture. Furthermore, the fact that Haynes' films are not as overtly graphic in their representation of the sexual act as several other films of the New Queer Cinema does not make him any less integral a contributor to this cinema's vitality; in fact, the ability to move beyond such matters as gay sexual representation and content enables Haynes to hypothesise the structure of queer desire more dynamically. Haynes' method fuses sexuality and politics, through the articulation of fantasy scenarios that arrange confrontations between past and present at the levels of the personal, sexual, and social. In the process, he politicises the human tendency to forget, as well as the inability of the sexual subject to release himself from the history of his own identifications and desires. The lessons he offers are vital not only to individual queer subjects struggling to engage the dynamics of their own sexual histories, but also to the history of a New Queer Cinema that, as B. Ruby Rich has intimated, has lost touch with its historical antecedents in a troublesome case of short-term memory.

NOTES

1 B. Ruby Rich, 'New Queer Cinema', *Sight and Sound*, 2:5 (September 1992): 32, reprinted in this book.
2 B. Ruby Rich, 'Queer and Present Danger', *Sight and Sound*, 10:3 (March 2000): 24.
3 Justin Wyatt, 'Cinematic/Sexual Transgression: An Interview with Todd Haynes', *Film Quarterly*, 46 (Spring 1993): 7.
4 Ibid., p. 8.
5 Sigmund Freud, 'A Child Is Being Beaten: A Contribution to the Study of the Origins of the Perversions', in James Strachey (trans.), *The Complete Psychological Works of Sigmund Freud*, Vol. 17 (London: The Hogarth Press, 1955). For a discussion of the definition of identification and its relation to object choice, see Sigmund Freud, 'Group Psychology and the Analysis of the Ego', in James Strachey (trans.), *The Complete Psychological Works of Sigmund Freud*, Vol. 18 (London: The Hogarth Press, 1955), p. 106.
6 See the chapter 'Fantasia', in Elisabeth Cowie, *Representing the Woman* (Minneapolis: University of Minnesota Press, 1997), pp. 123–65.
7 Ibid., p. 133.
8 In an insightful discussion of causality in Haynes' film *Safe* (1995), Roddey Reid suggests that 'the film queers and goes against the grain of what could be called "a politics of epistemology and visibility"' in that the film resists any clear explanation of the origins of its central protagonist's environmentally-related illness. See 'UnSafe at Any Distance: Todd Haynes' Visual Culture of Health and Risk', *Film Quarterly*, 51:3 (Spring 1998): 32–44.

9 Nick James, 'American Voyeur', *Sight and Sound*, 8:9 (September 1998): 8.
10 Leo Bersani, *Homos* (Cambridge, MA: Harvard University Press, 1995), p. 63.
11 In 'Fantasia', Elisabeth Cowie explains, 'The pleasure [in fantasy] is in how to *bring about* the consummation, is in the happening and continuing to happen; is how it will come about, and not in the moment of *having happened*, when it will fall back into loss, the past' (emphasis in the original). See *Representing the Woman*, p. 133.
12 Christopher Kelly, 'The Unbearable Lightness of Gay Movies', *Film Comment*, 35:2 (March–April 1999): 20.
13 Craig Seligman, 'All That Glitters', *Artforum International*, 37:2 (October 1998): 104.

5. CAMP AND QUEER AND THE NEW QUEER DIRECTOR: CASE STUDY – GREGG ARAKI

Glyn Davis

The first three New Queer Cinema films that I saw at the cinema in the early 1990s – Jarman's *Edward II*, Haynes' *Poison* (both 1991), and Kalin's *Swoon* (1992) – filled me with dread and disappointment. All three seemed relentlessly miserable, dry and pretentious. In the light of these viewings, one particular comment made by B. Ruby Rich about the New Queer Cinema movies – 'above all, they're full of pleasure' – just didn't make sense.[1] *What* pleasure? At that time, I'd already seen enough grim movies about homosexuals to know that, according to filmmakers, being gay is a pretty miserable state of affairs. Did we really need a bunch of 'queer' directors to tell us the same?

Of course, repeated viewings of the named trio of films enabled my recognition of their complexity and intelligence. More importantly, watching a much broader range of New Queer Cinema films allowed me to admit that Rich was correct: many of the titles identified as part of this movement were irreverent, parodic, silly, and (yes, dammit) fun. For me, what was interesting and notable about these films was that, very often, the humour and pleasure in them manifested itself through campness. The campness in these films was not solely about comedy; although the two are intimately connected, camp appears in the work of the New Queer Cinema directors in a more multifarious form. And yet discussions of New Queer Cinema rarely seem to mention camp. The main purpose of this chapter, then, is to begin to fill in this gap by providing an exploration of the status and importance of campness, in its broadest sense, within the New Queer Cinema corpus. A secondary (and clearly connected) aim is to examine the ways in which the forms and manifestations of camp have altered in recent years.

Rich herself recognised campness as a constituent component of these films: commenting on several videos by dyke directors – including *The Meeting of Two Queens* (Barriga, 1991) and *Dry Kisses Only* (Brooke and Cottis, 1990) – she said that 'their style is unlike almost anything that's come before. I would call it lesbian camp'.[2] However, as I have suggested, the presence of campness in New Queer Cinema films is much more widespread than this statement would seem to imply. It's there, rather obviously, in *Grief* (Glatzer, 1993), *Zero Patience* (Greyson, 1993), *Stonewall* (Finch, 1995), *Hedwig and the Angry Inch* (Mitchell, 2001), and others. But it also plays a key role in the movies of Bruce LaBruce (*Super 8½*, 1994; *Hustler White*, 1996), Todd Haynes (*Superstar: The Karen Carpenter Story*, 1987; *Velvet Goldmine*, 1998), and the director whose films this chapter will focus on, Gregg Araki (*The Living End*, 1992; *Totally Fucked Up*, 1994; *The Doom Generation*, 1995; *Nowhere*, 1997).[3] The presence of campness in these New Queer Cinema films (and others not listed), and the form that campness takes, tie them into a historical lineage of lesbian and gay independent filmmaking that stretches back at least as far as the 1940s. Juan Suárez, Richard Dyer, and Philip Core, among others, have all identified campness as a significant component of the work of notable 'underground' American gay filmmakers of earlier decades (Jack Smith, Andy Warhol, Kenneth Anger);[4] it is also prevalent in the films of such directors as Paul Morrissey and John Waters. The campness of the New Queer Cinema films not only perpetuates this tradition, but also, as we shall see, makes witty, parodic references and pays homage to its key films and directors.

But what *is* camp? Up to this point, I confess I have been assuming a certain level of knowledge and cultural awareness in this chapter's putative readers; however, for the benefit of those at the back, it is worth pausing here to examine in some detail exactly what camp *is*, and what it is *not*. It is almost *de rigueur* in academic accounts of camp to point out that it is a difficult concept to define. Susan Sontag's famous paper on camp – the first to take a serious, critical approach to the subject – argues on its first page that 'a sensibility . . . is one of the hardest things to talk about', and that because camp is 'something of a private code', 'to talk about camp is . . . to betray it'.[5] Other authors also have problems. Andy Medhurst, for instance, has stated that camp is 'a great big pink butterfly that just won't be pinned down'; 'trying to define camp', he writes, 'is like attempting to sit in the corner of a circular room'. The problem, he argues, 'is that [camp] is primarily an experiential rather than an analytical discourse. Camp is a set of attitudes, a gallery of snapshots, an inventory of postures . . . a shop-full of frocks'.[6] Despite the elusive nature of camp, Medhurst has claimed, in a different essay, that 'nonetheless, most of us know it when we see, hear, feel or do it'.[7]

The way in which some theorists manage to get around clearly defining camp is to supplement a range of elusive hints, suggestions and allusions with a list of items that they perceive as being outstanding examples of camp. (Indeed, as Medhurst writes, 'a banal attempt to define the meaning of camp might well start with "like the sixties' *Batman* series" '[8]). This listing is true of, among others, Jack Babuscio, Richard Dyer, Andy Medhurst, and the pantomime dame of the camp spectacular, Susan Sontag.[9] An extreme example is Philip Core's book on camp, which supplements an A to Z 'Who's Who and What's What of camp'[10] with an additional alphabetical list of 'camp to like', 'about which there is nothing to be said'.[11] Not to be outdone, my own list would include such items as: the photographs of Pierre et Giles; early Russ Meyer films; a number of British docusoaps, including *The Cruise* and *Airport*; the pop singles (and associated videos) of Kylie Minogue, Jennifer 'J-Lo' Lopez, and O-Town; James Cameron's *Titanic*; Channel 5; and everything ever touched by John Waters.[12]

Perhaps this all seems rather abstruse and ineffable; if so, here are more concrete definitions. Richard Dyer claims that there are 'two different interpretations' of camp. The first 'is a distinctive way of behaving and of relating to each other that [gay men] have evolved'. The second 'is a certain taste in art and entertainment, a certain sensibility'.[13] And that sensibility 'is a way of prising the form of something away from its content, of revelling in the style while dismissing the content as trivial'.[14] Bringing these two interpretations together, Andy Medhurst states that 'camp is not an entity but a relationship – a relationship between queens and their circumstances'.[15] In its association with a specific subcultural group – gay men – campness is usually seen as politically charged. Pre-Stonewall, queeny behaviour was an overt, defiant statement of one's identity; that queens were (allegedly) centrally involved in the Stonewall riots solidified the link between campness and subcultural politics. For many, campness still retains a political edge; as Medhurst has claimed, camp 'answers heterosexual disapproval [of queerness] through a strategy of defensive offensiveness . . . incarnating the homophobe's worst fears, confirming that not only do queers dare to exist but they actively flaunt and luxuriate in their queerness'.[16] However, as we will see shortly, others have contested this view.

The list of camp items I provided above is comprised almost wholly of contemporary examples. Mainly, they are drawn from mainstream (or mass) culture, rather than any form of independent production; and, although some of the items on the list have associations with gay culture (Kylie Minogue, Pierre et Giles, John Waters), others do not. This list, then, raises important questions that, hopefully, this chapter will succeed in answering. First, are there different types of camp manifest in 'mainstream' and 'independent' culture? For instance, is New Queer Cinema's campness distinct from that of Hollywood movies? And, second, are the items camp because they were intentionally produced to be so, or is it rather that they can be 'read' or 'consumed' in such a way? Or, to put it another way, is New Queer Cinema's campness 'really there'?

Given the diversity of (fairly recent) examples of camp goodies on my list, it is perhaps somewhat surprising that, in the past twenty years or so, a large number of authors have attempted to sound the death knell of camp. Specifically, it is the gay use of camp that they have tried to inter. Their reasons are many and various, but do not bear up to too much close scrutiny, partly because other authors, including Pamela Robertson and Alexander Doty, have argued exactly the opposite: that is, that the importance to, and position in, gay culture of campness have in recent years, been 'revitalized' and 'reinforced'.[17] However, some of the comments made by the pallbearers for gay camp raise topics of debate which can be used to highlight important points about New Queer Cinema's uses of campness, and thus are worth examining.

For several critics, camp has become too widespread, too socially and culturally prevalent, to have any effect or impact any longer: its political purpose and charge have been eroded. Thus, Andrew Britton states:

> camp is a house-trained version of the aristocratic, anarchistic ethic of transgression, a breach of decorum which no longer even shocks . . . What was once an affront has now become part of life's rich pageant. The threat has been defused.[18]

Similarly, Fran Liebowitz has claimed that the contemporary mainstreaming of camp has turned it into a 'smugness with no edges'.[19] And there is an echo of the same sentiment in Mark Simpson's comment that 'the days of speaking of camp as the "gay sensibility" are over forever'.[20] Certainly, camp is no longer solely a subcultural discourse. Since the 1960s, mainstream awareness of camp has grown and its presence has spread. However, this has tended to separate camp from its connection with gay culture (and, arguably, depoliticised it). Indeed, any account of camp's form and status since the 1960s needs to take into account the distinction between the gay use of camp, and the general widespread cultural dissemination of campness.

In recent years (in fact, since the appearance of 'queer' culture in the late 1980s, of which New Queer Cinema is a part), this segregation has been further complicated by the appearance of a specifically 'queer' form of camp. Chuck Kleinhans has written that '[o]ur understanding of Camp changes with the evolving history of gay subculture. The conditions and contexts for Camp differ in pre-Stonewall, post-Stonewall, post-AIDS, and contemporary Queer moments'.[21] It would seem that one part of the latter 'moment' is the emergence of 'queer camp'. Theorists who argue for a division between 'gay camp' and 'queer camp' maintain that the campness used by queer artists/filmmakers is qualitatively different to 'gay camp'; it would seem that 'gay camp' has become a system of signifiers that almost anyone can now use or mimic, including mercenary profit-oriented straight people. That is, whereas a division would formerly have been erected between 'gay' and 'straight' uses of camp, with gay men claiming that only the former had true meaning and purpose, in recent years this division has been mapped onto the separation of 'queer camp' and 'gay camp', now that gay camp has become prevalent in mainstream culture (and thus somewhat co-opted).[22]

Certainly, this would seem to be the crux of Honey Glass's argument about queer camp:

> Compare *The Adventures of Priscilla Queen of the Desert* (1994) and *To Wong Foo Thanks For Everything, Julie Newmar* (1995). The first uses camp to speak from a queer perspective to a queer audience; the second, Hollywood co-opting a sensibility and getting it wrong, merely aims to raise a laugh.[23]

'Queer camp', then, it would seem, is used by queers to speak to other queers, and although it may occasionally be humorous, is never 'merely' funny; such are the subtle intricacies of queer camp that it cannot be used by anyone from 'outside'. At the heart of this distinction, then, is the need to maintain alterity, to sustain the cohesion of the 'subculture', and to continue to assert camp's political status.[24] As Pamela Robertson argues, 'queer camp emphasizes . . . camp's ability to signal difference and alienation from the dominant. Here . . . queer camp recodes the subculture's own history to reconceive itself as adversarial'.[25]

This formulation neatly describes the form of New Queer Cinema's campness. Queer culture and politics, from the mid/late 1980s onwards, have often espoused a policy of non-assimilationism. Gay rights activists tried throughout the 1970s and 1980s to find (or earn) a place in mainstream life, making slow progress. In contrast, many self-styled queers saw this struggle as futile, and as antipathetic to the 'nature' of homosexuality; thus, they asserted their difference and separateness. As Brian McNair has put it, '[s]ome queers greeted growing acceptance of homosexuality by the straight world as a form of betrayal or collaboration, preferring to maintain a stance of rejectionism and anger'.[26] As part of queer culture, New Queer Cinema is thus wilfully 'different' and independent (and thus somewhat elitist) in form, address and production methods. And in being so, it is, as noted earlier, drawing on historical precedents provided by gay underground filmmakers, from Warhol to Waters, elements of whose films (including camp) New Queer Cinema reworks and revives. The films of these earlier directors – and the directors themselves – are seen as exemplary of what queerness's 'transgression', difference and alterity are all about.[27] Thus New Queer Cinema pays homage to their innovation, bloody-mindedness, and historical importance; yet it is also 'New' in its reflection of contemporary gay life and concerns.[28]

However, to argue that all queer theorists, activists and cultural producers agree on the political importance of maintaining campness as a strategic subcultural mode of operation would be false. There are a number of critics who see campness as outmoded, as a signifier of an older, closeted, pre-Stonewall version of homosexuality. For them, camp is a system of coding from the bad old days, that gay men used to identify and interact with each other. Since gay liberation, they argue, camp has become unnecessary. As Daniel Harris puts it: 'as the forces of social stigma and oppression dissipate and the factors that contributed to the making of the gay sensibility disappear, one of homosexuals' most significant contributions to American culture, camp, begins to lose its shape'.[29] Columnist Barbara Ellen reinforces this perspective: writing on Britain's second *Big Brother*, she characterised the 'Brian/Josh standoff' as 'Old Gay (camp; sexless; Larry Grayson) versus New Gay (swaggering; sexual; *Queer as Folk*)'.[30]

And yet, evident in the opinions of other writers and filmmakers there is a queer nostalgia for difference and alterity, as epitomised by 'old school', pre-Stonewall campness: that is, a nostalgia for an era before the mainstreaming of gay culture. This nostalgia is a crucial component of the queer use of camp. There is, it would seem, a queer desire for a time when being gay/lesbian was still dangerous, furtive, criminal. Clare Whatling describes this yearning for the 'good old bad old days' as a 'nostalgia for abjection', 'a nostalgia that operates as an antithesis to what often seems like the Laura-Ashleyisation of contemporary lesbian culture'.[31] As the swishy Bruce LaBruce argues, '[n]ew school means new strategy and, ironically, a nostalgia for certain old school values'; the commercialisation and widespread dissemination of gay culture, he argues, camp tongue in cheek, 'rob[s] all homosexual youths of their very birthright: an appreciation of latter-day Judy Garland, the fisting impulse, and the love of a good stiff drink, to name only a few'.[32]

If queer support for camp is not clear-cut, neither is the distinction between the campness of queer cinema and Hollywood's uses of gay camp. Campness in Hollywood product is most immediately recognisable in its representation of gay men; it is fair to say that the mainstream films that employ campness in characterisation tend to use it as shorthand to connote homosexuality. Neatly summing up this limited semiotic strategy, the lead gay character in *Three to Tango* (Santostefano, 1999) states that 'that's what we gay men do: hold dinner parties. That, and shop for small dogs.' However, to dismiss all of these camp characters as reductive stereotypes would also be to deny the potential pleasures of individual roles and narratives.[33] In addition, audiences are perhaps accustomed to the fact that mainstream cinema, as a mass medium trying to reach the largest audience possible, frequently works with broad brushstrokes, stock types and within the boundaries of genre. Although, arguably, this makes it politically more important, it may also mean that we are more lenient, less judgmental, and have lower expectations.

Hollywood also produces a range of films which seem to be saturated with a camp sensibility – recent examples include *Charlie's Angels* (McG, 2000), *Legally Blonde* (Luketic, 2001), and *Moulin Rouge* (Luhrmann, 2001) – and movies which are best appreciated through camp pink spectacles (*Legends of the Fall* [Zwick, 1994], for instance).[34] To what extent individual cultural texts/objects are inherently camp, or simply available to appropriation, is a longstanding debate in relation to campness: theorists disagree as to whether camp 'exists in the smirk of the beholder',[35] or whether it is a recognisable set of components within things (the answer, of course, lies somewhere between the two poles of the argument). The (elusively located) campness of these films – which may, of course, contain camp characters too – offers additional possibilities for pleasure to the queer spectator of mainstream cinema.

The uses of gay camp by mainstream cinema in the past decade, though, are most evident in characterisation. The camp gay men in Hollywood movies, drawn with broad brushstrokes, are usually used for comic purposes. Their 'safe' version of campness is usually associated with swishiness and effeminacy, and it is often essentialised (they can't help being this way). Mainstream films that feature camp gay characters are not necessarily (or even primarily) aimed at a gay audience, although they may be enjoyed by them. Further, the politics of these films may be questionable, neutral or uncertain (although it is difficult to tell how the films will be interpreted by their viewers).

The 'gay' campness of mainstream cinema, then, is fairly democratic and 'open'; in contrast, the queer camp of New Queer Cinema is somewhat elitist and exclusive. Paradoxically, the forms of queer camp are more expansive and subtle than those of Hollywood movies, incorporating historical allusions, political commentary, genre parody, *and* camp characterisation. In order to demonstrate this, and by way of example, I will use the remainder of this chapter to explore the forms queer campness takes in the films of Gregg Araki. The five aspects that I will identify here, if only because they are the most self-evident, are: (1) performance style; (2) the role of trashy ephemera; (3) the use of parody; (4) political aims; and (5) the references to earlier (queer) camp filmmakers.

Around twenty minutes into *Totally Fucked Up*, butch teenage stud Tommy (Roko Belic) faces down a video camera. 'Everything that homos are s'posed to like . . .', he grumbles, 'disco music, Joan Crawford, drag shows – I hate fuckin' Bette Midler'.[36] Although this commentary would seem to be an indictment of camp gay culture, the filming style is reminiscent of Andy Warhol's screen tests, and draws attention to Belic's (weak) acting style. This is one of the major camp aspects of Araki's filmmaking: an emphasis on performance, which exposes the supposed 'naturalness' of everyday behaviour and identity as a sham. Sontag observed that 'to perceive Camp in objects and persons is to understand Being-as-Playing-a-Role. It is the furthest extension, in sensibility, of the metaphor of life as theatre'. Further, she says, camp 'is the love of the exaggerated, the "off", of things-being-what-they-are-not'.[37] Araki's films keep reminding us that we are watching actors performing; they do this in different ways. In *The Living End* and *Totally Fucked Up*, for instance, the acting is terrible; by conventional standards, almost every performance is shoddy and embarrassing, lines poorly delivered in frequently bombastic or hyperbolic ways. However, it's not as though this acting style hasn't been seen before: it closely resembles that seen in several Paul Morrissey films – especially *Flesh* (1968), *Trash* (1970), and *Heat* (1971) - and various John Waters movies – including *Pink Flamingos* (1972), and *Polyester* (1981).[38] In *The Living End*, this performance style reaches its apotheosis in a scene in which a woman ('Barbie'), bedecked in a ridiculous black wig, returns home to find her husband ('Ken') in bed with a hustler. In an oddly flat tone, Barbie drones at Ken, 'It's not the seventies anymore, when being married to a bisexual was fashionable. Can't you see you're tearing me apart?', before hacking him to death with a large kitchen knife, fake blood liberally splattering everywhere.[39]

For *The Doom Generation* and *Nowhere*, Araki had larger budgets, and could afford more talented actors. However, the acting in these later films continues to draw attention to itself as performance. In both films, money and time have clearly been spent on the outlandish production design, the costumes are over-stylised and sometimes planned to co-ordinate with the sets, and the dialogue is an exaggerated, somewhat self-satisfied version of LA teenspeak.[40] As Liese Spencer has written, 'styled to the hilt in blue wigs, biker gear and other hip accessories, Araki's gorgeous bulimics, drug addicts, dominatrices and rape victims are not so much real characters as "drag" teens'.[41]

Performances that draw attention to themselves *as performance* are central to both gay camp and queer camp; what distinguishes them, I would argue, is the register in which they are executed. Whereas the delivery of the camp gay characters of mainstream cinema is usually shrieking, effeminate, and waiting for laughter, that of queer camp characters is 'fake', deadpan, redundant. And while the former can often suggest an essentialised association between homosexuality and campness, the latter, through exposing itself as performance, attempts to reveal that there is nothing underneath. This queer camp performance manifests itself in a specific acting style which historically links together the underground queer cinema: for instance, in a study of the films of Paul Morrissey, Yacowar refers to the 'unconventional acting' in *Heat*, *Flesh*, and *Trash*, which he describes as a key part of the 'Warhol aesthetic'.[42] In the realm of New Queer Cinema, this delivery style is also seen in, for example, Bruce LaBruce's performances in *Super 8½* and *Hustler White*, and Keanu Reeves' blank diction in *My Own Private Idaho* (Van Sant, 1991).

The second element worthy of note is Araki's pleasure in trashy ephemera. Sontag has commented that 'Camp doesn't reverse things. It doesn't argue that the good is bad, or the bad is good. What it does is to offer for art (and life) a different – a supplementary – set of standards'.[43] Campness often values highly that which mainstream, accepted culture denigrates. Andy Warhol's work is suffused with campness: it forces audiences to consider the beauty in everyday objects, and to recognise the importance of the marginal. Warhol's screenprints of popular cultural icons like Elizabeth Taylor, Mickey Mouse, and Elvis Presley raised such populist figures to the rarefied heights of the art world; at the same time, he made 'superstars' of street hustlers, social misfits and drag queens.[44] Standards of taste are trampled all over by camp. Thus, Araki's films are interesting for their mix of pop culture and high art references. The two protagonists of *The Living End* are called Jon and Luke, seemingly a reference to Jean-Luc Godard; however, the published screenplay makes clear that their names are also references to John Wayne and Luke Skywalker, names familiar to audiences from popular cinema. And even if his characters do self-reflexively write papers on 'The Death of Cinema' (*The Living End*), and take down telephone numbers whilst leaning on a copy of André Bazin's book *What is Cinema?* (*Totally Fucked Up*), they also surround themselves with disposable cultural trash. In Jon's apartment in *The Living End*, a poster for Godard's *Made in USA* (1966) is blocked from view by a large inflatable dinosaur; Jon poses next to a poster advertising a retrospective of Warhol's films, and then stands on a squeaky toy shaped like an arse. The teens in *Totally Fucked Up* play 'Heart-Throb', 'a board . . . game for hormone-mad pubescent 12–year-old girls'[45] ('Heterosexuality sucks', says Patricia, a teen dyke, 'even as a board game'), watch porn videos and Jon Moritsugu's *My Degeneration* (1989), and listen to records by bands like Dead Can Dance, Ministry, and Trash Can Sinatras. And in one sequence of *The Doom Generation*, Jordan buys a yo-yo and snack foods from a sinister 24-hour store, while his girlfriend Amy (wearing garish, tacky-cool jewelry) and tattooed drifter 'X' hang around in a motel room swamped in black-and-white checks, fucking and watching hair-product commercials.

How exactly we are supposed to interpret this rather scattershot array of products is questionable; indeed, the pleasure that Araki seems to take in trashy ephemera, like that expressed in Kenneth Anger's *Scorpio Rising* (1963), is somewhat ambiguous. On the one hand, popular culture is being celebrated by both directors for the 'openness' of its texts and the appropriative opportunities it affords for consumers; on the other, it is associated with delinquency, boredom, apathy, and, ultimately, death.[46]

Third, a camp form of parody is evident in Araki's films. His movies tend to send up specific genres – road movies, teen films – and mix them with other popular, and not-so-popular, cultural forms. (Araki himself described *Totally Fucked Up* as 'a kinda cross between avant-garde experimental cinema and a queer John Hughes flick';[47] Liese Spencer refers to *Nowhere* as 'like *The Breakfast Club* on acid'.[48]) Comic books and 1950s' science fiction and horror films are evident references: the violence in *The Living End*, *The Doom Generation*, and *Nowhere* is extreme, cartoonish, unrealistic (indeed, Liese Spencer describes the violence in *Nowhere* as 'cartoon camp'[49]); the reptilian alien and giant talking bug in *Nowhere* seem to have wandered in from other narratives; and the day-glo colours and design of Araki's later films are brash and Pop Art-inspired.

Fourth, unlike mainstream cinema's use of camp, queer camp is more explicitly harnessed to political ends. For all of its trashy references, genre parody and campy performances, *The Living End* is an angry little movie about AIDS and nihilism; after committing murder, the film's two HIV+ protagonists go on the run in Jon's car, which bears a 'Choose Death' bumper sticker. The targets of Jon and Luke – policemen, homophobes – are the figures that queer political organisations such as Queer Nation (metaphorically) attempt to 'gun down'. Indeed, figures of authority fare poorly throughout the diegesis. As Roy Grundmann has written, connecting this politicised critique with the film's queer camp:

> *The Living End* . . . [uses] a successful combination of straightforward pastiche and off beat camp . . . For example, a doctor tells Jon he is seropositive in the same laconically downbeat way you tell someone they've missed their commuter train. No doubt AIDS is the epicentre of the film's rage, but it is expressed mainly through a curious mix of *Dr. Strangelove* humour and the kind of campy horror of giant insect movies.[50]

If *The Living End* swiftly asserts its intentions, so does *Totally Fucked Up*; the latter opens with a press clipping on the high suicide rate of gay teenagers. In addition to highlighting the additional adolescent concerns faced by queer teens, Araki also uses the film to enact other queer political strategies. In one scene, for instance, the four boys in the film (and Araki himself, via intertitles, and the script) discuss film and music stars, the closet, and fandom: comments are passed on Michael Stipe and Tom Cruise that are tantamount to 'outing' strategies.

Politics are also present in *The Doom Generation*, which Robin Wood has referred to as a 'powerfully political film'; indeed, Wood goes so far as to suggest that the film's final scene 'represents one of the most radical statements in American cinema'.[51] In this scene, the film's three protagonists – Amy, Jordan, and 'X' – find themselves in a warehouse, where they tentatively embark on a *menage à trois*. However, they are disturbed by rednecks, who, to the strains of a patriotic ditty, rape Amy and castrate Jordan, before Amy shoots them dead:

> The bloodbath itself juxtaposes two images of 'America.' . . . the gang of healthy all-American boys displays the American flag (immediately juxtaposed, as its necessary complement, with the swastika painted on the leader's chest) and plays the 'Stars and Stripes Forever' . . . on a ghetto-blaster; these are presented as mere empty signifiers, drained long ago of all substance and meaning, relics of an always dubious patriotism that has lost whatever meaning it once had, reduced to a pretext for malicious and repressive violence . . . Against it is set Araki's America, exemplified by the essential purity of its three main characters.[52]

And it is the sexual 'triangle' that is destroyed by the hicks that Wood sees as the film's radical political message; for Wood, Araki's 'treatment of teen sex . . . is passionate and positive, deeply romantic, seeing sex as a positive force'.[53]

Finally, as James M. Moran has stated, (queer) campness is evident in Araki's films through his references and allusions, more and less explicit, to earlier filmmakers.[54] Warhol is a clear touchstone. In addition to the poster (mentioned above) which appears in *The Living End*, the film also features two murderous lesbians called Daisy and Fern (possibly a reference to such florally-named Warhol superstars as Holly Woodlawn, Ivy Nicholson, and Ultra Violet), who call Luke a 'lonesome cowboy' (Warhol made a film called *Lonesome Cowboys* in 1968). A billboard advert for cowboy boots that the camera lingers on recalls Warhol's many ('artistic' and 'commercial') images of footwear; TV news reportage of 'another death', unspooling on a screen in Jon's apartment, could be seen as an allusion to Warhol's 'tragedy' screenprint series of car crashes, suicides, and so on. In *Totally Fucked Up*, Steven's insistence on filming everything – Deric: 'I just don't feel like being videotaped while I'm having sex, alright?'; Tommy, in a separate scene: 'Get that fuckin' camera out of my face' – is reminiscent of Warhol's machinic desire to endlessly produce, store, and record. And in *Nowhere*, a party takes place which resembles a gathering at Warhol's Factory: during the bash, a biker named Elvis kills a drug dealer called Handjob with a tin of Campbell's soup, and Duckie, a boy stricken with grief at the suicide of his sister Egg, throws himself into a swimming pool on the surface of which float hundreds of silver balls (a reference, perhaps, to Warhol's silver pillow-balloons).

Of course, the brief summary above can only begin to unpick the wealth of detail and allusions that pepper Araki's glorious, tacky, extreme cinematic fantasies. However, hopefully it serves to indicate the layered, complex ways in which New Queer Cinema films work with campness. This 'queer camp' is distinctive in specific ways: it references, pays tribute to, and reworks 'radical' gay culture's camp history; it is more subtly textured and layered than mainstream cinema's campness is capable of; it is targeted almost exclusively at a knowledgeable queer audience (and is therefore rather elitist); and it is politicised, in both subtle and heavy-handed ways. New Queer Cinema's queer campness, then, is serious *and* silly, political *and* irreverent, contemporary *and* historically informed, elitist *and* open. In its contradictory nature, it is not too distant from other manifestations of camp ('camp thrives on paradoxes', writes Medhurst[55]); indeed, the form of mainstream cinema's campness intersects and blurs with the camp of cinema that is independently produced. Both provide distinct but overlapping pleasures for the queer spectator.

Arguably, New Queer Cinema is the 'postmodern moment' in the history of gay representation in film. As Honey Glass states, 'Queer cinema is a prime example of post-modern aesthetics – besides using irony and pastiche, it represents fragmented subjectivities and is often dystopian. The films are deliberately, sometimes flamboyantly stylish'.[56] Similarly, B. Ruby Rich refers to New Queer Cinema's 'common style', which she terms 'Homo Pomo': 'there are traces in all of them of appropriation and pastiche, irony, as well as a reworking of history with social constructionism very much in mind . . . these works are irreverent, energetic, alternately minimalist and excessive'.[57] What is astonishing is the extent to which these definitions could be describing the campness at work in the New Queer Cinema corpus; yet neither author considers or explores this connection.[58] Campness – which has *not* died out, which retains a significant position in queer culture, and which may even be increasing in prevalence – is a key aspect of many a New Queer Cinema film, but this has remained largely theoretically ignored. I hope this chapter at least begins to redress the balance.

NOTES

1 B. Ruby Rich, 'New Queer Cinema', *Sight and Sound*, 2:5 (September 1992): 32, reprinted in this book.

2 Ibid., p. 33. Generally, campness, as it is associated with gay/queer culture, is assumed to be the province of gay men; indeed, the focus of this chapter is primarily on cultural artefacts produced by gay men. However, a number of lesbian writers have argued for the existence and importance of lesbian camp. See, for instance: Andrea Weiss, *Vampires and Violets: Lesbians in the Cinema* (London: Jonathan Cape, 1992); Patricia Juliana Smith, ' "You Don't Have To Say You Love Me": The Camp Masquerades of Dusty Springfield', in David Bergman (ed.), *Camp Grounds: Style and Homosexuality* (Amherst, MA: University of Massachusetts Press, 1993); Sue-Ellen Case, 'Toward a Butch-Femme Aesthetic', in Fabio Cleto (ed.), *Camp: Aesthetics and the Performing Subject: A Reader* (Edinburgh: Edinburgh University Press, 1999); and Paula Graham, 'Girl's Camp?: The Politics of Parody', in Tamsin Wilton (ed.), *Immortal Invisible: Lesbians and the Moving Image* (London: Routledge, 1995). For a consideration of women's relationship to camp, see Pamela Robertson, *Guilty Pleasures: Feminist Camp from Mae West to Madonna* (London: I. B. Tauris, 1996).

3 I am sure this list of examples will cause problems for many, as defining the limits of the New Queer Cinema corpus is difficult. Is it composed only of the films that Rich mentions in her seminal essay, or those listed under the heading 'New Queer Cinema' by Raymond Murray in his book *Images in the Dark* (New York: Plume/Penguin, 1996), p. 589? Is there a date beyond which no film can be termed 'New Queer Cinema'? And what if the directors themselves reject the queer label? (See, for instance, LaBruce's stinging critique of the label/movement in his essay 'The Wild, Wild World of Fanzines: Notes from a Reluctant Pornographer', in Paul Burston and Colin Richardson (eds), *A Queer Romance: Lesbians, Gay Men and Popular Culture* (London: Routledge, 1995).) Perhaps the odd one out in my list is Nigel Finch's *Stonewall*, which was made in the UK. Can British films be seen as part of the New Queer Cinema movement? In relation to this chapter, and its discussion of camp, it *is* worth pointing out that there are notable differences in national configurations and manifestations of camp; and within nations, one also finds regional differences. However, I do not have space here to consider this in more depth; therefore, this chapter will focus almost wholly on North American culture.

4 Juan A. Suárez, *Bike Boys, Drag Queens and Superstars: Avant-Garde, Mass Culture, and Gay Identities in the 1960s Underground Cinema* (Bloomington

and Indianapolis: Indiana University Press, 1996); Richard Dyer, *Now You See It: Studies in Lesbian and Gay Film* (London: Routledge, 1990); Philip Core, *Camp: The Lie That Tells the Truth* (London: Plexus, 1984).

5 Susan Sontag, 'Notes on "Camp"', *Against Interpretation* (London: Eyre and Spottiswoode, 1967), p. 275.

6 Andy Medhurst, 'Batman, Deviance and Camp', in Roberta E. Pearson and William Uricchio (eds), *The Many Lives of the Batman: Critical Approaches to a Superhero and his Media* (London: BFI, 1991), pp. 154, 155.

7 Andy Medhurst, 'Camp', in Andy Medhurst and Sally R. Munt (eds), *Lesbian and Gay Studies: A Critical Introduction* (London: Cassell, 1997), p. 276.

8 Medhurst, 'Batman', p. 150.

9 Jack Babuscio, 'Camp and the Gay Sensibility', in Richard Dyer (ed.), *Gays and Film* (London: BFI, 1977); Richard Dyer, 'It's Being So Camp as Keeps Us Going', *Only Entertainment* (London: Routledge, 1992); Medhurst, 'Camp'; Susan Sontag, 'Notes'.

10 George Melly, 'Preface', in Core, *Camp*, p. 5.

11 Core, *Camp*, p. 208.

12 Even the tendency to provide lists has been criticised for concretising camp; Charles Ludlam has argued that lists '[nail camp] to the wall and [make] it very literal . . . The value of camp, the ability to perceive things in this unique way, is that it turns values upside down' (Ludlam, 'Camp', in Steven Samuels (ed.), *Ridiculous Theatre – Scourge of Folly: The Essays and Opinions of Charles Ludlam* (New York: Theatre Communications Group, 1992), p. 226.

13 Dyer, 'It's Being So Camp', p. 5.

14 Ibid., p. 136.

15 Medhurst, 'Camp', p. 276.

16 Ibid., p. 276.

17 As Pamela Robertson argues: 'Queer Nation's use of camp strategies, as well as the prominence of drag in Gay Pride parades, and other overt manifestations linked to gay identity politics, have redefined and revitalized camp within the gay community' (*Guilty*, p. 130). Similarly, Doty has written that 'camp . . . continue[s] to be [a] mainstay of queer humour, particularly as lesbian and gay producers and audiences have been [utilising this form/strategy] more and more since the 1970s' (*Flaming Classics: Queering the Canon* [New York: Routledge, 2000], p. 79).

18 Andrew Britton, 'For Interpretation: Notes against Camp', in Cleto, *Aesthetics*, p. 138.

19 Quoted in Caryl Flinn, 'The Deaths of Camp', in Cleto, *Aesthetics*, p. 433.

20 Mark Simpson, 'Camp for Beginners', *It's a Queer World* (London: Vintage, 1996), p. 92.

21 Chuck Kleinhans, 'Taking out the Trash: Camp and the Politics of Parody', in Moe Meyer, (ed.), *The Politics and Poetics of Camp* (London and New York: Routledge, 1994), p. 182.

22 Indeed, Fabio Cleto has noted that 'the whole tradition of critical writings' on camp 'can in fact be summarised in a series of oppositions, enacting . . . binary logic' ('Introduction: Queering the Camp', in Cleto, *Aesthetics*, p. 23).

23 Honey Glass, 'Q for Queer', *Sight and Sound*, 7:10 (1997): 38.

24 Perhaps the most militant proponent of this thesis is Moe Meyer: 'Camp is political; Camp is solely a queer (and/or sometimes gay and lesbian) discourse; and Camp embodies a specifically queer cultural critique . . . [T]he un-queer do not have access to the discourse of Camp, only to derivatives constructed through the act of appropriation' ('Introduction: Reclaiming the Discourse of Camp', in Meyer, *Politics*, p. 1).

25 Robertson, *Guilty*, p. 129. Similarly, Medhurst states that '[q]ueer activism sought to re-gay camp, to reclaim it from the widened-out heterosexualisation it had undergone in the years since Sontag, to imbue its subcultural codes with an overtly

ideological edge'. There is, says Medhurst, a '[q]ueer wish to insist on camp as an always-political statement' ('Camp', pp. 282, 280).

26 Brian McNair, *Striptease Culture: Sex, Media and the Democratisation of Desire* (London and New York: Routledge, 2002), p. 30.

27 Edward Lawrenson has described Andy Warhol's films as 'parlaying his fascination with old-style Hollywood glamour into gloriously camp studies of the beautiful people who wandered into the Factory'; he goes on to describe Warhol as 'the Queen mother of queer cinema' ('Soup Dreams', *Sight and Sound*, 12:3 (2002): 4.

28 Indeed, as Glass notes, 'what primarily differentiates New Queer Cinema . . . is its recognition of the transformative power of Aids' [*sic*] 'Q', p. 37. For more on the role of AIDS in New Queer Cinema, see José Arroyo, 'Death, Desire and Identity: The Political Unconscious of "New Queer Cinema" ', in Joseph Bristow and Angelia R. Wilson (eds), *Activating Theory: Lesbian, Gay, Bisexual Politics* (London: Lawrence and Wishart, 1993).

29 Daniel Harris, *The Rise and Fall of Gay Culture* (New York: Ballantine Books, 1997), p. 34.

30 Barbara Ellen, 'Putting the Sex in Homosexuality', *Observer Magazine*, 24 June 2001: 3. Ellen's binary division does not do justice to the complexity of the situation: first, brash twat Josh was hardly camp-free; and second, campness is hardly sanitary and 'sexless', as Julian Clary ably demonstrates. However, Brian Dowling's popularity (and eventual success) was undoubtedly influenced by his rather naïve, innocent (and therefore more 'harmless') campness.

31 Clare Whatling, *Screen Dreams: Fantasising Lesbians in Film* (Manchester: Manchester University Press, 1997), p. 82.

32 Bruce LaBruce, *The Reluctant Pornographer* (Toronto: Gutter Press, 1997), pp. 41, 45.

33 *My Best Friend's Wedding* (Hogan, 1997) is a gorgeous confection, even if it does leave a bad taste in the mouth. And Nathan Lane is to be commended for his ongoing contributions to Hollywood's representations of homosexuality; such is his acting prowess that he can make the most objectionable implications palatable.

34 In *Legends of the Fall*, argues José Arroyo, Brad Pitt's character, 'the gentle-savage warrior-within tree-hugger was over-written to such an extent it's camp' ('Brad Pitt: The Making of a Super-Icon', *Attitude*, 32 [December 1996]: 72).

35 Thomas Hess, 'J'Accuse Marcel Duchamp', *Art News*, 63:10 (1965): 53.

36 Gregg Araki, *The Living End/Totally Fucked Up* (New York: William Morrow & Co., 1994), p. 47. The wording in the film is marginally different.

37 Sontag, 'Camp', pp. 280, 279.

38 Indeed, as Chuck Kleinhans argues, in relation to the films of John Waters, '[c]amp pushes a poorly done form (poorly done by conventional standards of technique and social manners) to the limits so that its very badness is what the work is about' ('Trash', p. 189).

39 Similarly, in *Totally Fucked Up*, after Tommy has been kicked out of his parental home for being gay, and the narrative looks as though it might be taking itself too seriously, Araki inserts an intertitle which reads 'Can This World Really Be As Sad As It Seems?' His intention, clearly, is to (rather camply) undermine any heavy-handed message, and remind us that we are watching a movie.

40 These elements are all commented on by Geoffrey Macnab, in his review of the film; he also relates Araki's casting process to that of John Waters. See *Sight and Sound*, 6:6 (1996): 37–8.

41 Liese Spencer, 'Teenage Kicks All through the Night', *Sight and Sound*, 8:6 (1998): 36.

42 Maurice Yacowar, *The Films of Paul Morrissey* (Cambridge: Cambridge University Press, 1993), p. 29.

43 Sontag, 'Notes', p. 286.

44 For more on Andy Warhol's campness, see Peter Wollen, 'Notes from the Under-

ground: Andy Warhol', in *Raiding the Icebox: Reflections on Twentieth-Century Culture* (London: Verso, 1993), and Matthew Tinkcom, 'Warhol's Camp', in Colin MacCabe (ed.), *Who is Andy Warhol?* (London: BFI, 1997).

45 Araki, *The Living End*, p. 35.
46 For more on this tension in Anger's film, see Suárez, *Bike Boys*, pp. 141–80.
47 Quoted in Raymond Murray, *Images*, p. 12.
48 Spencer, 'Teenage', p. 36.
49 Ibid.
50 Roy Grundmann, 'The Fantasies We Live By: Bad Boys in *Swoon* and *The Living End*', *Cineaste*, March 1993: 26.
51 Robin Wood, *Sexual Politics and Narrative Film: Hollywood and Beyond* (New York: Columbia University Press, 1998), p. 339.
52 Ibid., p. 342.
53 Ibid., p. 338.
54 James M. Moran, 'Gregg Araki: Guerilla Film-maker for a Queer Generation', *Film Quarterly*, 50:1 (Fall 1996): 18–26.
55 Medhurst, 'Camp', p. 276.
56 Glass, 'Q', p. 37.
57 Rich, 'New', p. 32.
58 For more on the relationship between camp and postmodernism, see Andy Medhurst, 'Pitching Camp', *City Limits*, 10–17 May 1990: 19; Mark Simpson, 'Ooh, No Missus!', *It's a Queer World*; Anneke Smelik, 'Lesbian and Gay Criticism', in Pamela Church-Gibson and John Hill (eds), *The Oxford Guide to Film Studies* (Oxford: Oxford University Press, 1998); and Pamela Robertson, 'Introduction: What Makes the Feminist Camp?', in *Guilty Pleasures*.

6. ART CINEMA AND MURDEROUS LESBIANS

Anneke Smelik

The New Queer Wave in cinema has featured notoriously few women film-makers or films about lesbians.[1] Although some critics have included independent films and videos by women and some lesbian films were even quite successful, they have remained marginal in the critical work on New Queer Cinema.[2] This marginality is all the more conspicuous when compared to the critical attention devoted to lesbian chic in mainstream cinema.[3] In between these two poles of independent lesbian filmmaking and Hollywood lesbian flicks surged an unexpected small wave of art films in the mid-1990s featuring young lesbian couples who seal their affections for each other in blood: *Sister My Sister*, *La Cérémonie*, *Heavenly Creatures*, *Fun* and *Butterfly Kiss*.[4]

It is not easy to situate these five films *vis-à-vis* New Queer Cinema. If gay authorship is to be taken as a defining characteristic of New Queer Cinema, then the films certainly do not fit into the category of NQC because – to my knowledge – the directors are not gay; the films were certainly not promoted as queer in any way by the filmmakers or producers. Yet, the films partake in the popularisation of queer images and themes and could therefore be seen to be a product of NQC. They can be characterised as art movies with popular appeal and as queer products of straight directors simultaneously. This may raise the question how close these art films are then to New Queer Cinema. Although the films do not raise concerns about the commercialisation of queer images, as the films of NQC did, they do cause worries about the perpetuation of old stereotypes, *in casu* the stereotype of the murderous lesbian. In this chapter I will argue that this stereotype is deconstructed rather than reinforced. In the second half of the chapter I will discuss the disturbing association of lesbian sexuality with madness and violence in more depth, in order to analyse the representation of stereotypes and position the films in relation to NQC. I will do so within the context of Lacanian psychoanalytic theory for reasons that will become apparent later. But first I will introduce the narrative and visual pleasures of the five films.

DÉLIRE À DEUX

The films display a striking thematic and structural unity in its queer subject matter, focusing on the intense relationship between two girls or young women. A passionate love that leads to 'ceremonial killings' (as I will argue later); the sacrifice of the mother or a maternal figure on the altar of lesbian love.

Sister My Sister (UK 1994) is the only film made by women: directed by Nancy Meckler and written by Wendy Kesselman (based on her play *My Sister In This House* from 1981). It tells the 'true story' of two domestic servants, the sisters Christine and Léa Papin, who savagely killed their mistress and her daughter in a French provincial town in the 1930s.[5] The French film *La Cérémonie* tells a similar story (Claude Chabrol, Fr/Ger, 1995; based on the novel *A Judgement in Stone* by Ruth Rendell). Sophie is hired as a domestic servant to Madame Lelièvre in her remote mansion in the country-side. The introverted and illiterate Sophie befriends the volatile Jeanne. Together they shoot Madame Lelièvre and her husband and two children. *Heavenly Creatures* (Peter Jackson, NZ, 1994) is set in the 1950s in a provincial town in New Zealand. Like *Sister My Sister*, the story is based on a historical case: of Juliet Hulme and Pauline Parker who killed Pauline's mother when the friends were threatened to be separated. *Fun* (Rafael Zelinski, US/Canada, 1994) is not based on historical material, at least not more than that the film is loosely inspired by a sentence from a diary in a Californian murder case: 'Today we ran away and killed an old lady. It was lots of fun'. That is how Bonnie and Hilary finish a delirious day they have spent together. *Butterfly Kiss* (Michael Winterbottom, UK, 1994) differs from the other four films in that the friends Eunice (Eu, 'you') and Miriam (Mi, 'me') mainly kill men after the initial murder of a woman. Eunice is also the only serial killer of all these female characters.

In narrative structure and aesthetic imagery there are striking analogies between the films. The films based on historical matter, *Sister My Sister* and *Heavenly Creatures*, both start with a flashback of the murder, after which the story of a lesbian love relation unfolds. In contrast to *Sister My Sister* where the murder is filmed in slow motion, in the dark and by rapid montage, the murder in *Heavenly Creatures* is filmed hyperrealistically. In both cases the slaying is physically heavy and literally bloody work; passions exploding into a frenzied *délire à deux*.

The colourful luminosity of *La Cérémonie* shrilly contrasts with the dark imagery of *Sister My Sister*. The films are quite similar, however, in their psychological finesse and the reconstruction of seemingly meaningless details that acutely express the oppression and humiliation of the lower-class women and takes the stories to their macabre endings. *Heavenly Creatures* and *Fun* show remarkably similar imagery in the cinematic style. The filmmakers have looked for effects in colour and camera work to represent the unbridled energy of the adolescent girls up to the point of delirium. Finally, in *Fun* and *Butterfly Kiss* the stories are told in flashback structure by the surviving friend in prison, Hilary and Miriam respectively. Those scenes are filmed in black and white, while the love-and-murder story is filmed in colour.

Against the stereotype of the dangerous lesbian who is inevitably killed in Hollywood cinema as revenge or punishment,[6] the girls mostly survive the carnage. This does not necessarily bring the films closer to some of the more cheerful stories that came out of New Queer Cinema because the girls end up in prison or an asylum. When they die it is at their own hands. Bonnie commits suicide when she is separated from Hilary in prison. In *Butterfly Kiss* Eunice asks Miriam for the ultimate gesture of love and dedication in her desire for divine punishment and redemption: she wants to be killed by her. In a magical scene Miriam drowns Eunice in the sea – and we cannot tell whether it is suicide, murder or baptism.

EXCESS

The notion of excess may point to the way in which these films can be read as 'queer'. As Michele Aaron has convincingly argued, the films are a multi-genre mix of '[b]uddy movie, erotic thriller and lesbian love story . . . invested with the politics of documentary'.[7] I want to add that the films draw heavily upon art cinema aesthetics in their general foregrounding of cinematic means: superb acting by outstanding (mostly European) actresses, creative camera work, beautiful imagery and original scripts with a tendency for the gothic. The main attraction of the films, for this spectator at least, lies in the uncompromising passion of the girls. They are fascinating characters in their transgressive behaviour, carried away in the maelstrom of their passions. Admittedly, some of the women are bordering on the insane, but the films work to understand their complex psychic life rather than reject or despise them.

More importantly, narrative and visual pleasure never functions at the expense of the female characters, even in the love scenes – conventionally a set-up for erotic titillation of the (male) spectator. This kind of voyeuristic pleasure is denied in the films. We do see naked bodies, and we watch female bodies making love to one another, but the cinematic style privileges the depth of feeling and the excess of passion rather than the cheap thrills of sleazy sex. Also, the women are not conventionally beautiful according to Hollywood standards. Visual pleasure in these films lies elsewhere. The excess of the deep-felt emotions is visualised in a refined aesthetic style or cinematic spectacle. The first can be found in the desolate beauty of *Sister My Sister*, *La Cérémonie* and *Butterfly Kiss*; the latter in the colourful and vertiginous imagery of *Fun* and *Heavenly Creatures*. The films make the excess, whether in fantasy, emotion or sexuality, physically poignant, psychologically rich and visually spectacular.

The narrative point of view lies unambiguously with the female characters. Because the stories of the art films are told from the girls' perspective, the spectator aligns her sympathy with them. The films project a spectating position of identification with the female characters. We follow the girls' dreams, hopes, desires as well as their fears, nightmares, and pain. The female perspective can also be traced in the complex relation of the girls to the mother or mother substitute, a figure all too often neglected in our culture. Probably most spectators are put off by the carnage, but until then the films have produced an understanding if not sympathy for the intense inner lives of the female characters. By giving them full narrative and visual perspective, the films get across the complexity and vicissitudes of female identity and lesbian desire in a repressive society.

Bursting with life, overflowing with passions, alive with creativity, the women produce their own imaginative worlds. The key term here is, once again, excess. Actively desiring, refusing to be desired in heterosexual terms, transgressing the boundaries of their class and gender, the women's bodies become the site of struggle. Continually on the verge of exhilarated and often painful love and passion, and full of anger, the women resist 'established gender and sexuality categories'[8] and transgress into homoeroticism (*Fun* and *La Cérémonie*), explicit lesbianism (the other three films), or even into heterosexual sex (*Heavenly Creatures*, *Butterfly Kiss*), incest (*Sister My Sister*) and sadomasochism (*Butterfly Kiss*). 'Queer' indeed.

QUEER PARADOXES

Sister My Sister, *La Cérémonie*, *Heavenly Creatures*, *Fun* and *Butterfly Kiss* maintain the queer paradox that the female characters are not only 'heavenly creatures' but also dangerous misfits. To the gay spectator these are perturbing films because they connect adolescent female bodies and violence, lesbian desire and pathology, same-sex love and bloodthirstiness. A stereotypical image all too familiar from Hollywood movies, even more recent ones such as *Thelma and Louise*, *Basic Instinct* and *Bound*.[9] The burning question here is whether the films perpetuate the stereotype of the man-hating and murderous lesbian.

As Aaron has pointed out: 'So strong is the connection between woman's deviant or independent sexuality . . . and her deadliness, that it haunts all representations of strong women or of strong relationships between women'.[10] This is undoubtedly true and it is also true that in this sense the art films do little to counter the traditional stereotype lurking in the shady background. However, some redeeming factors make me consider the art films as *not* yet another repetition of the same old story. It seems to me that the films work against rather than with the stereotype of the dangerous lesbian. In that respect, the films are certainly closer to the work of lesbian and gay filmmakers within New Queer Cinema than to the lesbian chic of Hollywood movies.

Part of my argument has already been suggested above: the sustained visual and narrative perspective of the female characters, the intensity of the committed relationships between them, and the artistic aesthetics privileging excess and ecstasy. For these reasons I feel about those films (with maybe the exception of the sombre *Butterfly Kiss*) as Aaron about the queer film *Swoon*: 'Intoxicated by the beauty and the rarity of the image of *Swoon*'s lovers, one almost forgives, or rather forgets, their crime'.[11] Thus, the films' seductive powers invite an appreciation of moving and daring lesbian loves. As I have argued elsewhere, the question in queer cinema is not simply to get rid of stereotypes (as they are quite resilient), nor how to replace them with positive images (which leave the heterosexist imperative intact), but rather to achieve complexity and diversity.[12] I would like to point to a paradox here. Where New Queer Cinema has perhaps remained too close to the project of positive images in, for example, the lesbian romances like *Bar Girls*, *When Night Is Falling*, *Thin Ice*, *The Incredibly True Adventures of Two Girls in Love* and *Gazon Maudit* that came in its wake, these 'queer' art films have accomplished unsurpassed levels of complexity.

The other part of my argument lies in the nature of the killings. I want to argue that the killings are ceremonial rather than lustful. First of all, the killings lack the most important ingredient for the stereotype of the dangerous lesbian, and that is a *femme fatale*. Not only is the femme fatale conspicuously absent from the films I'm discussing here; so are men. The 'thrilling threat' of the dangerous lesbian is usually directed at men in the form of devastatingly beautiful women; their beauty defined in purely heterosexual terms.[13] Catherine Trammell in *Basic Instinct* is the perfect example of such a female figure. Second, the killings are not immediately connected to sexuality or to a sexual act, countering the intricate intimacy between sex and death in most Hollywood movies. Except for *Butterfly Kiss* the women don't 'fuck and kill'.

This is not to say that the killings are devoid of passion; they are excessively passionate. I would even go as far as to say that they are like a *crime passionnel*. This suggests that love is involved, or rather a love–hate relationship. If we look at the people who are killed by the girls, this may become more obvious. Again, *Butterfly Kiss* is the exception here. The other girls mainly kill somebody they know well: the mother in *Heavenly Creatures*, the mistress and her family (with whom the girls live in the same house) in *Sister My Sister* and *La Cérémonie*. In *Fun* the girls kill somebody they haven't met before; an older woman who is explicitly portrayed and positioned as a grandmother. The women may be psychologically unstable, but they are not criminals who are likely to repeat their murderous acts. That would not fit with the nature of a *crime passionnel*. In order to understand the cinematic representation of these killings, and make a further case for the deconstruction of the stereotype of the murderous lesbian, I will make a theoretical excursion into Lacanian psychoanalysis.

MIRRORS

Lacan took a great deal of interest in the crime of the sisters Papin and based part of his later reflections on the mirror phase on this case,[14] a concept which had a great influence on film theory.[15] In his early practice and perhaps all his life Lacan was fascinated by women who had committed a crime, especially by what he saw as the paranoid female criminal.[16] According to him, the paranoid structure means that the female criminal sees her mirror image reflected in her victim. Thus, the sisters Papin hated in their employers – mother and daughter – their own projected suffering. Lynda Hart points out that Lacan thought to observe a secret in female criminals: 'the danger of too much closeness'.[17] This proximity between two women is related to a notion of perfect love. It can have disastrous consequences and explode in aggression when the subjects are forced to allow the outside world into the relation or when they are forced to separate. Lacan attributes an 'erotomaniac' component to this kind of paranoia, consisting of repressed homosexuality.

The sisters Papin did cherish a homosexual love for each other, which points to a strong element of narcissism in that love. Lacan writes: 'But, it seems that between them the sisters were even unable to take the necessary distance to hurt the other. True Siamese souls, they formed a world that remained forever closed'.[18] Cathérine Clément argues that on the basis of this kind of case – the female paranoid criminal with repressed homosexuality – Lacan concluded that the 'correct distance is the opposite of the feminine'.[19] This implies that only the male subject can approximate the correct distance. Without the intervention of a third term, the male other, the two women are frightening *Doppelgänger*, copies of one single self.

In Lacanian psychoanalysis the mirror phase is the psychic phenomenon in which that 'correct distance' is established for the subject. This is the moment at which the young child begins to form an identity. The mirror phase is situated within the Imaginary, more or less between six and eighteen months of the earliest years in childhood. In Lacan's view, the child's first steps on its way to the formation of an identity are based on a 'misrecognition' (*méconnaissance*). This means that the child observes its body in the mirror – usually in its mother's arms – as an autonomous and complete unity, while the child does not yet control its own body and does not yet experience itself as a separate entity from the mother.

The newly acquired identity is, however, based on an optical illusion because the child 'misrecognises' itself as an autonomous whole. It identifies with the imago of its own body, an image which is all the more idealised because it holds a promise of control that the child does not yet experience in its own helpless body. The first identification is therefore already an alienation in which the child learns to identify (with) itself as an other, as well as through an other.

The process of the formation of the self during the mirror stage forms the basis for all later identifications. For Lacan each identification is therefore structurally imaginary, that is to say it is based on fictive imagos. This is where the relation to cinema can be made, because in cinema the spectator's identification is effectuated through imagos; through visual imagery. The subject's identity lies always under threat as it is dependent on a fundamental misrecognition within the mirror stage; identity is built upon a fiction, an imago. The Imaginary is not so much a stage, as a psychic register that remains influential throughout adulthood, especially in love relations.[20] Hence, the importance of visual representations like cinema in offering continuing opportunities for ideal yet imaginary identifications.

The identity of the self is in fact an identification with the other who is incorporated within the illusion of autonomy. Where there is a self, there is also an other. The fact that in the first instance this other usually is the mother or the maternal figure, is meaningful in the context of the films which I discuss in this chapter. However, the boundaries between self and other are still confused in the mirror stage. Because the child learns to identify as an other through the idealised mirror image, the distance between self and other is as fictional and imaginary as one's own identity. That distance, 'the correct distance', is a precarious balance which can be undone any moment. The subject has to continually play acrobatics in order to guard that boundary. Loss of the boundary between self and other will swallow up the subject.

Although narcissism is a necessary psychic structure for human well-being, narcissism easily connotes an infantile and diseased personality. It is quite telling that in Western culture narcissism has been intimately connected to a female subject position. To this almost automatic linking of women and narcissism, lesbianism is all too often added, and vice versa lesbian eroticism is all too often coupled with narcissism. However, it may be opportune to recall that the narcissistic structure of the mirror stage forms the foundation for all love relations, not only for homosexual love relations.

On the basis of the inseparability and the 'dangerous' closeness of the sisters Papin, Lacan theorised a psychical structure which he later conceptualised in the mirror stage. For Lacan the same-sex love between women equals the loss of boundary between self and other. Self and other are inextricably bound in a bond that will inevitably explode in violence when the 'law of the Father' intervenes and draws the boundaries between the Imaginary and the Symbolic. In this way Lacan unequivocally renders lesbian desire as the source of criminality and madness in women.

THE M/OTHER

The concept of the mirror stage may help to understand the love and violence of the girl characters in *Sister My Sister*, *La Cérémonie*, *Heavenly Creatures*, *Fun* and *Butterfly Kiss*. In these films there is definitely a high level of identification between the girls. Their physical friendship and love even completely exclude others. Although the boundary between self and other acquires vague contours within the friendship, the boundary with the outside world, on the contrary, is very sharply drawn. The girls do not allow the Other within their friendship and thus place themselves outside the Symbolic order. Yet, their friendship cannot be understood as a complete symbiosis because the girls feel desire for one another. And desire requires a distance between self and other. The girls move back and forth between identification (the wish to *be* the other) and sexual desire (the wish to *have* the other).[21]

This difference is hardly noticed by Lacan. In his theory he is so blinded by sexual difference between men and women that he is unable to recognise differences among women. Because the films fully represent the eroticism between the girls, the focus there is rather on desire than on identification and thus the difference among the female friends is not denied. In this context it is interesting that Aaron has noted that the girls in the films are visually contrasted: '[o]ne of the pair might be darker or taller, or they might also come from different classes as in *Heavenly Creatures*. Somehow they are pitted against each other'.[22] For Aaron the visual contrast is a way in which 'lesbianism is being heterosexualised by the play upon the pairs' visual and enduring differences'.[23] To me, however, these differences point precisely to a representation of active lesbian desire.

In all the five films the girls commit a murder when a forced separation is threatening or actually happening. In most films this is made explicitly clear. Even in *Butterfly Kiss* the story suggests that Eunice starts to kill after she has lost the only woman (Judith) who loved her. This characteristic, the explosion of violence when the friends' inseparability is threatened, corresponds to Lacan's observations about violent female patients. If we consider the object of the girls' violence, it is striking that the victims are by no means arbitrary. The victim in *Fun* may appear to be arbitrarily chosen, but the killed woman is an old, sweet, granny-like lady. Just before the murder Hilary and Bonnie express their disgust at the display of family portraits of children and grandchildren on the wall. In *Heavenly Creatures*, *Sister My Sister* and *Fun* the girls commit a matricide: they kill the mother or a mother figure. In *La Cérémonie* the women kill not only the mother but her whole family. Only in *Butterfly Kiss* is the violence mainly directed at men.[24]

As mentioned above, the girls do not allow others into their friendship. The friendship can be understood as the symbolic refusal to allow a third party into their mirroring relation. In other words, the girls refuse to enter an oedipal triangle. This still begs the question why the girls kill the mother or a mother substitute rather than the father or a father substitute. In some cases they have good reasons for patricide (in *Sister My Sister*, *Fun* and *La Cérémonie* there are suggestions of sexual abuse in early years by the father; in the last film it is even suggested that Sophie has actually killed her father). I think that the reason for the killing of the maternal figure can be found in the nature of the friendship of these girls.

In their relationship the girls adhere more meaning to the Imaginary than to the Symbolic. The narcissistic identification and the great role of fantasy both point to the primary function of the Imaginary. In this context it is important to realise that it is the mother who is the first person to be experienced and known as the other. The mirror stage is therefore one of the first conscious moments in which the I separates from the m/other. Thus, this is the moment which starts off the slow and painful process of breaking out of the symbiotic relation with the mother who is the first love object for the child. When at a later stage in life the threat of a second traumatic separation dawns, breaking off the intense and loving friendship with another girl, deep fear and pain of the initial trauma are awakened, that is the repudiation of the first love object. This is perhaps the reason why the girls direct their fury at the maternal body. The mother does not only stand for the symbolic order that breaks into the imaginary world of the girls, but also recalls the early trauma. A repetition of the trauma must be avoided at all pains. For the inseparable friends a permanent separation is unimaginable and must be averted by a ceremonial killing. The mother is the victim who has to be ceremonially offered on the altar of love between the girls.

There may be another motive at play as well. Lacan saw the sisters Papin as doubles with a shared ego-ideal. The ego-ideal is founded upon female figures within the unconscious. These are ambivalent imagos that may call forth hate as well as love within the mirroring relation of the Imaginary. In the films the girls reject this female ego-ideal. Whether it is because they belong to a lower class and hate the bourgeois ideal of femininity, or because of sexual abuse by the father, or because their repressed lesbian desires can find no outlet in society, the girls all refuse the heterosexual model of womanhood and its related role of mother and housewife. For them, the ideal is in fact an ordeal and the mother represents precisely that which they do not wish to become. The matricide can thus be read as a symbolic murder of traditional femininity and of the patriarchal family.

TRANSGRESSION

It is time to return to the question how *Sister My Sister*, *La Cérémonie*, *Heavenly Creatures*, *Fun* and *Butterfly Kiss* can be situated *vis-à-vis* New Queer Cinema. In my view, the small *hausse* in independent films embracing lesbianism in the context of violence and murder is part of the proliferation of queer images and themes within the mainstream in the 1990s. The films may be read as 'queer', but they are not part of New Queer Cinema. New Queer Cinema has brought along a certain popularisation of queerness in mainstream cinema. Not that I am necessarily against popularisation; the more images of gay and lesbian characters, stories and themes, the better. Invisibility is the greatest enemy for any marginalised social group.

A 'queer' film is generally understood to 'challenge or transgress established straight or gay and lesbian understandings of gender and sexuality'.[25] Sometimes I have the impression that queer politics have underestimated what it means to seriously challenge or transgress categories of gender and sexuality. Such transgressions, as we can witness in *Sister My Sister*, *La Cérémonie*, *Heavenly Creatures*, *Fun* and *Butterfly Kiss*, come necessarily with bewilderment, disorder and pain. Thus, the films that I have discussed in this chapter may well interrogate some of the celebratory aspects of New Queer Cinema. To deny the workings of the unconscious and to simply wish for a celebration of queerness seems to me a hopelessly idealistic and therefore unrealistic project. A Lacanian reading, as I have offered above and corrected for its normative readings of lesbian subjectivity, may not only point to a deconstruction of the stereotype of the murderous lesbian, but more importantly, may also help to understand the confusion and grief involved in processes of queer subjectivity and sexuality. As such, the art films may actually be a step beyond the mere positivity of some of the films in New Queer Cinema. This does not solve, however, the painful issue of stereotyping. I am not advocating an easy embracement of the films I discussed in this chapter, because the stereotype of the murderous lesbian is too vicious and enduring. The films move between the Scylla of perpetual stereotypes and the Charybdis of positive images, in deconstructing the very stereotypes they evoke. Given that they diverge widely from the slick representation of lesbian murderous chic in Hollywood movies, and that New Queer Cinema has given us a wide range of pleasing self-representations, maybe these art films can function to present us with passionate yet perturbing images of lesbian love. Such is the paradox of queer transgression.

NOTES

1 See B. Ruby Rich, 'New Queer Cinema', *Sight and Sound* 2:5 (September 1992), reprinted in this book.
2 See Martha Gever, John Greyson and Pratibha Parmar (eds), *Queer Looks: Perspectives on Lesbian and Gay Film and Video* (London: Routledge, 1993).
3 See, for example, the collections of Laura Doan (ed.), *The Lesbian Postmodern* (New York: Columbia University Press, 1994); Diane Hamer and Belinda Budge (eds), *The Good, the Bad and the Gorgeous: Popular Culture's Romance with Lesbianism* (London: Pandora, 1994); and Tamsin Wilton (ed.), *Immortal, Invisible: Lesbians and the Moving Image* (London: Routledge, 1995).
4 It is surprising that these films met with much more critical attention than lesbian romantic comedies released in the same period, such as *Go Fish* (Rose Troche, 1994), *Bar Girls* (Marita Giovanni, 1994), *When Night Is Falling* (Patricia Rozema,

1995), *Thin Ice* (Fiona Cunningham-Reid, 1995), *The Incredibly True Adventures of Two Girls in Love* (Maria Maggentie, 1995), *Gazon Maudit* (Josianna Balasko, aka *Bushwhacked* or *French Twist*, 1995), and *Love and Other Catastrophes* (Emma-Kate Croghan, 1996). In 1995 Jackie Stacey could still complain that *Desert Hearts* (Donna Deitch, 1985) had no followers, but the above list suggests that this genre is by now fairly established, still in vogue with later additions such as *Chutney Popcorn* (Nisha Ganatra, 1999). See Stacey, ' "If You Don't Play, You Can't Win": *Desert Hearts* and the Lesbian Romance Film', in Wilton, *Immortal*, pp. 92–114.

5 For many decades to come French intellectuals would spill their ink over this crime. The story inspired Jean Genet to write his famous play *The Maids*. Anarchists saw in the sisters Papin 'the angels of the revolution'. Existentialists de Beauvoir and Sartre understood this crime as the uprising of the labourers against the bourgeoisie. de Beauvoir also saw it as the rebellion of female servants against maternal authority. Psychoanalyst Jacques Lacan analysed the murder as 'paranoia caused by repressed lesbian desires' ('Motifs du crime paranoïaque: le crime des sœurs Papin', in *de la Psychose: paranoïque et ses rapports avec la personnalité. Suivi de premiers écrits sur la paranoïa* [Paris: Editions de Seuil, 1975], pp. 389–98). Later in this chapter I will discuss his well-known theory of the mirror phase which is said to be founded on this case. More recently the Papin case became subject of feminist reflection: see Lynda Hart, *Fatal Women: Lesbian Sexuality and the Mark of Aggression* (Princeton, NJ: Princeton University Press 1994); and C. Lane, ' "The Delirium of Interpretation": Writing the Papin Affair', *Differences*, 5:2 (1993): 24–61; and Nicole Jouve-Ward, 'An Eye for an Eye: The Case of the Papin Sisters', in Helen Birch (ed.), *Moving Targets: Women, Murder and Representation* (Berkeley, CA: University of California Press, 1994), pp. 7–31.

6 See Vito Russo, *The Celluloid Closet: Homosexuality in the Closet* (New York: Harper & Row, 1981).

7 Michele Aaron, ' 'Til Death Us Do Part: Cinema's Queer Couples Who Kill', in Michele Aaron (ed.), *The Body's Perilous Pleasures: Dangerous Desires and Contemporary Culture* (Edinburgh: Edinburgh University Press, 1999), p. 77.

8 Alexander Doty, 'Queer Theory', in John Hill and Pamela Church Gibson (eds), *The Oxford Guide to Film Studies* (Oxford: Oxford University Press, 1998), p. 150.

9 See Cathy Griggers, 'Phantom and Reel Projections: Lesbians and the (Serial) Killing-Machine', in Judith Halberstam and Ira Livingston (eds), *Posthuman Bodies*. (Bloomington, IN: Indiana University Press, 1995), pp. 162–76; Christine Holmland, 'A Decade of Deadly Dolls: Hollywood and the Woman Killer', in Birch, *Moving*, pp. 127–51; R. C. Hoogland, *Lesbian Configurations* (Cambridge: Polity Press, 1997); Deborah Jermyn, 'Rereading the Bitches from Hell: A Feminist Appropriation of the Female Psychopath', *Screen*, 37: 3 (1996): 251–67; Yvonne Tasker, *Spectacular Bodies: Gender, Genre and the Action Cinema* (London: Routledge, 1993) and Lee Wallace, 'Continuous Sex: The Editing of Homosexuality in *Bound* and *Rope*', *Screen*, 41:4 (2000): 369–87.

10 Aaron, 'Death', p. 74.

11 Ibid., p. 68.

12 See Anneke Smelik, 'Gay and Lesbian Criticism', in Hill and Gibson, *Oxford Guide*, pp. 135–47.

13 Aaron, 'Death', p. 69.

14 See Jacques Lacan, 'The Mirror Stage as Formative of the Function of the I', in *Écrits: A Selection* (London: Norton, 1966), pp. 1–7.

15 See Jean-Louis Baudry, 'Ideological Effects of the Basic Cinematographic Apparatus', in Gerald Mast et al. (eds), *Film Theory and Criticism* (Oxford: Oxford University Press, 1992), pp. 302–12; and 'The Apparatus: Metaphysical Approaches to Ideology', in ibid., pp. 690–707; and Christian Metz, *Psychoanalysis and Cinema: The Imaginary Signifier* (London: Macmillan, 1982).

16 See Lacan, 'Motifs du crime paranoïaque: le crime des sœurs Papin', *De la Psychose*, pp. 389–98.

17 Hart, *Fatal*, p. 146.
18 Lacan, 'Motifs', p. 397. Translation by author.
19 Quoted in Hart, *Fatal*, p. 146.
20 See Robert Stam et al. *New Vocabularies in Film Semiotics: Structuralism, Post-Structuralism and Beyond* (London: Routledge, 1992), p. 129.
21 Jackie Stacey worked out the difference between these two forms of desire for female friendship in film and the lesbian spectator in 'Desperately Seeking Difference', *Screen*, 28:1 (1987): 48–61.
22 Aaron, 'Death', p. 76.
23 Ibid., p. 76.
24 Eunice's violence is, however, part and parcel of a complex sadomasochistic game in which she both executes and receives punishment. The killings are a far cry from the rape-revenge fury that is ruthlessly depicted in the nihilist film *Baise Moi* (*Fuck Me*; mysteriously released in the US as *Rape Me*). This recent variation on the female buddy movie (France, 2000) in which two soulmates bond and kill a range of men was made by two women filmmakers (Virginie Despentes and Coralie Trin Thi). The film met with angry criticisms at its supposed hatred of men and was censored in many countries for its explicit portrayal of sex. Its critical reception recalls the angry reactions of male audiences to earlier feminist films in which women 'arbitrarily' kill men, such as *A Question of Silence* (Marleen Gorris, 1982). The fact that the five films which I discuss in this chapter have not met with such an angry outcry may have to do with the fact that the girls kill women rather than men (with the exception of *Butterfly Kiss*).
25 Doty, 'Queer', p. 149.

7. NEW QUEER CINEMA AND EXPERIMENTAL VIDEO

Julianne Pidduck

Barbara Hammer insists, polemically, that 'radical content deserves radical form'.[1] This statement marks a longstanding association between feminist and lesbian and gay filmmakers and the avant-garde. Some ten or fifteen years into the 'New Queer Cinema', the word 'radical' is provocative. What is 'radical' about new queer form and content? Can we concur with B. Ruby Rich when in 2000 she proclaims New Queer Cinema's 'short sweet climb from radical impulse to niche market'?[2] Such a narrative affords concise periodisation, where this cycle emerges in the 1980s through AIDS and queer activism and the independent festival circuit, and dies a tragic death with *Boys Don't Cry* (Kimberly Peirce) and *Happy Together* (Wong Kar-Wai) in 1999. However, rather than relinquish the 'radical impulse' to the niche market, I'd like to argue, somewhat polemically, for the continuing relevance of formal experimention as an irritant and a source of renewal for New Queer Cinema.

As a point of departure, it is worth returning to Rich's initial characterisation of the movement:

> Call it 'Homo Pomo': there are traces in all of [these films] of appropriation and pastiche, irony, as well as a reworking of history with social constructionism very much in mind. Definitively breaking with older humanist approaches and the films and tapes that accompanied identity politics, these works are irreverent, energetic, alternately minimalist and excessive. Above all, they're full of pleasure.[3]

In this chapter, I use Rich's suggestive passage to consider several 'experimental' videos by Mike Hoolboom, Richard Fung, Sadie Benning and Cathy

Sisler. Aside from Benning who is American, the other three makers work in a Canadian context, and all four have screened their works in queer milieux while receiving acclaim in fine arts circles. These videos are not selected as 'representative' of the diverse field of queer art video, although I point to some common elements. Indeed, I would suggest that queer art video is characterised by a singularity of form and content that unravels pat discourses of identity, politics and relationality. In this chapter, I use the singularity of each project to interrogate the terms 'new', 'queer', 'cinema'.

'New': Mike Hoolboom's *Tom*

'Newness' is part of the mythology of this cycle. Drawing from the momentum of American independent cinema, the first wave of New Queer Cinema boldly appropriated elements from existing traditions: excessive surrealist imagery from Kenneth Anger and the American underground (*Poison*, Todd Haynes, 1991); the European avant-garde (the works of Ulrike Ottinger and Rosa Von Praunheim); a flamboyant performativity and excessive costuming reminiscent of Warhol and Jack Smith's 1963 *Flaming Creatures* (*Paris is Burning* [Jennie Livingstone, 1990], *Velvet Goldmine* [Todd Haynes, 1998]); the erotic rewriting of genres such as the road movie from Jack Kerouac to *My Own Private Idaho* (Gus Van Sant, 1991), *The Living End* (Gregg Araki, 1992) and Isaac Julien's video installation *The Long Road to Mazatlán* (1999); an amoral 'criminal' expression of desire that may be traced back to Genet, Pasolini, Rimbaud (*Swoon* [Tom Kalin, 1991], *Edward II* [Derek Jarman, 1991], *Les Nuits Fauves* [Cyril Collard, 1992], *Head On* [Ana Kokkinos, 1998]); the queer legacy of the Harlem Renaissance and American 'race' movies of the 1930s and 1940s evoked in *Looking for Langston* (Isaac Julien, 1989) and *The Watermelon Woman* (Cheryl Dunye, 1996) respectively. Such extensive borrowing underscores how New Queer Cinema is rooted in earlier aesthetic traditions, notably an auteurist legacy that is almost exclusively male.

Mike Hoolboom's 75-minute video *Tom* (2002) makes explicit this legacy in a homage to New York filmmaker Tom Chomont. Richard Dyer situates Chomont within a 1970s' avant-garde aftermath to the gay American underground, noting that his films (*Oblivion* [1969], *Love Objects* [1971], *Minor Revisions* [1979] and *Razor Head* [1984]) accentuate the intimate qualities to be found in the works of Jack Smith or Gregory Markopolous; however, the personal qualities of Chomont's films are offset by a certain 'strangeness in the filmmaking, much use of negative reversal, superimposition or remarkable set-ups'.[4] Hoolboom's *Tom* takes up some of these strategies to create a vivid and densely intertextual portrait that incorporates historical documentary, fictional and surrealist film footage, home movies, and recent digital video footage of the ageing filmmaker. A rapidly morphing image track is often treated through negative reversal, colour treatment, repetition and speed

Mike Hoolboom's *Tom*: homage to gay American
Underground filmmaker Tom Chomont (Mike Hoolboom)

variation. Meanwhile, an equally complex soundtrack layers extensive interviews with Chomont, industrial noise, and sudden bursts of music: a sultry jazz saxophone line, sampled single notes and arpeggios on the piano.

An established and prolific Canadian 'fringe' filmmaker and writer, Hoolboom's sexuality is often almost incidental to his work (as with Chomont's films). In keeping with a queer preference for oblique accounts of subjectivity, *Tom*'s palimpsest imagery and breadth of cultural reference serves to disassemble rather than reify 'identity'. Geoff Pevere observes that Hoolboom's 'primary aesthetic is the exposure of the limits of discourse . . . how narrative film practice represents the systematic elimination of . . . [the photographic image's] infinite, unknowable, ambiguity'.[5] Hoolboom situates his own 'fringe film' practice within a tradition where 'from [the cinema's] very inception, a scatter of artists have trained their sights to other ends – sometimes as provocation, or political exposition, or material demonstration'.[6] Tracing a continuity from the auteurist (gay) underground to Hoolboom's own practice, clips from Chomont's films are cut into the video, as are images of Hoolboom filming, or simply observing just off-frame.[7] A recurring sequence of Chomont editing 16mm film stock on a table on a New York sidewalk insists on filmmaking as an artisanal and creative industrial practice.

Hoolboom's work shares New Queer Cinema's strategies of pastiche and the social constructionist reworking of history. *Tom* presents a meditation on the intersection of history, (cinematic) representation and the ephemeral qualities of human memory and corporeality. Hoolboom creates a sound/image canvas, a 'portrait' that does not follow a standard biographical trajectory, but is rather anchored in Chomont's face, voice, and fragmented recollections. After a brief opening sequence in Chomont's apartment, the film cuts to a wide-angle shot close in on his bald, elfin face with the Manhattan skyline in the background. In voiceover, Chomont declares: 'My name is Tom and this is my city.' Cut to an aerial shot, soaring over the Statue of Liberty towards Manhattan. This shot introduces a structuring analogy between the human body and the modern city – not just any city, but New York in 2001. Hoolboom comments:

> Manhattan is a small island which changes constantly in its quest for the new . . . it rips down buildings and makes new ones. The destruction of New York has been imagined many times, not only in cinema, and the September 11 attacks are [a particularly horrible] part of this continuum . . . The body of Tom is framed by images of New York's destruction . . . And in this image of a city constantly refigured lies a metaphor for personality itself, as we see Tom incarnated as a drag queen, as S/M top, S/M bottom, as brother and son, as film then video maker, always changing appearance, interests, sexual predilections.[8]

The dialectic between destruction and renewal is integral to *Tom*, which incorporates clips from disaster movies, documentary footage of skyscraper construction and building demolition, and early twentieth-century Lower East Side street scenes. The resulting visceral but abstract portrait of the city is a time-travelling version of the great modernist 'city symphony' films *Man with a Movie Camera* (Dziga Vertov, 1929) and *Berlin, Symphony of a Great City* (Walter Ruttmann, 1927). Juxtaposed with Chomont's voiceover childhood recollections and sampled industrial sounds, the soundscape and narration are non-synchronous with the image track. Parallels between memory and experience and the city are at once broadly historical and oddly intimate.

Something strange happens to time in Hoolboom's films. The linear logic of event-as-sequence – conventional history, narrative, biography – dissolves here. New Queer Cinema's claim to the 'new', at least if read through the logic of just-in-time production and niche marketing, is incommensurable with *Tom*'s rich temporality. Gilles Deleuze claims that narrative cinema (what he calls the 'movement-image') unfolds in a perpetual present governed by a vision of human intentionality and agency. Within this system, 'aberrant movements' (cinematic aspects that exceed or digress from causal sequence) are suppressed to preserve the hegemony of 'normal movement'. The dominant form of the 'action-image' centres the human body in the frame as transformative agent within a determined milieu. Aberrant movement stands for the transformative capacity of time as both *before* and *after* the perpetual present of the movement-image: 'There is no present which is not haunted by a past and a future, by a past which is not reducible to a former present, by a future which does not consist of a present to come'.[9] For Deleuze, the 'time-image' describes a different cinematic trajectory, where the spatial ordering of narrative time gives way to 'pure optical and sound situations' where 'time is no longer the measure of movement but movement is the perspective of time'.[10]

Hoolboom's work deploys several aspects of the time-image.[11] 'False continuities' of surrealist editing abound, where the splicing together of incommensurable fragments creates unexpected articulations of memory, causality and meaning. Juxtaposed with Chomont's narration, the 'city symphony' dialectic of disintegration and frantic rebuilding personalises the cinematic residue of historical social space and long-dead citizens, while depersonalising and extending the peculiarities of individual recollection. Most germane to new queer cinema, *Tom* jumbles what might loosely be called 'the history of sexuality'. For instance, the frequent use of surrealist 'dream-images' (dissolves, super-impositions, deframings, special effects) transfigures objective perception into a subjective modality. In *Tom*, the reconfiguration of saturated symbolism and banal popular culture creates a disturbing and unexpected account of mortality, generation, and (queer) corporeality. The dissolution of cinematic 'sense' through a barrage of the time-image's 'pure sound and optical situations' corresponds to a disintegration of corporeal and biographical boundaries.

Pale, wizened, balding and suffering from Parkinson's disease and HIV/ AIDS, Chomont's hands and body are unsteady and his quavering voice often is overcome with emotion. Hoolboom intercuts his alternately gnome-like and childlike subject with foetuses, martians, microscopic organisms and children. The co-presence of Tom's childhood, young adulthood and present parallels the restless city sequences, where different decades collide without respect for generic convention or temporal sequence. For instance, in voiceover Chomont links his homosexuality with an intense relationship with his brother who was his main companion in an itinerant childhood. The boys were lovers briefly as teenagers, and Chomont's account of this relationship coincides with a montage of historical footage of boys playing in the street and exploring an empty farmhouse. This imagery is made strange through compulsive repetition and speed variation, overwriting found historical footage with same-sex desire and the taint of incest. In a cumulative editing strategy, *Tom* incorporates many shots of children and adults entering and leaving rooms, opening and closing doors and windows – a simple scenario suggesting exploration, transgression, voyeurism, or more broadly the life cycle as a series of thresholds and passages.

Chomont describes how his brother explored S/M and fetish sexuality before him, and recounts the scene of his brother's death from AIDS, a scene that foreshadows his own imminent death. In *Tom*, the rapidly morphing, fragile subject evokes most of all the unsteady passage of time – the haunting duration of the recollection-image, the fragile corporeal temporality of illness and everyday experience. For Deleuze, cinematic forms are equated with 'images of thought', and Hoolboom's reassembled moving image form generates fresh ways of conceiving illness, corporeality, desire and history.

'QUEER': RICHARD FUNG'S *SEA IN THE BLOOD*

The 'queerness' of new queer cinema derives centrally from an activist response to the AIDS crisis and the rise of the New Right from the mid-1980s,[12] primarily in Anglo-American, European and antipodean contexts. 'Queer' is often associated with a generational structure of feeling, what José Arroyo identifies as an 'epistemic shift' in gay culture. More specifically, he suggests that AIDS is the 'political unconscious' of the new queer cinema. Although AIDS does not figure explicitly in films such as *My Own Private Idaho* and *Edward II*, they 'depict the context of the pandemic through their use of style, their romanticism, their representation of sexuality and time, and their dystopic viewpoint'.[13] Films like *Swoon*, *The Living End* or *Frisk* (Todd Verow, 1995) project the intensity of gay desire in the face of death. It might be argued that the eclipse of New Queer Cinema coincides with another epistemic shift in queer culture where HIV/AIDS is imagined (if not necessarily experienced) as 'past', a 'chronic manageable condition' in Western countries;

at this juncture the encounter with death and loss requires a different analytic and affective register.

I would suggest that Arroyo's argument still has resonance for contemporary queer culture: Does AIDS as political unconscious imply an ethical ground for New Queer Cinema as it spins into a post-political, purely for-profit orbit? Part of what is at stake with an increasingly commercial queer cinema is an edge associated with the AIDS crisis and its impact on a generation of gay men and lesbians. In *Letters from Home* (1996), Hoolboom's narrator asks: 'Because we already know how we're going to die. What we don't know, what we're asking you now, is how we're going to *live*?' Hoolboom's work begs the broader question: How are we to represent AIDS now? *Tom*, like the AIDS-specific works *Frank's Cock* (1994), *Letters from Home* and *Panic Bodies* (1998) are saturated with the personal and social implications of AIDS, but they are not 'about' AIDS in any simple way. Hoolboom's work is inflected by his public HIV+ status, and his films and videos articulate queer experience and corporeality in unexpected ways with personal memory and historical change. 'Unexpected' is the pivotal term here, for experimental form has the capacity to challenge the generic and affective orders that both comfort and capture us. Films like *Longtime Companion* (Norman René, 1990), *An Early Frost* (John Erman, 1985) or *Philadelphia* (Jonathan Demme, 1993) represent important victories for gay self-representation within the arenas of independent film, television, and Hollywood cinema respectively; but their melodramatic modality does not address Hoolboom's question: 'How are we going to *live*?' Another recent video that addresses 'living with AIDS' unexpectedly is Richard Fung's *Sea in the Blood* (2001).

Sea blends the two major strands of Fung's 20–year video *œuvre*, post-colonial Asian history and queer Asian identity. Like *The Way to My Father's Village* (1988) and *My Mother's Place* (1990), *Sea* interrogates family history alongside colonial histories and codes of representation. Fung uses the metaphor of fluids to juxtapose his lover's struggle with HIV/AIDS with his sister's rare blood disorder (thalassaemia, meaning 'sea in the blood'). This metaphor is anchored in recurring footage of water and swimmers. *Sea* begins with underwater imagery featuring Fung and his lover Tim McCaskell. Each swims gracefully through the inverted 'V' of the other's spread legs, their faces and bodies almost brushing the camera as they glide up to the surface of the water. Tinted with ambers and reds and shot through with rays of light, this footage is speed altered to accentuate a dreamlike fluidity of motion. Nayan Shah describes this *leitmotif* as follows: 'The rose-tinted waters dilute and refract the blood everywhere. The color of the water recalls the blood of heredity: the blood that carries illness, the blood that can cause distress, and the blood of intimacy'.[14]

In this quiet and intricate video essay of 26 minutes, Fung traces parallels and tensions between his birth family and his longstanding gay relationship.

The tape begins with a romance, a series of snapshots and slides held up to the camera depicting Richard and Tim's travels as young lovers, and in voiceover, Fung describes his family's disapproval of their travels to Europe and Asia. The next segment of the tape describes Fung's Trinidadian childhood with his sister Nan as his constant companion. Through home movies, photographs and Fung's voiceover narration, a tender sibling relationship emerges; the swimming motif returns in home movie footage of a boy and girl playing on a beach. Gradually through intercutting the two narratives, the tension between Fung's gay relationship and family ties culminates as he returns from his trip too late, after Nan's death. *Sea* deftly intertwines memoir and conflict using Fung's and other family members' voiceover recollections, personal photographs, documentary footage, and a line of red text that comments silently along the bottom of the screen. For instance, Fung describes in voiceover how 'Nan would talk about how she could never lead a normal life, never have a boyfriend', while the text states: 'I couldn't tell her that I wanted a boyfriend'. Later, as Fung's mother Rita describes Nan's death to him (the voicetrack non-synchronous with close-ups of her face and hands as she works in the garden), the written text reveals: 'It took 20 years for me to ask my mother to describe Nan's death.'

Richard Fung's *Sea in the Blood*: swimmers and metaphorical fluids (V tape)

In an e-mail typed, ghostlike, onto the screen, Fung confides to his sister Arlene: 'I have always lived with illness, first with Nan, now with Tim'. This moment exemplifies Fung's carefully polyphonic account of the sometimes painful negotiation between his Chinese-Trinidadian family and a gay political/intimate circle. José Muñoz suggests that Fung practises 'autoethnography', a method that

> in many ways [seeks] to reclaim the past and put it in direct relation with the present. Autoethnography is not interested in searching for some lost and essential experience, because it understands the relationship that subjects have with their own pasts as complicated yet necessary fictions.[15]

In this respect, *Sea* exemplifies what I would call the utopian theoretical and political valence of 'queer' suggested by Lisa Duggan: 'The continuing work of queer politics and theory is to open up possibilities for coalition across barriers of class, race, and gender'.[16] Fung traces the complexity of conflicting 'queer' allegiances across gaps in time/space, and ethnic and sexual experience, seeking to heal rifts without denying dissonance.

Duggan's explicitly activist notion of queer 'coalition' is transfigured in *Sea* along the more intimate lines of 'allegiance'. The tape offers a meditative account of AIDS that diverges from the urgency of Fung's earlier *Fighting Chance* (1990), a documentary about gay Asians living with AIDS. Building on the AIDS activist video tradition, Fung cuts into *Sea* a sequence from John Greyson's *The World is Sick (Sic)* (1989), where activists storm the 1989 World AIDS conference in Montreal, and McCaskell (Fung's lover) opens the conference in the name of people living with AIDS. This video cameo *personalises* the retrospective moment of AIDS activism, prompting a more lateral thinking about death, memory, responsibility. *Sea* extends insights about the social construction of AIDS to another place, another time, another illness. Images of Nan as an Asian-Trinidadian child in the 1960s are intercut with clinical images and voiceover from a pedagogical slide show about thalassaemia. While Fung's scrutiny born of AIDS activism interrogates the ethnic, colonial and class implications of the illness, his family gratefully acknowledges the pro bono treatment that Nan received from a renowned English haemotologist.

Rather than the crisis temporality of AIDS activist video that declares the urgency of immediate action (SILENCE = DEATH), some years later *Sea* addresses AIDS differently through the 'recollection-image', another aspect of Deleuze's time-image. Eschewing the pedagogical cause-and-effect narrative essential to strategic media and political intervention, the recollection-image filters 'chains of associations and memories of past experience' associated with the image, and in the process, 'the object depicted is de-framed and created anew'.[17] The swimming sequences, home movies and photographs evoke the resonance of the moment in memory – Richard and Tim's travels as young lovers, an afternoon swimming in the sea, the last photo taken of Nan by Richard. But these vivid moments tinged with memory, bereavement and hope are constantly, gently interrogated by competing accounts and through the intersection of intimacy and history. *Sea* negotiates living with the ephemeral nature of the body, and the fragility of intimate ties within families and between lovers.

'CINEMA': SADIE BENNING'S *IT WASN'T LOVE* (BUT IT WAS SOMETHING)

The term 'cinema' begs the question of medium, inclusivity and context. If lesbian/gay/queer film and video consist of overlapping circuits of production and consumption, the community-based film and video festivals that arose in the 1980s have been tremendously generative. AIDS and queer activism of the 1980s and 1990s were pivotal to the development of this independent circuit – an aesthetic, institutional and cultural basis for self-representation not directly reliant on commercial funding. Many of the new queer 'auteurs' (Tom Kalin, Todd Haynes, Cheryl Dunye, Lisa Cholodenko, John Greyson, Midi Onodera, Richard Kwietnioski, Pratibha Parmar, Isaac Julien) began with shorts, documentary, and experimental and activist video. Festivals and feminist/queer distributors facilitated innovative self-representation and assembled engaged audiences. The audiences, aesthetics and expertise that developed in these contexts have been pivotal to the genesis of the New Queer Cinema phenomenon.

Community-based festivals are part of a 'queer public sphere' where, as Martha Gever suggests, lesbians and gay men forge our identities – 'the names we give ourselves' – be they 'ordinary', outrageous, ambivalent.[18] Urban activist and arts contexts that include film festivals and other media have inspired *new ways of looking, acting and being* that fuel the distinctive energy of the New Queer Cinema. It is my contention that experimental form has the unique capacity to stretch the limits of intelligibility for queer identity, relationality and politics. On this theme, the organisers of the New York Experimental Lesbian and Gay Film Festival (now Mix) wrote in 1987:

> The experimental process mirrors, in many ways, the process of understanding a gay identity; both demand an endless re-imagining of the self and the world in order to envision and create what the mainstream believes should not and must not exist.[19]

Hybrid documentaries, dramatic shorts, experimental film and especially video have been rich formats for the rescripting of identity and sexuality – what Deleuze might call 'aberrant movements'. This is especially true for lesbians and makers of colour who have historically had less access to the means of production for features, and generally these groups are marginal to the New Queer Cinema canon.[20] The availability of portable, inexpensive video technology has been an important factor in the proliferation of queer art and activist video. In Canada where Hoolboom, Fung and Sisler are based, artist-run centres have historically facilitated the use of video for political expression by marginal groups.[21] For Rich, from the outset New Queer Cinema featured 'a new kind of lesbian video' that expresses a 'new type of lesbian sensibility'.[22] Sadie Benning's works were among the few videos, or indeed lesbian-authored and themed works of the New Queer Cinema 'roll of honour' from the early 1990s; even so, her videos are unavailable outside of the US. Although some feminist and queer community-based distributors still handle non-commercial video,[23] it is increasingly the case that formats other than feature-length narrative cinema elude the networks of distribution associated with the recent rise of the niche market. In 1999, Rich reported that 80–90 per cent of festival programming was (still) not distributed outside of this context.[24] Moreover, shorts, documentaries and experimental film and video mostly fall below the radar of critical reception, including lesbian and gay media and academic criticism.

Shot on a Fisher-Price Pixelvision camera, teen-aged Benning's no budget, low-tech works exemplify the resourceful deployment of video, where the camera becomes generative in its technical limitations.

> Because the camera doesn't have a zoom lens, Benning pushes her face close to its aperture, achieving an eerie fish-eyed sense of presence . . . [Meanwhile] the length of the shots, a consequence of the camera's weak batteries, becomes a stylistic asset as the piece careens dizzily from one suggestive fragment to the next.[25]

Benning's videos are characterised by a 'handmade' aesthetic shared by Cathy Sisler, whose work I will return to below. In this low-resolution, flattened out aesthetic, the camera scans text scrawled on paper, fragmented images of Benning's face and body and cut-out dolls; these elements are edited in-camera with snippets of music, and the anchoring address of Benning's voice. Benning uses a common 'video diary' form that emphasises the medium's capacity to represent 'visceral sensations and interior speech'.[26] Like Fung's contemplative voiceovers, the maker's personal address produces 'autoethnography' – in Benning's case, the self-conscious performance of an emergent teen dyke sensibility.

Benning's pixie face features centrally, her unblinking eye pressed in close to the camera as she recounts a series of 'tall tales' in *It Wasn't Love* (1992). Like Hoolboom, Benning delights in quoting from popular culture. But the teen-aged maker is much closer to the erotic charge of dominant mythology, and also much more direct in her critique. In *It Wasn't Love*, Benning queers the coming of age narrative, playing with and against the all-American mythology of the open road. Benning confides to the camera how a 'glamourous chick' took her away: 'She said: "Get in the car, we're going to Hollywood"'. Cut to

Benning, in close to the camera with a spotlight behind her head, lip-synching with a vintage microphone: 'I Found My Thrill on Blueberry Hill'. Later, she continues: 'She said, "Let's go to Detroit. On the way we'll rob some liquor stores. And when we get there, we'll lay low" '. Cut to gangster movie footage and Benning in drag playing out the phallic possibilities of a cigar and a cane to the song 'Why Must I Be a Teenager in Love?'. Pointedly, the road trip to Hollywood is indicated by a shot of a hand pushing a toy car along the floor. Benning's hand-made form is revindicated in a dyke counterculture manifesto at the end of the tape as she 'confesses':

> We didn't make it to Detroit, much less Hollywood. Instead, we pulled into a fried chicken parking lot and made out . . . And then it happened, she dropped me off at home. You know, I wanted to feel sorry for myself, like I was missing out on something. And yet, in that parking lot, I felt like I had seen the whole world. She had this way of making me feel like I was the goddam Nile River or something. We didn't need Holly-wood, we *were* Hollywood. She was the most glamourous chick I'd ever seen, and that made us both famous.

Cut to a hand-made intertitle: 'IT WASN'T LOVE, BUT IT WAS SOME-THING'.

Sadie Benning's *It Wasn't Love*: 'We're going to Hollywood' (Video Data Bank)

Benning's episodic, quirky works present the self-conscious unfolding of a generational political and sexual outlook. An anomaly among short or experimental queer video makers, Benning is something of a fairy tale. Described by Rich as a 'Wunderkind' who wowed the critics at Sundance, her videos have been widely screened in queer film festivals and art galleries alike (including the prestigious New York Museum of Modern Art).[27] Without taking anything away from these brilliant tapes, part of the cachet of Benning's videos arises from their encapsulation of a playful, sexy, irreverent sensibility celebrated by queer activists and theorists of the period. Benning's fluid account of identity correlates perfectly with Judith Butler's account of 'gender as performance' (as does *Paris is Burning* which features centrally in *Bodies that Matter*). This perfect homology underscores the cultural and generational specificity of the New Queer Cinema moment. However, part of the ongoing 'radical' project of experimental video and critical queer thought alike is to question the limits of emergent cultural discourses as they arise (unexpectedly), become almost self-evident, then even commercially viable.

In an era of self-conscious performances of queer identity, Cathy Sisler's work literally staggers over recalcitrant obstacles of normative femininity, substance abuse and corrosive self-doubt. Her work offers a reminder that the market forces and taste formations that enable the New Queer Cinema also exclude many of the more politically edgy – and less *photogenic* – aspects of lesbian/queer identity. On the 'minimal' rather than the 'excessive' end of New Queer Cinema's aesthetics, Sisler's work, like Benning's, is resolutely unfinished, rough around the edges. As with Hoolboom's imploding sound and imagescapes or Fung's unexpected parallels, Sisler's and Benning's minimal realms of make-believe demand an attentive, thinking viewer. Experimental form is the legacy of modernism and the avant-garde, but it would be too easy to dismiss these unfamiliar video trajectories as élitist. The fact that these works do not command a 'mass' audience does not eliminate the significance of the *process* of multiple, dissonant self-representations by disenfranchised subjects. Against the airbrushed homogeneity of queer consumer culture, these artists continue to articulate what is 'singular', indigestible, strange, ugly and powerful in queer existence.

PUSHING THE LIMITS: CATHY SISLER'S *ABERRANT MOTION #4*

Sharing with Benning the use of performance, storytelling and an improvised, low resolution aesthetic, Sisler places her own body at the centre of a series of video experiments that scathingly interrogate normative codes of behaviour and identity. In *The Better Me* (1994), she mocks 'self-help' discourses, where a TV presenter (Sisler) wearing a loud flowered blouse asks the audience: 'Want a better career, a better body, a better memory, better relationships, a better prediction for your future? Sure, we all do'. But Sisler's mockery of the pat soundbites of self-improvement is not without ambivalence. In this video,

Sisler carts around with her on the street a painted, life-sized flat replica of an 'improved' self. Painted from a photograph of herself as a teen-ager (unsullied feminine potentiality), her 'better me' is a life-sized reminder of the perennial pain and disappointment of failed femininity.

In a series of four short, arresting videos entitled *Aberrant Motion*, Sisler explores the powers and dangers of deviant movement as *interruption*. Sisler's videos record performances where she uses her (lesbian) body as an intervention in the everyday flow of 'normal' traffic, pedestrians, thought. *Aberrant Motion #1* (1993) begins with a figure of a spinning woman (the artist) at a busy Montreal intersection. The degraded video image, strangely arresting, documents the pedestrians' responses to Sisler's large body clothed in an oversized man's coat, her short haircut and 'aberrant motion'. As the spinning woman on a busy street corner, or in a series of failed attempts at 'public speaking' (*Aberrant Public Speaking*, 1994), Sisler seeks to imprint her aberrant body and ideas in the 'normal movement' of urban public space. But the passers-by hasten past this woman with her disorderly gait and oversized hand-made props. Pedestrians skirt the soapbox orator, and her words are barely audible, drowned out by the noise of passing traffic. Sisler's *Aberrant Public Speaking* self-consciously evokes the pathos of minority expression – even, at a stretch, the absurd courage of video and performance as public intervention.

Jean-François Lyotard describes cinematography as 'the inscription of movement, a writing with movements'.[28] For Lyotard, as for Deleuze, cinematic movement implies *intensity*, potential. The production of cinematic meaning involves a process of ordering and selection where certain bodies and movements are foregrounded while others are backgrounded, or simply excluded. This 'ordering' economy, where intensities are channelled into repeatable narrative and generic forms feeds an economy of consumption and exchange. This logic of 'selection and ordering of movements' for the purposes of exchange ultimately seeks to 'eliminate aberrant movements, useless expenditures'.[29] Lyotard explicitly relates the regulation of the pleasures of cinematic movement with the ordering of the drives toward 'normal genital sexuality' in a capitalist/patriarchal society.

Aberrant Motion #4 (1994) extends the spinning theme into a stagger. For Sisler, walking/staggering is more than a metaphor – an ontology, the deployment of the (deviant) body in space, a series of unpredictable, awkward and beautiful, sometimes hostile interactions. In the second segment of the tape entitled *Stagger Stories*, Sisler's confessions – 'I am a recovering alcoholic and drug user' . . . 'I am a lesbian' . . . 'I am fat' – seem to precipitate a twelve-step recovery trajectory. But the stagger of the drug user and the alcoholic resists 'cure', containment, stability:

> Staggering involves a disruption of the learned, repeated movements of walking . . . Disrupting the rhythm . . . These disruptions of the con-

vention of linear walking do not stop the motion of a person through space, rather, a whole new form of more complex movement is achieved. But this form of motion is seen as a deviation, and the staggerer is stigmatized in our society.

This text is read rapidly in Sisler's characteristic urgent monotone over a striking slow motion image of the artist staggering and stumbling down a green corridor towards the camera. Blurred, as in a hallucination, the staggering figure is weirdly graceful – a deviant kinesis that kilters between subjective disintegration and a fragile equilibrium.

Cathy Sisler's *Aberrant Motion #4*:
a staggering ontology (Groupe Intervention Video)

Where many heroes of New Queer Cinema (for instance, in *Swoon* and *The Living End*) revel in a renegade outsider status, Sisler's aberrant movements of spinning and staggering present *unfashionable* modes of deviation and risk. Sisler reveals the pain and, literally, fancy footwork, involved in surviving as a deviant. For Kim Sawchuk,

Sisler's work thus deviates from reflections on the subject in the city that romanticize homelessness, nomadism, or itinerant subjectivity. Some subjects do not have a choice. Some subjects have histories inscribed on and through their bodies. The body, her body, is the locus of these actions, but it is not depicted as a privileged site of knowledge or control, or as a place of empowerment and pleasure, but as well, as a site of potential trauma and injury.[30]

If *It Wasn't Love* confidently defies the allure of Hollywood – *We didn't need Hollywood, we WERE Hollywood* – in Sisler's universe, coherent identity, expression, belonging and beauty are disassembled. Sisler's 'aberrant motion' is not only corporeal movement through space, but an unassimilable vaga-bond femininity that is smart, funny and above all, angry. The stumbling, spinning body, and the articulate, thinking voice undertake a restless, search-ing trajectory fuelled by the rage of the dispossessed. Towards the end of *Aberrant Motion #4*, Sisler states: 'Now I am addicted to walking. Having to be normal so much of the time drives me crazy. But no matter how long I walk I always stay angry.' Corrosive to the gloss of commercial queer culture, Sisler's rage raises questions about pleasure and the more troubling aspects of queer self-representation.

'Above all', Rich reminds us, new queer films and videos are 'full of pleasure'. In an era where 'pleasure' and the radical reclaiming of popular culture have become something of a mantra for cultural studies, I would like to argue for pleasures that are not 'easy'. Barbara Hammer insists on 'work which allows the maker and the viewer the *pleasure of discovery*. Meaning is not apparent at first glance, and often requires repeated screenings, promising *challenge*'.[31] Sisler's work, like Hammer's, expresses 'perceptual, intellectual, and emotional con-figurations that provoke pain and give pleasure'.[32] For many, the term 'art video' conjures sensations of radical *displeasure*. This is not my own response to Sisler's videos or any of the works discussed here, and I find in them many moments of sublime beauty, acerbic humour, quirky erudition. As commercial viability overtakes 'aberrant motion' for New Queer Cinema, the challenge is to facilitate the radical exploration that comes with experimental form.

ACKNOWLEDGEMENTS

I would like to thank the following people for their generous input at different stages of this project: José Arroyo, Richard Dyer, Mike Hoolboom, Ger Zielinski, Bertie Mandelblatt, Anne Golden, Michele Aaron, Jo-Anne Pickel, Kim Sawchuk. Also, thanks to V tape, Video Data Bank and Groupe Intervention Vidéo for supplying preview tapes and images.

NOTES

1 Barbara Hammer, 'The Politics of Abstraction', in Martha Gever, John Greyson and Pratibha Parmar (eds), *Queer Looks: Perspectives on Lesbian and Gay Film and Video* (London: Routledge, 1993), p. 70.
2 B. Ruby Rich, 'Queer and Present Danger', *Sight and Sound*, 10:3 (March 2000): 23.
3 B. Ruby Rich, 'New Queer Cinema', *Sight and Sound*, 2:5 (September 1992): 32, reprinted in this book.

4 Richard Dyer, *Now You See It: Studies on Lesbian and Gay Film* (London: Routledge, 1990), p. 166.

5 Geoff Pevere, 'Outer Limits: The Cinema of Mike Hoolboom', *Take One*, 4:9 (September 1995): 22–7 [Internet InfoTrac Web version], p. 2.

6 Mike Hoolboom, *Inside the Pleasure Dome: Fringe Film in Canada* (Toronto: A Pages Book for Gutter Press, 1997), p. 4. See also Mike Hoolboom, 'Thoughts on Short Films', *Take One* 4 (9) 1995: Internet InfoTrac Web version.

7 In an e-mail interview (21 May 2002), Hoolboom describes the tape as 'a *memento mori* [to Chomont] as well as a self-portrait in a way'.

8 Ibid.

9 Gilles Deleuze, *Cinema 2: The Time-Image* (Minneapolis: University of Minnesota Press, 1989), p. 37.

10 Ibid., p. 22.

11 For a reading of the spatiality of Hoolboom's *Panic Bodies* with reference to Deleuze's time-image, see Darrell Varga, '*Panic Bodies* and the Performance of Space', *Canadian Journal of Film Studies*, 10:2 (February 2002): 80–101.

12 See Cherry Smyth, *Lesbians Talk Queer Notions* (London: Scarlet Press, 1992).

13 José Arroyo, 'Death, Desire and Identity: The Political Unconscious of "New Queer Cinema"', in Joseph Bristow and Angelia Wilson (eds), *Activating Theory* (London: Lawrence & Wishart, 1993), p. 80.

14 Nayan Shah, 'Undertow', in Helen Lee and Kerri Sakamoto (eds), *Like Mangoes in July: The Work of Richard Fung* (Toronto: Insomniac Press/Images Festival, 2002), p. 102.

15 José Muñoz, 'The Autoethnographic Performance: Reading Richard Fung's Queer Hybridity', *Screen*, 36:2 (February 1995): 89.

16 Lisa Duggan, 'Making It Perfectly Queer', *Socialist Review*, 22:1 (January 1992): 26.

17 D.N. Rodowick, *Gilles Deleuze's Time Machine* (Durham, NC: Duke University Press, 1997), p. 90.

18 Martha Gever, 'The Names We Give Ourselves', in Russell Ferguson et al. (eds), *Out There: Marginalization and Contemporary Culture* (New York: The New Museum of Contemporary Art, 1991), pp. 191–202. On lesbian/gay/queer film festivals, see also Patricia White (ed.), 'Queer Publicity: A Dossier on Lesbian and Gay Film Festivals', *Gay and Lesbian Quarterly*, 5:1 (January 1999): 73–93.

19 Cited in Joshua Gamson, 'The Organizational Shaping of Collective Identity: The Case of Lesbian and Gay Film Festivals in New York', in Martin Duberman (ed.), *A Queer World* (New York: New York University Press, 1997), p. 529.

20 Amy Taubin argues that the 'transgressive' violence and desire of the new queer cinema (especially its first wave) are resolutely masculinist, in 'Beyond the Sons of Scorsese', *Sight and Sound* (September 1992): 37. Part of a longstanding tradition that tends to sideline if not villify women, this tradition may be traced back to the Beat generation, Genet, Rimbaud, Cocteau, Pasolini. See Elizabeth Wilson, 'Is Transgression Transgressive?', in Bristow and Wilson, *Activating*, pp. 107–17.

21 See Janine Marchessault (ed.), *Mirror Machine: Video and Identity* (Toronto: YYZ Books and The Centre for Research on Canadian Cultural Industries and Institutions, 1995) and Peggy Gale and Lisa Steele (eds), *Video re/View* (Toronto: Art Metropole and V tape, 1996).

22 Rich, 'New', p. 33, reprinted in this book.

23 Video Data Bank (Chicago) and Women Make Movies (New York) distribute Benning's work, and V tape (Toronto) and Groupe Intervention Vidéo (Montreal) distribute Fung's and Sisler's work respectively. It is disturbing to note the fragility of these networks of distribution, as for instance, the British queer distributor 'Dangerous to Know' has folded and London-based feminist distributor Cinenova, like other feminist distributors, struggles to continue.

24 B. Ruby Rich, 'Collision, Catastrophe, Celebration: The Relationship between Gay and Lesbian Film Festivals and Their Publics', *Gay and Lesbian Quarterly*, 5:1 (1999): 82.

25 Christine Tamblyn, 'Qualifying the Quotidian: Artist's Video and the Production of Social Space', in Michael Renov and Erika Suderburg (eds), *Resolutions: Contemporary Video Practices* (Minneapolis: University of Minnesota Press, 1996), p. 22.

26 Ibid., p. 13.

27 Benning has gone on to make work for MTV, but significantly has not taken the feature filmmaking route of many stars of the New Queer Cinema. Benning's later works such as *The Judy Spots* (1995) and *Flat is Beautiful* (1998) continue a wryly dystopian interrogation of the conventions of gender and American teen-aged suburban experience.

28 Jean-François Lyotard, 'Acinema', *Wide Angle*, 2:3 (March 1978): 53.

29 Ibid., p. 55.

30 Kim Sawchuk, 'Out of Step: Cathy Sisler's Risky Deviations', *Inversions*, (1998): 15–16. On Sisler, see also Nicole Gingras and Cathy Sisler, *La Femme Écran/The Reflexive Woman* (Montréal: Les Éditions Nicole Gingras/Oboro/the Centre d'Art Contemporain de Basse-Normandie, 1996).

31 Hammer, 'The Politics of Abstraction', p. 73, original emphasis.

32 Ibid., p. 73.

PART III

LOCATING NEW QUEER CINEMA

OVERVIEW

Was New Queer Cinema an exclusively male, white and Anglo-American phenomenon? How was it influenced by, or influential for, lesbian film, black queer work, or non-US cinemas? How has the identity and geography of its filmmakers impacted upon NQC's emergence and progression? Through consideration of a range of narrative and national contexts, this part scrutinises those troubling limitations that NQC, and its reception, initially enacted to provide a crucial but less visible trajectory of the evolution of (New) Queer Cinema.

The first three chapters pursue the dynamic between NQC and gender and racial difference. For Anat Pick in Chapter 8, NQC provides a single but unsatisfying context for understanding the development of lesbian film in the 1990s. Combining this with discussions of postmodernism, lesbianism, and feminism, Pick is able to expose the 'breadth of lesbian filmmaking within and beyond the New Queer project'. She finds that the popularity of queer images have shaken the definitions, pleasures, and understandings of lesbian cinema, but, at the same time, lesbian cinema can perform a similarly critical role within our developing understanding of queer film. Race, like lesbianism, was also sidelined within NQC and, similarly again, the relationship between black queer film and NQC appears symbiotic, as both Daniel Contreras and Louise Wallenberg imply. For Contreras in Chapter 9, *Paris is Burning*, in its exceptional articulation of race *and* queerness, embodied all that was radical about NQC, but, ultimately, also, all that it failed to achieve. The film symbolised the utopian aspirations of the queering of race, but, at the same time, critiqued the euphoria surrounding NQC. For Wallenberg in Chapter 10, Isaac Julien's *Looking for Langston* (1989) and Marlon Riggs's *Tongues Untied* (1990) did not just represent what was radical about NQC but prefigured it. Exploring the two films' poetic and political expressions of the hybridity of queer black experience, Wallenberg positions them at, but also as, the very beginning of NQC.

The final two chapters in this part turn their attention to world cinemas to temper the privileging of the white-American-male aesthetic that dominated NQC, to substantiate the movement's global impact and to suggest its enduring productivity and relevance for film theory. For Ros Jennings and Loykie Lominé in Chapter 11, Ana Kokkinos' 1997 film, *Head On* represents Australia's answer to NQC in that it offers queer themes, characters and realistic representations of queer life. More than this, the authors suggest, it broadens the debate on the limitations of the US model of NQC, and reopens the critical potential of queer: 'Australian identities are constructed from such diverse and competing sets of co-ordinates that the notion "queer" takes on a wider emphasis than usually considered'. In Chapter 12 Helen Hok-Sze Leung finds the connections between NQC and Third Cinema extremely fruitful for a reconsideration of the political project of the former and the queer potential of the latter. Using Chinese cinema as a case study, she distinguishes films that are 'queer' both in their anti-normative depiction of sexual and gender practices, and their disruption of conventional notions of history, politics, and filmmaking: 'As China veers away from the political path of Third Worldist radicalism, thus eclipsing the climate once favourable to Third Cinema practices, queer cinema arrives on the scene to become the new icon of rebellion'.

8. NEW QUEER CINEMA
AND LESBIAN FILMS

Anat Pick

Introduction: 'Q' for Curious

The immediate aim of this chapter is to provide a critical overview of the place of lesbian films within New Queer Cinema. The task is not an easy one in a field which is as contentious as it is broad. The main difficulty seems to be how best to approach a range of definitions, from 'new' to 'queer' to 'lesbian', since with every one of them, we risk biting off more than we can chew. As often happens with formal titles, so with the New Queer Cinema, its lifespan ('officially' 1992–2000) now seems to have been a great deal shorter than that of the movies that first gave it its name. The same goes for its filmic legacies, which have outlived it. What, then, is New Queer Cinema? Is there, correspondingly, a New Lesbian Cinema? And if so, how does lesbian film fit into the New Queer framework? I hope to be able to offer some helpful complications, if not positive replies to these questions.

It was critic B. Ruby Rich who pin-pointed an influx of films made by and about gays that were redefining queer filmmaking in pre-Millennial, AIDS-affected America. These films, for example Todd Haynes' *Poison* (1991), Tom Kalin's *Swoon* (1991), Christopher Münch's *The Hours and Times* (1991), Marlon Riggs' *Tongues Untied* (1991), Gregg Araki's *The Living End* (1992), or Jennie Livingston's *Paris is Burning* (1990), were all low budget and formally inventive films, temperamentally confrontational, and deliciously transgressive.[1] Rich dubbed this sensibility 'Homo Pomo': homosexual (significantly male, and, we might add predominantly American and white), and postmodern. By the year 2000, however, Rich declared that New Queer Cinema did not constitute a 'movement' but, as it turns out, a 'moment'.[2]

I do not wish to embark on an ontological debate concerning New Queer Cinema. I shall argue instead that New Queer Cinema enabled new ways of screening female intimacy as well as facilitated the transition of lesbianism into a more popular cultural arena. At the same time, however, New Queer Cinema's near exclusive emphasis on male narratives of desire failed to foreground lesbian cinema on its own terms. Lesbian cinema in the 1990s must therefore be thought of both within and beyond the domain of the New Queer, in the broader context of feminist and lesbian films of the 1970s, and the popular cinema of the 1980s.

The other problem with New Queer cinema lies in the discourses of postmodernity, which hungrily appropriate 'marginal' positions and redistribute them to a mainstream public. Such postmodern 'inclusiveness' also risks erasing the specificity of lesbianism by turning it into a version of desire no different to heterosexual desire. And if this is the case, what would be the point of 'lesbian cinema'? Lesbian cinema in the new queer age, then, walks the tightrope between marginality and mainstream, between a broader (even promotional) appeal, and its assertion of a counter-cultural position.

By the New Lesbian Cinema I am not invoking an essentially lesbian perspective from which films are made and viewed. What unites the lesbian films I discuss below is, politically, a strong sense of a female community with sexuality as a major component; and aesthetically, a level of cinematic literacy coupled with formal audaciousness. I do not, then, intend to narrow down definitions of lesbian cinema. Lesbianism at the movies means, conversely, an opening up of aesthetic, political, fictional and psychological horizons that extend traditional narrative boundaries. How different films achieve this remains, fortunately, unforeseeable.

I begin with an analysis of New Queer Cinema and its limitations in the two principal contexts of *lesbianism* and *postmodernism*. A number of examples – from romantic comedies like Rose Troche and Guinevere Turner's *Go Fish* (1994) and Cheryl Dunye's *The Watermelon Woman* (1996), to the experimental video work of Sadie Benning, the 'post-queer' utopias of Monika Treut, and Lisa Cholodenko's art-house feature *High Art* (1998) – will then illustrate the breadth of lesbian filmmaking within and beyond the New Queer project.

Cherchez La Femme: Women in the New Queer Cinema

The fact that a group of very talented white gay men are getting exposure and access to budgets is to be welcomed, but we also need to consider the difficulties, through gender inequality, of access to economic and marketing resources for lesbian film-makers. (Pratibha Parmar)[3]

What or who is 'queer'? Are gay men necessarily queer? Are all lesbians? And what about those free-thinking, cool straight people? Where queer is concerned, it seems, it is easier to recognise who *isn't* rather than who *is*. More importantly, where do lesbians fit into a queer perspective? 'Queer' is most compelling, I think, when it signifies a 'making strange', odd or controversial. But as we shall see, such a generalised definition is not without its complications, especially for lesbians.

While 'queer' ideally signals an emancipated (and potentially limitless) range of sexual and social relations, most of the products identified as 'new' and 'queer' were in contrast overwhelmingly male. Does queer, or for that matter 'new' queer positively signal a democratic equality between gay men and lesbians?[4] Or does 'queer' stand for an eradication of differences, and the reintroduction of male hegemony, through the back door as it were?

In 'Fishing for Girls: Romancing Lesbians in the New Queer Cinema', Maria Pramaggiore contends that lesbian desire remains dangerously undefined within the New Queer paradigm: '[I]t is important to acknowledge that lesbian cinema participates in New Queer Cinema and to recognize that contemporary lesbian filmmaking is not characterized with enough precision or specificity by such a term'.[5] This is because queer cinema, as Amy Taubin powerfully argues, 'is figured in terms of sexual desire and the desire it constructs is exclusively male'.[6] Taubin sums up matters as follows:

> Like Akerman, Haynes, Kalin, Münch, Livingston, Riggs and Araki incorporate the formal and sexual transgressions of the avant-garde within a narrative of queer desire. *As long as that desire remains exclusively male, however, it's only queer by half.*[7]

Consequently, as Tamsin Wilton points out, what is at stake for lesbians is not just heterosexuality but 'the hegemony of the male narrative', heterosexual and homosexual alike.[8] But if a gender-neutral queer fails to adequately acknowledge a lesbian presence, neither do the gendered categories of 'woman' and 'feminism': 'lesbians and gay men may not easily be incorporated into a generic (gender-resistant) queer. On the other hand, neither may we be incorporated into a generic "woman", nor into feminism'.[9] If this account of the lesbian absence within the cultural discourses of queer and feminism sounds unduly forlorn, it also illustrates the relative weakness of cultural paradigms to at once contain and enable (to simultaneously account for or legislate, and to liberate) particular desires. This does not mean that we need to either abdicate feminist or queer, or, in turn, to resort to some idealised lesbian realm. It does suggest that feminism, queer, and women studies need to be confronted with *specific* cases that both challenge and enrich them, and that a dialogue between the different paradigms should take place.

There are (at present) stark differences between male and female visions. Pornography, for example, functions differently within the two communities. The stormy reception of Sheila McLaughlin's 1987 lesbian S/M film *She Must Be Seeing Things*, or of Monika Treut's work, demonstrates that pornography is still a bone of contention among feminists and lesbians alike. Less so in male gay circles where pornography is more legitimate.[10] So does queer risk becoming yet another false universal masking a peculiarly masculine ethos?

Perhaps. But there are some telling exceptions to indicate that reality is more complex. Unlike Gregg Araki, for instance, *Poison*'s director Todd Haynes has no qualms about drawing on, even belonging to a tradition of women's films. Not only does Haynes regularly collaborate with women (*über*-producer Christine Vachon, and *Poison*'s cinematographer Maryse Alberti), Haynes' themes are emphatically inclusive of, even exclusive to, women. His (now banned) 1987 *Superstar: The Karen Carpenter Story* is a biopic about Karen Carpenter's life and death from anorexia that uses the (invariably 'girlie') Ken and Barbie dolls. When, in her 1990 video *Jollies*, Sadie Benning uses 'gay' Barbie dolls, she is alluding to Haynes' earlier gesture. Both Haynes and Benning use Barbie to critique a heavily gendered consumer culture. Haynes returned to women's (and to European art-house) cinema in his 1995 masterpiece *Safe*, a film explicitly inspired by Chantal Akerman's *Jeanne Dielman* (1975), and his most recent *Far from Heaven* (2002) returns to the women's film once again.[11] *Safe* is a profoundly queer film that is emphatically also a women's film.[12] Haynes described *Safe* as 'hetero-phobic', but *Safe* is no less critical of patriarchal (straight or gay) practices. Haynes may be an exception among male queer directors, but he nonetheless exemplifies New Queer Cinema at its best, not least because he enables queer to function inclusively of women.

GENERATION 'GO GIRL': LESBIAN ROMANCE IN POSTMODERN TIMES

[T]he *popular lesbian romance* film is a virtual contradiction in terms. (Jackie Stacey)[13]

If 'homo' proved at best indifferent to a lesbian perspective, then what about 'pomo'? How does postmodernism treat lesbians? Since the 1980s lesbianism has become an increasingly ubiquitous cultural presence. Much of today's popular culture is served with a good dash of Sapphic seasoning. For over a decade television has been parading a near ceaseless array of dykes, from *Ally McBeal* to *Sex and the City* and *Buffy the Vampire Slayer*. In Britain the 2002 BBC2 adaptation of Sarah Walter's Victorian lesbian novel *Tipping the Velvet* has spurned much debate about the kind of lesbian visibility it promoted. Hollywood's dubious affair with lesbians peaked with Paul Verhoeven's *Basic Instinct* (1992), which prompted gay picketing (and apparently caused great distress to a conscientious Michael Douglas, as the anniversary DVD reveals).

Despite readings of *Basic Instinct* in terms of a backlash, the film is, in my view (as Rich puts it) a lot of fun. As the concept of lesbian spectatorship becomes more complex, so does the question of made-for-male titillation. What matters most, I think, is the ways in which same-sex female desire can be configured into mainstream texts to create new narrative, aesthetic, and political possibilities.

What does this new-found visibility tell us about the marketing of lesbianism in the new queer age? Lesbian 'marginality' could now be commodified, packaged, and gobbled by the masses. This demonstrates aptly the dilemma of evaluating lesbian films within the New Queer Cinema, which almost from its very inception had one foot within, the other outside the film establishment. With the growing prevalence of lesbians in mainstream culture, then, questions about queer art are far from settled. They concern the nature of postmodern assimilation, and assert the need for a radically lesbian position *vis-à-vis* mainstream culture.

Alongside the experimentalism of feminist and lesbian filmmakers since the 1970s, from Chantal Akerman and Yvonne Rainer to Su Friedrich and Abigail Child, lesbian cinema also pursued a resolutely popular path. The broad appeal of the 1990s lesbian comedies, like *Go Fish, The Watermelon Woman*, or Patricia Rozema's glossier *When Night is Falling* (1995) and Maria Maggenti's *The Incredibly True Adventures of Two Girls in Love* (1995), did not materialise out of thin air.

Go Fish officially kick-started the New Lesbian film wave of the mid-1990s. With its black, white and grainy aesthetic, its urban chic and American cheek, *Go Fish* spelled out new possibilities for the 'go girl!' generation. It gave a fresh image to lesbians beyond their familiar portrayals as psycho-killers, depressives, vampires, or victims, and engaged in playful genre-bending. The film's success not only confirmed the existence of a specifically lesbian market, but the possible appeal of lesbian movies to a heterosexual public. In the pizzazz of the moment *Go Fish*'s particular qualities seemed less important than its overall cultural resonance. A flurry of lesbian movies, of varying qualities and budgets, soon followed suit.[14]

Go Fish both continues and moves away from two lesbian traditions: the popular lesbian romance, and the coming out film. While earlier films, like Robert Towne's *Personal Best* (1982), Diane Kurys' *Entre Nous* (1983), or Beeban Kidron's *Oranges are Not the Only Fruit* (1989), tended to focus on the (often painful) rite of passage of coming out, *Go Fish* takes place in an already 'outed' universe in which girls seek girls for fun, sex, and romance. *Go Fish* also takes a particular stance on the problem of identity. Declaring oneself a 'lesbian' is mainly strategic. In one scene, Daria, the free-thinking womaniser, is confronted by an angry (presumably '*old* lesbian') mob after she has sex with a man. In her mock trial Daria argues that having sex with a man does not make her any less of a woman's woman. She refuses to call herself bisexual and insists that she is a lesbian *by choice*. Tamsin Wilton explains: 'An anti-essentialist, social-constructionist perspective on sexual "identity" does not make "lesbian" a redundant label, rather it obliges us to recognize and *deploy "lesbian" as an avowedly strategic* sign'.[15] *Go Fish* makes 'lesbian' a powerful fiction *and* a political fact by presenting a self-sufficient, sociable and professional world of women. This world is not hung up on definitions; it merely, and joyfully, exists.

It is easy initially to contrast *Go Fish* with the sugary aesthetic of an earlier lesbian 'classic', Donna Deitch's *Desert Hearts* (1985). Whereas *Go Fish* offers an 'independent' version of the lesbian romantic quest, *Desert Hearts* operates from within the conventions of Hollywood romance (the romantic formula by which an actively masculine subject wins over the reluctant feminine object). Consequently, *Desert Hearts* and *Go Fish* carve out different trajectories for lesbian viewing pleasure: the former makes pleasure the effect of replacing the traditional male with a woman while keeping the rigid conventions of romance intact, while *Go Fish* relocates romance to a female world that resists the masculine/feminine or butch/femme clichés. That both *Go Fish* and *Desert Hearts* were purchased for distribution by Goldwyn, however, shows them to be perhaps closer than one first assumed.[16]

At the same time as being an 'inside job' created by and for a sub-cultural lesbian 'scene', *Go Fish* also belongs to that all-American (sub)urban youth movie, captured so well in Kevin Smith's New Jersey films. When Rich argues that Smith's *Chasing Amy* (1997) is but an imitation of New Queer films, she is, I suspect, telling only half the story.[17] *Chasing Amy* (which aggravated some lesbian filmgoers) is about a lesbian, Alyssa (Joey Lauren Adams), falling in love with Holden (a typically smug Ben Affleck), or rather about a straight man who falls in love with a lesbian. As Rich noted, *Chasing Amy* has a lot in common with *Go Fish*. Indeed, Guinevere Turner makes a cameo appearance as a member of Alyssa's rock band. Despite its straight ending, however, *Chasing Amy* asserts the singularity of love and the unpredictability of desire – both of which are very much in keeping with queer theory's understanding of the dynamic nature of sexuality, of identity, and of the veritable anarchism of desire. To be sure, Smith provokes his critics, but he keeps ahead of the game, mainly through Holden's best friend, the wonderfully obnoxious Banky (Jason Lee), whose jealousy of Alyssa and Holden receives an explicit homoerotic turn.

In the spirit of *Go Fish*, Smith, and the black cinema of Spike Lee, came Dunye's spoof docu-comedy *The Watermelon Woman* (1996). Aspiring filmmaker Cheryl (Dunye) and her friend Tamara (Valarie Walker) work together in a *Clerks*-style video store. When Cheryl is drawn to the melancholy look of a Mammy in the 1930s' Hollywood melodramas known only as the Watermelon Woman, she goes in search of the actress with the sad eyes. Her inquiry yields some remarkable findings: the Watermelon Woman was involved with her white (and butch) female Hollywood director. In a parallel storyline, the film follows Cheryl's own liaison with the white Diana (Guinevere Turner again). Like other New Queer films (e.g. Tom Kalin's *Swoon*), *The Watermelon Woman* takes on the issue of historiography. The difficulty of uncovering a lesbian – and moreover a black lesbian – heritage means that this history needs to be (re)constructed from scratch. Dunye invents it in the form of a fictional character in a faux-documentary. Dunye is also interested in the intersection between lesbianism and race, a subject she explored in her earlier *Greetings from Africa*: is lesbian desire inherently 'raced'? Is this desire always white? What is at stake in female interracial attraction?[18]

So what to make of Hollywood's recent coveting of these low budget all-girl flicks? New Queer Cinema was part and parcel of the ephemeral extension of 'Hollywood' on the one hand, and of the growth of independent filmmaking on the other, a development which resulted in a gradual decentralisation of the old Hollywood hegemony. Consequently, Pramaggiore explains:

> 'Hollywood' is an increasingly problematic framework to use to describe an industry populated by a few voracious entertainment conglomerates, a growing number of small production companies, and a fashionable Indie circuit experiencing a frenzy as a result of profitable (queer and non-queer) small films.[19]

Such restructuring invariably affects the manner and frequency with which lesbians appear on screen. This is not to say that ampler budgets and mainstream distribution are synonymous with stereotypical, unimaginative, or negative portrayals of lesbians, only that delineating a space for truly 'independent' filmmaking is now more problematic.

Postmodernism and neo-liberal markets promote a 'universalising' portrayal of lesbian desire, which makes it a desire 'like any other'. This liberal-humanist tendency is welcomed by many gays and lesbians as well as by heterosexuals, but it does see lesbian desire as incidental, private, and thus as politically inconsequential. The message is one of inclusion, but it is also inclined to 'phase out' the specificity of lesbian (and I would add more generally of female) intimacy. Postmodernism, then, is a double-edged sword: it promotes lesbian visibility, yet at the same time inhibits the emergence of a specifically lesbian consciousness.

Do these New Lesbian comedies articulate a lesbian sphere of desire that challenges the rhetoric not merely of heterosexism but of masculinity? As Jackie Stacey suggests above, imagining lesbianism in new ways within a popular generic framework is a contradictory enterprise in which some films fare better than others. A radicalised version of deviancy and/as oppositionalism, on a par with the tradition of male sexual dissidence from Genet to Foucault, Jarman and Bruce LaBruce, has yet to fully materialise in its specifically lesbian guise. It is more often found in the transgender, sadomasochistic, and pornographic subcultures explored in the films of Monika Treut or the postfeminism of Camille Paglia. For LaBruce, queer nostalgically signals a 'repository of lost souls, and all the excess and conceits of style and political radicalism'.[20] But if there is a sexual dissident among lesbians whose vision is as unique as it is experimental, her name is Sadie Benning.

From 'Go Girl' to 'Riot Grrrl': The Videos of Sadie Benning[21]

Some people are sick, and I'm one of them . . . (Sadie Benning, *Jollies*)

Filmmaker James Benning's *The California Trilogy* (2002) is a mesmerising documentation of the spatial and metaphysical expanses of the United States. In direct juxtaposition to this panoramic exploration, his daughter, Sadie Benning, trails the confines of her own bedroom armed with a toy Pixelvision camera. The results are formally inventive, spunky commentaries on lesbianism, sexuality, and on the ways in which consumer culture intervenes in the formation of identities.

Benning's work is both confrontational and funny. It readily belongs to New Queer Cinema's no budget, up-front attitude. The Pixelvision films of *Videoworks Volume 1* are grainy, their frames choppy, and defy a classical narrative structure. Benning provides the first person narration, but there are other voices too: a friend on the answering machine or messages scribbled on scraps of paper. Popular music is an important backdrop to the visuals and scribbled notes. Benning's early work may be spatially restricted, but it is culturally and artistically dense. What may initially seem like intensely autobiographical work quickly becomes strangely impersonal. Benning assumes a variety of postures. Her self-presence is never fully disclosed either visually or psychologically – the frequent use of close-ups, zoom, and wide-angle shots of Benning's body and face keep her from coming fully into view – and she thus remains a playfully ambiguous figure. Benning does not, then, try to create the illusion of autobiographical transparency. In the ironic, pastiched manner that Rich describes, Benning critiques the notion of an accessible and verifiable personal history. Instead, she opts for a richly constructed account of selfhood, which is as playful as it is opaque. This allows Benning to conflate personal revelation with a broader socio-cultural critique. As Chris Holmlund explains: 'Benning also positions her "self" as representative of a larger group, fluidly composed of other young lesbian, alienated teens, riot grrrls. Her expressive, highly personal videos acquire polemical, quasi-ethnographic resonance in consequence'.[22]

In her later works Benning moved more resolutely away from the personal mode. Other actors begin to appear in her films. In *It Wasn't Love* (1992) an unidentified narrator tells of his/her sexual encounter with a stranger. The 1998 five shorts, *The Judy Spots* (shown on MTV), featured a papier-mâché teenage doll. *Flat is Beautiful* (1998) has the actors' faces masked.

Benning knows her popular culture. The use of ordinary props (from Barbie dolls to plastic combs, shaving cream, pornographic pictures, or television broadcasts) re-appropriates the mundane, 'bending' it into a specifically lesbian context. In *Jollies*, for example, Benning is seen casually shaving. Benning also quotes amply from 'high culture'. When in *Jollies* she recounts: 'it started in 1978 when I was in kindergarten. They were twins and I was a tomboy. I always thought of real clever things to say, like, like I love you', Diane Arbus' famous picture of the twins appears on screen. Benning's work incorporates popular music from Aretha Franklin to Doris Day, rock 'n' roll, and blues. *If Every Girl Had a Diary* (1990) ends with the more avant-garde sounds of Laurie Anderson's 'The Day the Devil Comes to Get You' (the song is taken from the album *Strange Angels*, Anderson's postmodern elegy to queer photographer Robert Mapplethorpe). Of particular importance in Benning's films is the 'riot grrrl' philosophy of contentious and highly politicised feminism. Benning uses the music of riot grrrl bands like Bikini Kill (in the 1992 *Girl Power* for example) to drive out the notion that girls need to be 'nice', and appear in equally 'neat' narrative forms. This places her firmly alongside New Queer male artists like LaBruce.

Since her Pixlevision days, Benning has worked in animation (*Flat is Beautiful*, 1998), Super-8 (*German Song*, 1995), and music videos (*Aerobicide – Julie Ruin*, 1998). Throughout this diverse career, Benning has resisted turning to conventional storytelling, and her work thus continues to occupy an uncompromisingly radical slot. Working as both filmmaker and video-artist, Benning's contribution to lesbian filmmaking to date has been immense. It is only regrettable that her work is not more readily (and more cheaply) available.

Spare Parts: Bodies and Machines in Monika Treut's Post-Queer Utopias

> lesbians bearing arms, lesbians bearing children, lesbians becoming fashion, becoming commodity subjects, becoming Hollywood, becoming the sex industry, or becoming cyborg human-machine assemblages. And from an alternative point of view, we are also bearing witness to the military becoming lesbian, the mother becoming lesbian, straight women becoming lesbian, fashion and Hollywood and the sex-industry becoming lesbian, middle-class women, corporate America, and technoculture becoming lesbian. (Cathy Griggers)[23]

Griggers describes the 'schizophrenic' subjectivities that populate an age in which bodies as well as personalities are in a state of constant becoming, reassembling, and flux. 'Lesbian' now permeates culture in a variety of ways, and is, in turn, affected by the hegemonic practices which previously excluded it. Moreover, with body-altering technologies (sex-change operations, hormone treatment, and sex-toys), organic tissue now merges with mechanical artefact. We are getting ever closer to what cultural critic Donna Haraway called the 'cyborg': a human-machine assemblage. By marrying technology with flesh, identity and desire can be directed along ever renewable trajectories.[24]

Negotiating technology and queer bodies is at the very heart of Monika Treut's work. From her early films, such as *Seduction: The Cruel Woman* (1985), *The Virgin Machine* (1988), *My Father is Coming* (1991) and *Female Misbehaviour* (1992), Treut examined a range of contentious themes from female S/M to the sex-industry, postfeminism and transsexuality. Because, as Julia Knight has shown, Treut refrains from privileging a specifically lesbian (or gay) sexuality her work has been labelled 'post-queer'.[25] Treut not only predates New Queer Cinema, she resists advancing a specifically queer position. Treut is most interested in 'sexual choice' as such, and that choice may be identifiably 'lesbian', 'gay', 'straight', or all those at once. I want briefly to discuss Treut's ability to both reinforce and unsettle lesbian filmmaking through her invocation of an *excessively* queer position.

Gendernauts (1999), Treut's documentary about San Francisco's transgendered community apparently aspires towards an idealised intersexual space of hermaphrodite existence. Despite this, the film is not a coherent piece. Early on in the film, cyber-critic Sandy Stone preaches polysexual mobility. She reminds us that many individuals born with more than one sexual organ are violently 'reduced' to a single sex by the removal of one of their genitals. This (literal and metaphorical) reductionism is rigorously practised throughout our culture. It renders the true multiplicity of genders invisible. We need to relearn how to see, Stone says.

Interestingly, many of the female to male transgenders who Treut interviews *choose* to undergo a similar kind of surgical (and hormonal) 'violence'. This opens up some fascinating questions: while advanced technology enables a remodelling of the body, what are the cultural codes that define these possibilities, and do they not risk repeating the very binary logic that is used to eliminate the sexual ambiguity of hermaphrodites? The in-betweenness of Stafford – born a woman who for a limited period of time took testosterone but now seems bored with definitions – may be *Gendernauts'* preferred position. When asked if she would rather be called 'he' or 'she', Stafford shrugs and says she does not really care. Others, like video-artists Jordi Jones and Texas Tomboy strive to become more definitively male. We may ask why they do, and what this entails for a truly polysexual future.

What might have been a polemic against the intervention of medical science to (re)determine gender and sex, in *Gendernauts* becomes a discussion about mastery over nature and the body, and the promises of cyborg culture. Crucially, nearly all of those Treut speaks to are sworn 'techies'. They work with, and feel comfortable around new technologies. Treut herself seems firmly on the pro-technology side (there is a relatively brief mention of the possible side-effects of hormone treatment, and of the fact that risks are currently under-researched). Sandy Stone shares an anecdote about a friend who wished to be uploaded onto the net, and not have a body. 'I would rather exist on the net, but have my body in San Francisco', Stone retorts. For all its 'cyborgian' abstractionism, Treut's work is very much about locale. Her American Dream is a utopian one. Treut looks to America, and particularly to the physical entity that is San Francisco, as a place of liberation. To the great chagrin of the Founding Fathers, Treut sees America not only as an ideally democratic space, but as a Queer New World.[26]

STILLNESS AND MOTION IN *HIGH ART*

All those young photographers who are at work in the world, determined upon the capture of actuality, do not know that they are agents of
Death. (Roland Barthes)[27]

As dusk was falling over 'the decade of the dyke', Lisa Cholodenko released her independent feature *High Art* (1998).[28] Rich did not consider *High Art* as New Queer, although it was directed by a lesbian and is certainly 'homo' and 'pomo' in equal measures. *High Art* is both an art-house movie that looks back to the German New Wave, and an American independent at the height of the indie-boom. *High Art*'s slowed-down theatricals and its zonked-out milieu evoke the high camp aesthetic of Rainer Werner Fassbinder by way of a queer homage.

High Art explores the themes of female ambition, desire, and loss. It tells the story of Syd, an assistant editor at the fine art magazine *Frame* who becomes involved, artistically and romantically with a lesbian (and Jewish) photo-grapher, Lucy Berliner. Berliner was briefly the darling of New York's art circle, but, disillusioned and unstable, she 'retired' from a life in the limelight. Lucy lives with her heroin addicted German lover Greta, a former actress in Fassbinder's films. A chance meeting brings Syd and Lucy together. Syd arranges Lucy's 'comeback', and secures her own promotion to editor. Both women recognise in each other a way out of personal and professional stagnation, but Lucy finally succumbs to her destructive relationship with Greta and with heroin. At the end of the film, Lucy dies, and her photos, depicting her affair with Syd, appear on the cover of *Frame*, an odd *memento mori*.

High Art is a conceptual piece on the nature of artistic representation, particularly the mediums of photography and film. It experiments with the 'motionality' of pictures, and with the opposite 'frozenness' of narratives, which makes the film's own narrative practices one of its prime concerns. As its name suggests, *High Art* also revolves around the connection between art and drugs. The film's style mimics the muffled spasms of a heroin rush, and thus offers much more than mere 'heroin chic'. Lucy's friends, permanently gathered in her living room consuming the drug, form a photographic *tableau vivant*. If Lucy specialises in freezing moments with her camera, she is herself caught up in a petrified existence. *High Art* lingers between the deathly passivity of photographs, and the life-like motion of cinema: it narrates the still lives of its characters, yet reveals how this stillness itself yields a vital pulse. How does this meditation on stillness and motion inform a specifically lesbian perspective?

High Art eroticises the relationship between the artist and her subject. The flashes between stillness and motion reveal Syd's growing fascination with Lucy, and finally her falling in love with her. In this oscillation between movement and stasis, passion and exhaustion, *High Art* rewrites the male/female, butch/femme dichotomies. This is not a coming out story about the straight femme falling for the butch dyke. Syd may look like a lipstick lesbian, but she is the one who is actively and upwardly mobile, and the one who more resolutely pursues Lucy. Syd is no feminine muse for the tormented (male-identified) artist. It is the more masculine Lucy who is self-confessedly 'passive'. This subversion of roles is obvious from the women's respective names: the feminine Syd has a man's name, while the more boyish Lucy has a 'girlie' one. *High Art*'s undoing of the traditional division between a feminised passivity and masculine activity makes the attraction between Syd and Lucy all the more compelling.[29]

Returning from Lucy's flat, Syd has sex with her boyfriend. But this straight sex scene feels very much like substitution. We clearly sense that Syd is acting out her desire for Lucy, thereby reversing the convention that sees lesbian desire as 'second best'. *High Art* is not a tragedy that either victimises or elevates its lesbian heroines. Neither apologetic nor celebratory, *High Art*'s import comes from the unflinching portrayal of its characters, its reworking of the conventions of desire, and the seriousness with which it treats its artistic subject matter. *High Art* manages to be several things at once: a New Queer film that places female desire centre stage, an independent film on the nature of art, and finally, a film which draws the two themes of female sexuality and creativity intimately together.[30]

CONCLUSION: GIRL-GAZING, CRYSTAL QUEER

It's one thing to criticize codes of representation and another to say that lesbians don't exist or that women don't exist . . . we're trying to construct a representation that is not simply one using the dominant codes . . . I think we are trying to develop, whether as women critics or film- and video-makers, representations that are simultaneously decon-structions of dominant codes. But this can only be done through codes of representation; otherwise it would be an entirely solipsistic endeavour. (Teresa de Lauretis)[31]

Screening lesbianism is not simply a matter of making the invisible visible, but of negotiating different *regimes of visibility*. The conceptual shift from 'gay' and 'lesbian' to 'queer', and then to 'new queer', has propelled discussions of what makes a lesbian text, a lesbian perspective, or a lesbian auteur. It has also invigorated thinking about the relation between the 'margin' and the 'centre'. Liz Kotz writes that lesbians need to 'interrogate marginal sexual identities not only as subject matter but also as *stance*, as a *process* of reinscription, as a way of situating oneself in relation to sets of images, experiences, and historical formations'.[32] Rather than invoking a grand 'Lesbian Subject', then, Kotz urges us to think lesbianism dynamically as something 'considerably wider, less stable, and less clearly defined than a more realist-defined (and content-oriented) model'.[33]

My readings of New Lesbian films here tried to show how 'lesbian' functions in culturally and formally sophisticated ways, to unsettle our more habitual (and lazy) ways of reading and of seeing. At its most powerful lesbianism is just that: an opening up of the possibilities of thinking and seeing otherwise. Teresa de Lauretis calls this changing the 'conditions of vision', not only creating new objects of vision, but mapping out new ways of perceiving old ones.[34] For lesbians, in this respect, New Queer Cinema has been a mixed blessing. Redefining the conditions of vision signals becoming conscious of the ways in which all male discourses ignore and affect women and lesbians. Lesbian art can yield the uncanniness of these discourses and make them speak anew, as if they were a foreign language.

What, then, are the concrete possibilities and responsibilities of lesbian cinema? I have suggested that answers partly lie at the level of individual texts. In 'Queer and Present Danger', Rich surmises that 'it all comes down to genius after all, despite all your labels of sexual identity'.[35] I would add that it comes down to politics too. De Lauretis says 'it takes two women, not one, to make a lesbian'.[36] I think it takes at least three. The need is ever greater for a wealth of works that are both lesbian and queer. If New Queer Cinema momentarily embodied the contradictions of counter-culturalism and appropriation, its passing should herald new ways of thinking, being, and screening lesbian and queer.

NOTES

1 For a quick working definition for New Queer Cinema see Honey Glass, 'Q for Queer', *Sight and Sound*, 7:10 (October 1997): 36–9.

2 See Rich's 'Queer and Present Danger', reprinted in Jim Hillier (ed.), *American Independent Cinema: A Sight and Sound Reader* (London: BFI, 2001), pp. 114–18. The fate of New Queer Cinema resembles that of other cinematic 'movements' first hailed as unprecedented yet soon after surpassed. The Danish 'Dogme '95' school, for example, made waves in its home country of Denmark, in the United States (with maverick filmmakers like Harmony Korine), and in the field of documentary. But the Dogme manifesto is arguably less important than some of the films that were made in its name, and its novelty transpired into commonplace. Like Dogme, then, New

Queer Cinema stands more for a burst of creative energy and less for a wholly new kind of filmmaking.

3 Pratibha Parmar, *Sight and Sound*, 2:5 (September 1992): 35.

4 On 'queer democracy', see Derek Jarman in 'Queer Questions', *Sight and Sound*, 2:5 (1992): 34–5.

5 Maria Pramaggiore, 'Fishing for Girls: Romancing Lesbians and the New Queer Cinema', in *College Literature*, special issue on *Queer Utilities: Textual Studies, Theory, Pedagogy, Praxis*, 24:1 (1997): 65.

6 Amy Taubin's 'Beyond the Sons of Scorsese' first appeared in *Sight and Sound*'s September 1992 issue. It is reprinted in Hillier, *Independent*, p. 91.

7 Ibid., p. 92, emphasis added. Chantal Akerman, the experimental Belgian filmmaker directed important feminist films such as *Je, Tu, Il, Elle* (1974) and *Jeanne Dielman* (1975).

8 Tamsin Wilton (ed.), *Immortal Invisible: Lesbians and the Moving Image* (London: Routledge, 1995), p. 8.

9 Ibid., p.9.

10 Attitudes have shifted since the angry reactions to McLaughlin's film. The New Queer emphasis on sexuality meant that lesbian films could now explore more freely sexual undergrounds like S/M or the sex-toy industry. Figures like Annie Sprinkle or Susie Bright have become more of a household name among lesbians, and Guinevere Turner tackled S/M culture in *Preaching to the Perverted* (Stuart Urban, 1997). Conversely, Tom Kalin warns against over-simplifying male gay attitudes towards pornography, since some gay men are as uneasy about it as women, see 'Concluding Discussion', in Bad Object-Choice (ed.), *How Do I Look? Queer Film and Video* (Seattle: Bay Press, 1991), p. 278.

11 On *Far from Heaven* as part of the tradition of women's films, and particularly Sirkian melodrama, see Dennis Lim's interview 'Heaven Sent', *Village Voice*, Oct. 30–November 5 2002: available on: http://www.villagevoice.com/issues/0244/lim.php; and J. Hoberman's 'Signs of the Time', *Village Voice*, 6–12 November (2002): available on: http://www.villagevoice.com/issues/0245/hoberman.php.

12 An exception is Roy Grundmann who argued that *Safe* betrays a certain (male gay) misogynistic bias. See 'How Clean Was My Valley', *Cineaste*, 21:4 (April 1995): 22–5. For replies to Grundmann, see Roddey Reid's 'UnSafe at Any Distance: Todd Haynes' Visual Culture of Health and Risk', *Film Quarterly*, 51.3 (March 1996): 32–44, and my own 'No Callous Shell: The Fate of Selfhood from Walt Whitman to Todd Haynes', *Film and Philosophy*, 7 (2003): 1–21.

13 Jackie Stacey, ' "If You Don't Play, You Can't Win": *Desert Hearts* and the Lesbian Romance Film', in Wilton, *Immortal*, pp. 92–114.

14 These include: *Heavenly Creatures* (1994); *Bar Girls* (1994); *The Incredibly True Adventures of Two Girls in Love* (1995); *Stone* (1995) which later mutated into the Oscar-winning *Boys Don't Cry* (1999); *When Night is Falling* (1995); *Thin Ice* (1995); *Gazon Maudit* (1995); *Butterfly Kiss* (1995); *The Watermelon Woman* (1996); *Bound* (1996); *I Shot Andy Warhol* (1996); *Love and Other Catastrophes* (1996); *All Over Me* (1997); *Chasing Amy* (1997); *High Art* (1998); *Fucking Amal* (1998, released as *Show Me Love* for the soft-spoken Anglo-American communities); *The Girl* (1999); *Better than Chocolate* (1999); *Chutney Popcorn* (1999); *But I'm a Cheerleader* (1999); *Kissing Jessica Stein* (2001); and *Mulholland Dr.* (2001). On the new lesbian explosion in filmmaking, see Rachel Abramowitz's online article 'Lesbian Filmmakers are Telling Stories of Wit, Wonder, and Wide-eyed Romance' at: http://ww.angelfire.com/ms/amhomes/article1.html

15 Wilton, *Immortal*, p. 5, emphasis added.

16 The jury on *Desert Hearts* has been out, in, and back out again for quite some time. For an overall favourable reading of *Desert Hearts*, see Stacey's 'Don't Play', pp. 92–114. Teresa de Lauretis is much less sympathetic in 'Film and the Visible', in Bad Object-Choice, *How*, pp. 223–64.

17 Rich, 'Queer Present', p. 115.
18 The connection between the discourses of race, postcolonialism and lesbianism are increasingly important. See, for example, Lynda Goldstein's 'Getting into Lesbian Shorts: White Spectators and Performative Documentaries by Makers of Colour', in Chris Holmlund and Cynthia Fuchs (eds), *Between the Sheets, In the Streets: Queer, Lesbian, Gay Documentary* (Minneapolis: University of Minnesota Press, 1997). *College Literature*'s special issue on 'Queer Utilities' devoted a section to lesbian desire in conjunction with race and postcolonialism. See Jean Walton's 'Introduction: Radicalized Lesbian Desire on the Transnational Scene', *College Literature* 24:1 (1997): 78–82.
19 Pramaggiore, 'Fishing', p. 62.
20 Bruce LaBruce quoted. in ibid., p. 74.
21 Like the New Queer, 'riot grrrls' was a 1990s' phenomenon. Originally from Olympia, WA, riot grrrls blended feminist theory, art, and punk. Bands included Bikini Kill, Babes in Toyland (with an album cover by photographer Cindy Sherman), and the not quite California-girls band L-7 (seen in John Waters' *Serial Mom*). Courtney Love's Hole was an early contender, but Love soon moved to slicker, more lucrative musical pastures. Riot grrrl music is uncompromisingly 'ugly', aggressive, and foul-mouthed. The message is political, critical of mass, male-oriented culture, and the music industry (the albums of the now defunct Bikini Kill are entitled *Pussy Whipped* and *Reject All American*). In 1996 Benning joined Kathaleen Hannah's (former Bikini Kill) new band Le Tigre for one album. If LaBruce sees Punk as the ally of (male) 'queer', riot grrrls make their own connection between rock 'n' roll, punk, lesbianism, and feminist empowerment. For background on the riot grrrl movement (or was it a 'moment'?) see Cherie Turner, *Everything You Need to Know About the Riot Grrrl Movement: The Feminism of a New Generation* (New York: Rosen Publishing Group, 2001).
22 Holmlund, *Between*, p. 131.
23 Cathy₁ Griggers, 'Lesbian Bodies in the Age of (Post)mechanical Reproduction', in Michael Warner (ed.), *Fear of a Queer Planet: Queer Politics and Social Theory* (Minneapolis: University of Minnesota Press, 1993), pp. 183–4.
24 Griggers' discussion draws on Donna Haraway's 'A Cyborg Manifesto', in Donna Haraway, *Simians, Cyborgs, and Women: The Reinvention of Nature* (New York: Routledge, 1991).
25 Julia Knight, 'The Meaning of Treut?', in Wilton, *Immortal*, pp. 39, 48.
26 On Treut's love affair with America see Steve Fox's 'Coming to America: An Interview with Monika Treut', *Cineaste*, 19:1 (1992): 63–4.
27 Roland Barthes, *Camera Lucida: Reflections on Photography*, trans. Richard Howard (London: Cape, 1982), p. 92.
28 Rich, 'Queer Present', p. 97.
29 A similar subversion of roles is brilliantly played out in the Wachowski Brothers' *Bound* (1996). For an excellent reading of *Bound* vis-à-vis lesbian and popular culture, see Paula Graham's *Lesbian Subculture and Popular Cinema* (online book) on Graham's website 'Women and Cult: Female Bonding – from Subculture to Network' at: http://liquid2k.net/pgraham/index.htm.
30 I am reminded here of another film which links lesbianism and high art, Patricia Rozema's *I've Heard the Mermaids Singing* (1987). Teresa de Lauretis is unconvinced by Rozema's blend of lesbianism and art. She sees it as the sort of tokenism that treats lesbianism as a marketable spectacle. My own feeling is that *I've Heard the Mermaids Singing* is more closely connected to the tradition of arthouse and queer filmmaking than de Lauretis allows. But the difference with *High Art* is nonetheless instructive: for unlike Polly in Rozema's film, Syd is not the passive or fantasising observer and she is profoundly transformed by her affair with Lucy.
31 De Lauretis, 'Film and the Visible', p. 281.

32 Liz Kotz, 'An Unrequited Desire for the Sublime: Looking at Lesbian Representation Across the Works of Abigail Child, Cecilia Dougherty, and Su Friedrich', in Martha Gever, Pratibha Parmar, and John Greyson (eds), *Queer Looks: Perspectives on Lesbian and Gay Film and Video* (London: Routledge, 1993), p. 87, emphasis in original.
33 Ibid., p. 88.
34 de Lauretis, 'Film and the Visible', p. 224.
35 Rich, 'Queer Present', p. 116.
36 de Lauretis, 'Film and the Visible', p. 264.

9. NEW QUEER CINEMA: SPECTACLE, RACE, UTOPIA

Daniel T. Contreras

Paris is Burning, a documentary directed by Jennie Livingston, was the art house hit of 1990 and became an important example of what was becoming defined as the New Queer Cinema. Film critic B. Ruby Rich in her foundational essay, while describing the films and videos as not sharing a 'single aesthetic vocabulary or strategy or concern', pointed out that

> there are traces in all of them of appropriation and pastiche, irony, as well as a reworking of history with social constructionism very much in mind. Definitively breaking with previous humanist approaches and the films and tapes that accompanied identity politics, these works are irreverent, energetic, alternately minimalist and excessive. Above all they're full of pleasure.[1]

Rich's piece released a celebratory energy about these new forms of representation and an optimism about what they could achieve, challenge, and create in the cinema and in society. Partibha Parmar responded to Rich's enthusiasm with a measured critique which emphasised the racial homogeneity of the New Queer Cinema and its self-conception:

> I am wary of talking about an overarching queer aesthetic, as my sensibility comes as much from my culture and race as from my queerness. In queer discourses generally there is a worrying tendency to create an essentialist, so-called authentic queer gaze. My personal style is determined by diverse aesthetic influences, from Indian cinema and cultural iconography to pop promos and 70s avant-garde films.[2]

This direct critique would (rightfully) haunt ongoing discussions of the New Queer Cinema's accomplishments and its claims of representational revolution and inclusion. Parmar's critique served as a reality check on the invisibility of queer filmmakers of colour: in fact, only two major ones emerged as important artistic forces in the incontestably rich terrain of race and sexuality. Isaac Julien (*Looking for Langston*) in the UK and Marlon Riggs (*Tongues Untied*) in the USA represent for me two of the more productive filmmakers of this new politics of difference. In their films, Julien and Riggs not only presented new forms of queer visibility but also presented new forms of narrative, mixing documentary, history, and testimony to present less coherent or linear perspectives – a 'mix' that was queer in the broadest sense of the word. But these filmmakers were not often brought into the larger discourse of the New Queer Cinema and instead were relegated to specific discussions about race and representation and not the more general discussion on queer film itself.

I would argue that *Paris is Burning* is one of the very few New Queer Cinema films that directly and complexly dealt with race at all in an unavoidably queer context. Released almost simultaneously with Madonna's hit single, 'Vogue', *Paris is Burning* celebrates Black and Latino drag queens and transsexuals who held 'voguing' balls and competitions in Harlem in the late 1980s and early 1990s. Voguing is a dance form that consists of a series of poses struck by the performer in campy imitation of a high fashion catwalk. The dance fad achieved its widest circulation through Madonna's accompanying video, but it was Livingston's film which offered a more meaningful context for the art form and the complexities of race, class, and, gender that accompanied it.

Furthermore, *Paris is Burning* could be thought of as functioning as a type of critique of the euphoria around queer representation in the New Queer Cinema – it offered a more sobering and artistically complicated vision of queer urban life than that offered by many of the other New Queer Cinema filmmakers. I would like to discuss *Paris is Burning* in detail as a way to explore how at least one film in this movement dealt with issues of race *and* queerness at the same time, in a decidedly non-essentialist way. While at times bleak, the film's portrait of race has utopian aspirations that mirror for me the utopian gestures of the New Queer Cinema itself.

GENDER AND RACE TROUBLES

The New Queer Cinema emerged in the milieu of the identity politics and Culture Wars of the late 1980s and early 1990s, where questions of identity and race were hotly debated both in the academy and other cultural and artistic institutions. Arguably, a key characteristic of the New Queer Cinema was its interest in destabilising the notion of a single fixed (queer) identity. One of the most influential works on the subject of identity was Judith Butler's

(1991) book, *Gender Trouble: Feminism and the Subversion of Identity*. On the opening page Butler argued: 'For the most part, feminist theory has assumed that there is some existing identity, understood through the category of women, who not only initiates feminist interests and goals within discourse, but constitutes the subject for whom political representation is pursued'.[3] Butler goes on to point out that gender is not consistently constructed in different historical contexts, especially considering that gender intersects with other constituted identities such as race, class, and sexuality.

Regarding the issues of race and identity as they play out in the New Queer Cinema, what I find productive in Butler is her consideration that Queer practices such as drag, which seem to mimic heterosexual institutions such as 'femininity' and 'masculinity', may in fact be reshaping and transforming familiar gender roles. These practices may only superficially resemble heterosexual representations; therefore, drag can be liberatory in its derailing of gender assumptions even if it often partakes in oppressive narratives of gender, race, and class. This point provides *Paris is Burning* with its spectatorial charge that still gives it an oppositional stance more than ten years later. In 1990 and 1991, issues of race, gender, and queerness aligned in a particularly urgent way in many cultural texts, and *Paris is Burning* provided visible and entertaining representations of these cultural questions.

In fact, by de-centring essentialist readings of gender identities, by suggesting that 'we dispense with the priority of "man" and "woman" as abiding substances', Butler opens up different contexts in which to consider *Paris is Burning*.[4] If, for example, we detach, however imaginatively, the concept of masculinity from men, we draw upon the ability of queer people to fashion and refashion identities and practices that may only superficially resemble heterosexual constructs. In this case, a gay marriage may not simply be an imitation of a heterosexual legal and religious union. It may draw upon some (or most) of the elements of convention but also may re-invent ways to construct a commitment or imagine heretofore unimagined forms a relationship could take. This way of re-working heterosexual meanings allows us to re-consider, for example, a gay man's claim that he only wants to find a husband, cook for him, and live in a house with a white picket fence. The very conventionality of this wish, and its reliance upon bourgeois standards of contentment, takes on an entirely different inflection in *Paris is Burning*, which provides ambivalent representations of material dreams of wealth and stardom. Considering that Livingston struggled for at least six years to assemble footage and funding, simply the release of the film itself was a triumph of determination and visibility, which resembles the struggles depicted in the film to achieve 'stardom'.

The participants in the film are clearly shown in a drag environment: dressing up, sewing clothes, applying make-up, and gossiping about each other. The film, of course, has many displays of voguing, but the larger context is that of the competitive atmosphere of the drag ball itself. The cultural sensationalism of drag attracted many viewers to the film, but I think it was the racial and class dynamics of the performers that gave the film its gravity, and provided the greatest attraction for cultural critics in the academy.

In the film, not one person is marked visibly as white. The only white images are quick edit clips of rich New Yorkers walking on Park Avenue, glossy magazine photographs, and the cast of TV's *Dynasty*. The juxtaposition between how the queens in the film 'really' live and the fantasies they live inside of provides a charge, and not always a positive one. For example, a prominent character in the film is Octavia, a young black transsexual, who describes her life and dreams quite frankly:

> I'd always see the way rich people live, and I'd feel it more, you know, it would slap me in the face, I'd say, 'I have to have that', because I never felt comfortable being poor, I just don't, or even middle-class doesn't suit me. Seeing the riches, seeing the way people on *Dynasty* lived, these huge houses and I would think, these people have forty-two rooms in their house, Oh my God, what kind of house is that, and we've got three. So why is it that they can have that and I didn't? I always felt cheated. I always felt cheated out of things like that.

Another seeker of fame and fortune, Venus Xtravaganza, a young Latina transsexual, is also clear about her dreams:

> I want to be a spoiled rich white girl . . . I don't want to have to struggle for finances . . . I want a car. I want to be with the man I love. I want a nice home away from New York . . . I want my sex change.

A veteran of the ball scene, Dorian Carey remarks that 'some of these kids don't even eat – they come to the ball starving . . . but whatever you want to be, you be'. Carey's remark is notable because it connects a material reality of physical suffering with the fantasy of dreaming up another identity, one that is not starving. This contradiction of consciousness that the participants in the film express received different critical responses ranging from cheering to condemnation. The conflicting views that met the film were determined by the reviewer's perspective on whether the film was radical in its representational visibility or conservative in its perpetuation of normative consumerist dreams.

Of the latter view was bell hooks, in *Z* magazine, who was especially piqued by Livingston's film:

> Within the world of the black gay drag ball culture she depicts, the idea of womanness and femininity is totally personified by whiteness . . . This combination of class and race longing that privileges the 'femininity' of the ruling-class white woman, adored and kept, shrouded in luxury, does not imply a critique of patriarchy.[5]

In fact, hooks sees the entire cultural structure of the drag balls as 'contaminated' by a colonising whiteness, she continues: 'The whiteness celebrated in *Paris is Burning* is not just any old brand of whiteness but rather that brutal imperial ruling-class patriarchal whiteness that presents itself – its way of life – as the only meaningful life there is'. hooks reads the participants' claims straightforwardly and seeks to expose the buried reactionary contexts of their dreams. From the opposing point of view, John Champagne wrote in his 1995 book, *The Ethics of Marginality: A New Approach to Gay Studies*, that:

> The film's relationship to this common-sense desire for wealth and fame is necessarily ambiguous and complicated. Although the interviewed subjects often speak of their desires for wealth and glamour, the film portrays, in what this context seems a highly critical light, white consumer culture, its distance from their 'real' lives; and the lures that it continues to hold out and to deny to them.[6]

Since hooks views the film as *cinéma vérité*, she sees the fantasies as retrograde and as evidence of a flawed consciousness; Champagne, on the other hand, sees the film as primarily symbolic of the social order, and therefore, too elusive to provide evidence of reactionary politics. These two positions can be seen as two sides of the same coin: they both look through the film, wanting to see critical value in what are basically quite tawdry and commercial dreams contained in a small and under-budgeted film.

Judith Butler, in her sequel to *Gender Trouble*, *Bodies That Matter: The Limitations of 'Sex'*, devotes an entire chapter to *Paris is Burning*. Drawing upon Foucault's formulation of the productivity of power, Butler looks at the film for 'what it suggests about the simultaneous production and subjugation of subjects in a culture which appears to arrange always and in every way for the annihilation of queers, but [also for] . . . those killing ideals of gender and race [to be] mimed, reworded, resignified'.[7] Butler recognises that the oppression(s) caused by racial and economic exploitation can produce a counter-narrative; the creativity displayed in the drag pageants is made possible by the very exploitation that makes them necessary. At the end of the film, the viewer discovers that Venus Xtravaganza was brutally murdered by one of her tricks and not found for three days, which leads Butler to question whether parodying the dominant norms is enough to displace them. Butler in fact is suggesting that the very displacement of gender norms can lead to a strengthening of those norms. Here, Venus' murder is a means for thinking through the limitations of drag as a 'political' response.

> There is no necessary relation between drag and subversion . . . Drag is a site of certain ambivalence, one which reflects the more general situation of being implicated in the regimes of power by which one is constituted and, hence, of being implicated in the very regimes of power one opposes.[8]

hooks, too, noted this ambivalence in the film, claiming that it was seen as 'inherently oppositional because of its subject matter and the identity of the filmmaker'. hooks' point is well taken, but she describes ambivalence as a negative criticism: 'Yet the film's politics of race, gender, and class are played out in ways both progressive and reactionary'.[9] (It is worth wondering what film, or any cultural production, would not contain elements that could be considered both 'progressive and reactionary'.)

Champagne, meanwhile, criticises hooks for not privileging this ambiguity in the film and feels that her reading fails to recognise how drag's very idealised, fetishised sexist version of femininity is what Livingston's film both celebrates and critiques. Champagne then offers his own critique of drag: 'I would suggest here that drag is not a politically oppositional practice, but one that might be mobilized in the service of, and connected up to, struggles both politically oppositional and reactionary'.[10] What seems to be irksome for these critics is that the fantasies in the film feel far from revolutionary. Instead, it is the content of the dreams and the aspirations expressed that are most provocative. For me, both the above positions are over-determined in their conclusions and, as I will discuss later, ignore the utopian possibilities present in the film.

RACIAL DREAMS/RACIAL NIGHTMARES

What is at stake in *Paris is Burning* is the question of the value of sheer fantasy and of wish fulfilment on the part of queers of colour. When Venus says she wants to be a 'rich spoiled white girl', her wish is compounded not only by her economic and racial subjugation, but also by her gender: she knows she needs her sex change to be a 'total woman'. This does not fit into the critical context of drag, but to that of transgender politics, which is ignored by all the critics that I have read, who are distracted by the familiar drag theatricality of the film. But Venus' wish to be white is harshly criticised by hooks as purely symptomatic of a colonised Fanonian consciousness, and, further, this is seen as her retrograde wish to be a white woman. But in Venus' eyes, this is the same thing. In terms of the film, this is not to say that all those who want to dress up or want to be a woman also want to be white, but that the identity of race becomes as unfixed as a masquerade. In *Paris is Burning*, it is not just gender that is being de-naturalised but also race at the same time. To me, this signalled its importance not only to the New Queer Cinema, but also to the debates and activism of the early 1990s around queer politics.

I wish that hooks, Champagne, and other commentators and critics of the film had not ignored one of its most visible and winning aspects – the relationship of race to fashion and fashionableness. They take it for granted that the participants in the balls are simply practising a type of parody of high fashion catwalking instead of actually *creating* it. Towards the end of the film, Venus goes to an open call by Eileen Ford for new models looking pretty and a little forlorn, but she clearly holds her own with the gaggle of eager white women. This little moment is important to me, as it shows the clearest mixture of dreams and reality. The highly stylised strut of the fashion runway in fact does not seem so removed from the highly stylised world the 'kids' live in, as they theatrically insult each other, haughtily proclaim their 'realness', and generally make mischief. Passing over the texture of the film and the possibility that these kids of colour would have followed the fashion world, these critics respond, instead, in a spirit of either bemused or indignant condescension that doesn't recognise young queers' ability to fantasise without futility.

One of the lessons for me of Cultural Studies is that mass culture spreads information along with its relentless advertising, and it is entirely conceivable that some of the kids would read *Vogue*, be able to identify with various supermodels, have a fairly sophisticated sense of how fame and publicity work, and want to be considered fashionable. It is often difficult for US 'white' culture to conceive of people of colour as having sophisticated relationships with fashion, beauty, and the arts. Although these fields are structured along a generally white supremacist ethos, they often can be reappropriated and consumed in unpredictable ways by people of colour. This is one of the missed joys of the film – the courageous, inventive creativity of queers of colour in the most abject of circumstances.

The relationship of fashion to the street and fashion to the avant-garde is not an entirely degraded one – I am willing to hold that the legitimacy the kids seek from the grammar of the fashion world is not entirely one-sided. Fashion has also historically drawn legitimacy and relevancy from the streets and youth culture. Isaac Mizrahi in the 1993 documentary, *Unzipped*, made the connection between gay male camp and high fashion explicitly clear. In fact, around 1989, the lines between the fashion world, the art world, and mass culture may have been a bit more blurred than they are now: figures such as Keith Haring, Peter Hujar, Nan Goldin, Robert Mapplethorpe, Felix Gonzalez-Torres, Andres Serrano, and David Wojarnowicz were all creating work which pushed the parameters of Queer Art into new social contexts. Most sensationally, Mapplethorpe's photographs of black male nudes were exploding boundaries in the artistic and political spheres, leading to their denunciation in the US Senate. And by 1990, ACT UP had achieved its maximum exposure point, using the language and graphics of publicity, fashion, and advertising in its most effective interventions. Queer Nation also took up these tactics, and worked to incorporate race at the centre of queer debates and activism.

It was for Madonna that such acts of appropriation proved so commercially advantageous, and her widely publicised and visible uses of race were richly documented. Madonna was not only spreading the word about voguing, though; she seemed to embody an approachable text of race and gender, with the extra charge of obscenity her image carried then. Madonna played publicly with *Paris is Burning* figures like Willie Ninja and furthered the kids' dreams of stardom. But if there was something naïve and giddy in her approach to people of colour's 'realness' and 'eroticism' (as demonstrated in the documentary *Truth or Dare*), it was characteristic of a current in popular culture, which found something appealing in the visibility and 'expressiveness' of people of colour. Madonna represented a commercial manifestation of this 'new' multiculturalism.

The New Queer Cinema carried this trend and seemed to promise that new representations of queers and queers of colour could lead the vanguard and that the deliberate 'play' of racial stereotyping in films like Livingston's could clear the air of racial repression. But, as Partibha Parmar noted, what did not change was that all of the major figures that achieved wide circulation from the *Paris is Burning* phenomenon were white. But importantly, some film-makers of colour like Julien and Riggs did emerge as forces in the queer avant-garde and, however mediated, texts like *Paris is Burning* did offer new possibilities for different narratives. It is interesting, then, to consider how depressing the film's texture actually is. AIDS is not explicit in the film, but its ravages are there in the subtext, adding to the material and emotional suffering. When confronted with the drag queens and transsexuals of colour in *Paris is Burning*, one is confronted with the collision of race and sexuality – and poverty. The kinds of wishful aspirations that are produced in this context are necessarily formed and reformed and deformed by exploitation. In fact, the gritty sheen of the film's texture contributes to its ambience not just as 'reality', but as a resourceful use of materials at hand.

RACIAL UTOPIA

I argue that if drag is an instance of gender de-naturalisation, and a site of affective investment and historical context, in *Paris is Burning*, race becomes a signifier of utopian longings. The wish to be 'white', seems in this case, not simply a psychological pathology, but also a sense of not wanting to be what one is – poor, abject. How exactly gender as an aspiration is imprecated cannot be made entirely clear, but I do think that in this film, race contains its own fantasies of displacement and escape. In the film, it is *stardom* which is supposed to fulfil all the longings that poverty and racism create.

For me, the longings for stardom in the film, for comfort from suffering, remain unrequited. To want to change what one is, to inhabit another space more comfortable and beautiful, a place that may contain forty-two rooms and where a boy is a girl and a girl is a boy is not simply a reactionary wish. In fact, it seems a fairly reasonable one. That in this film these wishes take place in a space of racial marginalisation, through race and gender, makes them much more poignant, and perhaps more impossible to fulfil. The film's longing for something better and for something different is particularly resonant for me in terms of AIDS. The memory of losses known and unknown, recorded and unrecorded are practically unspeakable for queers of colour.

Perhaps sexual identities feel different when expressed through desires and race; racial identities may feel different when experienced through poverty and sexuality. What *Paris is Burning* makes poetically clear is that wish fulfilment cannot follow any straightforward political trajectory. This is what makes longing and dream-making such potent and dangerous cultural tools and why the promises of the New Queer Cinema and representations of queers of colour are important to maintain. That these dreams of the New Queer Cinema failed to maximise their potential regarding race and were at times co-opted by the media was unfortunate, since these expressions were then dependent on the temporality and obsolescence of fashion and trends. But visibility and queer media attention also ensured that these images could achieve their widest audience, perhaps still leading to unpredictable new manifestations of utopian possibilities and new considerations of queer identities.

It would be difficult to argue, more than ten years on, that the New Queer Cinema developed a critical *racial* perspective, but it would also be difficult to argue that the space it inhabited did *not* contain a racial component at all. If it fell short of the radical possibilities that critics like Rich hoped for, a type of erasure takes place to suggest that it simply remained a purely white gay male aesthetic. *Paris is Burning* remains as a reminder of the New Queer Cinema's racial and utopian potentialities.

NOTES

1 B. Ruby Rich, 'Homo Pomo: The New Queer Cinema', in Pam Cook and Philip Dodd (eds), *Women and Film: A Sight and Sound Reader* (Philadelphia, PA: Temple University Press, 1993), p. 166. Reprinted in this book.
2 Pratibha Parmar, 'A Response to B. Ruby Rich', in Cook and Dodd, *Women*, p. 175.
3 Judith Butler, *Gender Trouble: Feminism and the Subversion of 'Identity'* (New York: Routledge, 1991), p. 1.
4 Judith Butler, *Bodies that Matter: On the Discursive Limits of 'Sex'* (New York: Routledge, 1993), p. 124.
5 bell hooks, 'Paris is Burning', Z, July 1991.
6 John Champagne, *The Ethics of Marginality: A New Approach to Gay Studies* (Minneapolis: University of Minnesota Press, 1995), p. 108.
7 Butler, *Bodies*, pp. 124–5.
8 Ibid., p. 125.
9 hooks, 'Paris'.
10 Champagne, *Ethics*, p. 120.

10. NEW BLACK QUEER CINEMA

Louise Wallenberg

In 1989, three years before the New Queer Wave was even invented or discovered, two very different yet interconnected films were produced on either side of the Atlantic. Both soon became critically successful and both would win a number of prizes at different international film festivals and venues. In retrospect, these two films have come to constitute the very incitement to the Wave. British filmmaker Isaac Julien's *Looking for Langston* premiered in early 1989 and American filmmaker Marlon Riggs's *Tongues Untied* premiered later that same year, the latter including a still photo from the former so as to pay homage to Julien while also connecting the two films. Differing widely in film form, they share the same urgent topics: the making visible of black male queerness and its plurality, the search for forefathers and the expression of a voice of one's own. Furthermore, the two films erupted from specific socio-cultural milieu that differed yet shared a simultaneous coming to terms with what has been referred to as diasporic or even hybridic experiences.

British art critic Kobena Mercer, who has written extensively on the work of both filmmakers, points out how the postmodern and postcolonial situation, together with the AIDS crisis, has come to change both British and American society in that it has brought with it the 'dislocation of national identity'.[1] Describing the transatlantic diasporic situation, Mercer's words can also be read as descriptive of the two filmmakers' situation and focus:

> [I]t is precisely the differential specificity of their historical and national formation that must be recognized in order to grasp what is at stake in the diasporic resonance of the metaphors of being silenced, or invisible, or marginal – namely, the struggle over representation that inevitably comes with the territory wherever societies organize themselves around the metaphor of 'race'.[2]

Still, in their struggle over representation, both Julien and Riggs have given blackness a close companion, queerness. Not in terms of an either/or, but in terms of an inclusive *and*, thus stressing that black queerness, or queer blackness, cannot be divided so as to serve or represent different communities at different times. And by embracing the plural, both filmmakers have moved away from the simplistic negative/positive binary informing not only earlier representations of blackness but the early theoretical analysis of those representations. 'Increasingly', Valerie Smith writes, 'black cultural criticism in general and film criticism in particular have been concerned more with the diversity than with the homogeneity of black experience'.[3] This emphasis on diversity has opened up the possibility for black queerness to be heard and seen. The two films discussed here constitute prime examples of new black queer cinema (or, since there are so few, prime examples of non-white queer films in general.) Alongside Jennie Livingston's *Paris is Burning* (USA, 1990), these films emphasised affirmations of both blackness and queerness. As Michelle Parkerson writes, '[t]hese films imposed diversity upon the lily-white, largely male stereotype of gay experience'.[4]

While white dominant culture has left little space for black representations in general, it needs pointing out that homophobic attitudes informing black communities constitute another reason why there have been so few gay and lesbian representations produced. Critiquing black homophobia, Ron Simmons has stressed how black gays have been ridiculed and how the prevailing view on homosexuality as pathology resulting from white racist oppression has made impossible any serious discussion of it.[5] It remains a 'sin' against the race.[6] Presenting black gayness from within, creating previously lacking representations, Riggs' and Julien's texts are therefore politically crucial in more than one way; not only to the New Queer Wave, or to Black Cinema, but to cinema and Blackness as a whole. Yet, the 1990s would see few film texts dealing with black or other non-white gayness: just like queer theory and activism, the New Queer Wave soon found itself deeply 'immersed in vanilla'.[7]

This chapter examines the two film texts and the cultural contexts from which they emerged. My intention is to place both films at the very beginning of the New Queer Wave, or rather, *as* its very beginning, emphasising the pioneering status they deserve. Combining the poetic with the political, the personal with the collective, the past with the present, these films can be understood to have set the framing for what queer films could be like: 'fresh, edgy, low-budget, inventive, unapologetic, sexy and stylistically daring'.[8] That few queer films made after 1989 would actually manage to incorporate all of the characteristics, B. Ruby Rich's crucial definition, quoted from here, seems almost to describe *Looking for Langston* and *Tongues Untied* themselves.

Cultural, Intellectual and Political Contexts

From what cultural, intellectual and political contexts did these texts emerge? They did not come out of a vacuum but are indeed related to a larger setting: that of various contemporary cultural productions, discussions and expressions that focused on black and queer experiences in the diaspora. Hence, these films were not sole expressions of male black queerness, but two among many within a larger cultural and political continuum. As José Esteban Muñoz points out, black gay male cultural productions experienced a boom in the late 1980s and early 1990s and were united by their urge and desire towards a '(re)telling of elided histories that need to be both excavated and (re)imagined'.[9] It was during the 1980s that a (new) black cinema would constitute itself within British filmmaking and that black representation in film and television saw a major increase in the USA (albeit often one-sided and stereotypical). The violent uprisings of 1981, demanding black representation within public institutions as a basic right, triggered various measures to be taken by the British government including consistent funding of Black British art. Money was put into different cultural venues, and a number of film and video collectives were founded, including the Sankofa Film and Video Collective of which Julien was a member.[10] These demands and changes took place in the context of what Mercer and Julien have described as 'a re-articulation of the category "black" as a political term of identification among diverse minority communities of Asian, African and Caribbean origin, rather than as a biological or "racial" category'.[11] The 1980s, then, saw 'prolific activity of the black independent film movement', which meant the emergence of a younger generation of black British filmmakers and widened circulation of black film in the public domain.[12] The new cinema emphasised race, ethnicity and class while in some cases also taking gender and sexuality into account.[13] Not sharing one single aesthetic, they dwelled on the vast, boundless heterogeneity of 'diasporic being' as well as on the movement from centre to margin. Hence, the plurality of experiences in the formation of black British identity – and the contradictions informing this 'identity' – can be said to make up a consistent thematic concern running through black British filmmaking in the 1980s. With an apparent theoretical base in cultural studies and poststructuralism, identity was now analysed and understood as fragmented, pluralistic and diverse, yet mutual and centralised. Commenting on black British cinema, Mercer wrote that 'as it expands and becomes progressively de-marginalised, its oppositional perspectives reveal that traditional structures of cultural value and national identity are themselves becoming increasingly fractured, fragmented and de-centred'.[14]

The notion of a postmodern condition of the Western subject opened up a change in positionings between those assumed to be centred and those assumed to be marginalised. Whereas the Western subject started seeing itself as fragmented, the marginalised subject (as non-white and/or queer) could start seeing itself as centralised. Stuart Hall, in an almost ironic comment on the paradoxical nature of being migrated from colonial periphery to post-colonial metropolis, exclaimed that: 'Now that, in the postmodern age, you all feel so dispersed, I become centred. What I've thought of as dispersed and fragmented comes, paradoxically, to be *the* representative modern experience!'[15] Describing cultural identity and how it comes to be constituted in the diaspora, he argued that cultural identity 'is a matter of "becoming" as well as of "being"', and that identity belongs both to the past and to the future because it is always in the making, always and forever changing the 'I'. 'Cultural identities come from somewhere, have histories', he writes, '[b]ut, like everything which is historical, they undergo constant transformation'.[16]

It is within this intellectual and socio-cultural – and economic – context that *Looking for Langston* must be seen. Julien had co-produced and co-directed a number of critically acclaimed films before starting to work on *Looking for Langston*. However, this was the first film over which he was to have complete control, both as a director and producer.[17] For Riggs, the situation was somewhat different. Having received his master's degree from University of California Berkeley's Graduate School of Journalism in 1981, he set out to raise money for *Ethnic Notions*, a documentary dealing with the impact of negative African-American stereotyping in Western culture. It took Riggs five years to raise the money, and it was the first time he enjoyed total control as producer and director. The film had an enormous impact within a variety of cultural venues and it was shown twice on public television in the USA. Moreover, it won an Emmy Award, and subsequently helped establish Riggs as one of the foremost contemporary producers of historical video production.[18] More importantly, it was his ticket into making *Tongues Untied*. As Bill Nichols states, while *Ethnic Notions* was filmed in a traditional expository mode, with omniscient voiceovers and evidentiary editing, *Tongues Untied* breaks, or 'shatters', the traditional and conventional film styles 'in complex and unexpected ways'.[19] Describing both *Tongues Untied* and *Looking for Langston* in terms of performativity (as opposed to more 'referential' modes), Nichols would emphasise the poetic and expressive as well as the spectator's position in relation to the text and its social actors. These films, then, 'address us . . . with a sense of emphatic engagement that overshadows their reference to the historical world'.[20] Hence, performative documentary frees 'expressive elements from their subordination to a logic'.[21] Instead, realist representation is suspended and the viewer is invited to partake in the construction of what is presented: in *Looking for Langston* by re-constructing the imaginary space of the Harlem Renaissance, and in *Tongues Untied*, by constructing the visibility of a contemporary and diverse black male queerness. Postponing realism, the films offer a possibility of knowing difference differently. While emphasising the performative, Nichols, however, failed in connecting this new poetic 'anti-mode' with queer, not seeing performativity as a crucial element – formal as well as ideological – of queer cinematic expression. Poststructurally informed queer theory has argued for the performativity of gender and sex, queer cinema follows a similar trajectory: it upsets these supposedly natural categories through a recurrence of what Thomas Waugh has called 'performance-based techniques' (initially descriptive of the post-Stonewall cinema). These include a mixture of 'particular inflections of standard interviewing, editing, and expert testimony styles . . . reconstruction, statements and monologues based on preparation and rehearsal, and non verbal performances of music, dance, gesture, and corporal movement'.[22] While explicitly presenting the performative character of queer(-ing), these techniques can also be said to queer film form by their insistence on transgressing conventional boundaries and rules for film structure and representation.

Performative self-representation – to visualise and speak up in plural – constituted the form of early black queer cinema (as well as of all queer cinema.) As Mercer points out, 'coming to voice involved participation in the discursive construction of a new, hybrid form of "imagined community", in an in-between space that drew on elements from different origins and sources'.[23] The hybridic which takes place on various levels is highly significant. Not only does the black diaspora as a whole consist of various nationalities and cultures, but the individual is also hybridic in his or her transnationalism, i.e. being bicultural and black in a predominantly white society. This plurality, this hybridity, refers also to the two films use of time and place. The black gay identities speaking in *Tongues Untied* are present here and now. The here is the USA, and more specifically, Los Angeles, San Francisco and New York, and the now is the time of the making of the film, 1989. *Looking for Langston*, on the other hand, speaks of identities both in the past (the Harlem Renaissance) and the present, and it speaks of identities on both sides of the Atlantic. It stretches its own spectrum to include voices that for long have been gone, and by doing so, it invites us to imagine a transhistorical identity that is also transatlantic. The many identities spoken of are both imaginatively rediscovered and produced within the film, and they are therefore not presented as if grounded in a certain archaeology or an essential truth. Rather, they *become* in the re-telling of the past, a re-telling that is imaginary and open-ended. In this re-telling, there is no one truth to be told, no essential core that gives a shared essential identity to the transhistorical and the transatlantic. Still, there is, in Mercer's words, 'unity-in-diversity'.[24] And clearly, both films engage in a politically conscious move that shifts from a focus on 'othernesses' to a focus on 'differences'.

REFUSING THE EITHER/OR

Like sexuality, 'race' has come to be understood in terms of essentialism and constructionism, and like sexuality, the different ways in which we tend to read race hold a number of different political implications. As postcolonial theory has argued, 'race' is to a large extent constructed by a dominant white ideology, and this ideology ascribes race and specific 'racial traits' only to non-white people(s).[25] Whiteness, then, creates and perpetuates itself as non-race while turning its others into races.

Following the African-American separatist W. E. B. Du Bois's early definition of race as invention, one can assume that there is little that is 'natural' about race and racial cultural traits and that there is no essential truth connecting all individuals sharing the same race.[26] At the turn of the last century, Du Bois proposed to resolve the dilemma of African-American double consciousness by appealing to a revisionist analysis of the concept of race that set out to eschew a biological essentialist account of racial identity. The power to invent or reconstruct a concept of black identity that was to be freed from the oppressive and racist construction imposed upon it by white culture, Du Bois argued, was in the hands of black people themselves. Thus, he inscribed the process of making, or, to use Hall's term, the process of becoming identity, with conscious will and power.[27] And in thinking of race as a socio-historical construction, it would be accurate to assume that race is changeable over time and that 'racial identity' to a certain extent must be fluid. As with sexuality, there are always plural characteristics combining or shaping identity. Since various aspects of our being intersect, identity is never uniform. About being gay and black and not wanting to choose one over the other, even though one might feel compelled to as a black queer in a white (straight) society, Riggs once said:

> The way to break loose of the schizophrenia in trying to define identity is to realize that you are many things within a person. Don't try to arrange a hierarchy of things that are virtuous in your character and say 'This is more important than that'. Realize that both are equally important; they both inform your character.[28]

In line with Riggs, Mercer mentions the duality that during the past decades has come to define black queer struggles. This duality, he says, informs the working on both fronts at all times. These fronts are of course the racist white gay community and the homophobia of the black community, two fronts that in themselves create 'the difficulty of constantly negotiating our relationships to the different communities to which we equally belong'.[29] This constant twofold struggle, the consequence of this dual belonging, means that the queer black subject has to locate her- or himself 'in the spaces *between* different communities – at the intersections of power relations determined by race, class, gender, and sexuality'.[30] Similarly, having to choose between two 'sides' of one's being means, according to Hall, an 'essentializing of difference into two opposed either/or's'.[31] Following Paul Gilroy, who has argued that black people in the diaspora must refuse the binary black *or* British, Hall asserts that any such binary must be made invalid. He writes: 'They must refuse it because the "or" remains the sight of *constant contestation* when the aim of the struggle must be, instead, to replace the "or" with the potentiality of an "and" '.[32] The potentiality of 'and' is palpable, given that we are *'always in negotiation*, not with a single set of oppositions that place us always in the same relation to others, but with a series of different positionalities'.[33] Mercer, however, finds the question of whether one is either black *or* queer unhelpful because no one can separate different aspects of her identity, certainly not if the individual values both or all of these aspects.[34] None of us 'belong exclusively to one homogenous and monolithic community' (even though some of us are definitively less aware of our hybridised belonging than are others). Hence, for many people 'everyday life is a matter of passing through, travelling between, and negotiating a plurality of different spaces'.[35] This binary, and the transgression of it, can also be understood as central to queerness in general: queer identities take place or come to be between the accidental spaces where all identity variables intersect with one another. It is also applicable to the films. Manthia Diawara, in his analysis of *Looking for Langston*, stresses that race must be included in every reading of it: to see it only in terms of gayness means establishing it as 'gay essentialist' and this risks emptying it of its black content.[36] Hence, Diawara attempts to bring blackness and gayness together in a way that points towards the need to see gayness as part of blackness, and hence, to queer blackness. The same argument must be made about *Tongues Untied*: it is not about either/or, it is about both, constantly refusing to separate the two.

ESSENTIALISM AND INTER-RACIAL DESIRES

While not denying race or ethnicity as constructions, racial essentialism still occupies a central role in both films as they deal explicitly with the puzzling question of black essentialism and the politics involved in such a stance. The essentialist discourses enacted in the texts, however, are most interesting because they avoid any one-sided and ready-made image of what racial essentialism must – or can – be like. On the contrary, they openly complicate the need for racial unity in their refusal to follow the presupposed consensus about what a positive or negative image of black subjecthood should be. Rather, diversity and multiplicity are taken into consideration. The essentialism advocated in these films, then, takes different forms, celebrating plurality and breaking with the more single-minded, uniformed essentialism. However, while advocating black collective gayness, they also point towards another possible reality where gayness does not have to have a race (and vice versa). Hence, while emphasising the need to support identity politics, both films simultaneously demonstrate the need to question fixed notions of identity. Breaking with white gay culture and how it positions black gay men as others, the films point towards new definitions of self by offering a multitude of images and possible positions within the black gay community.

For example, the many different social actors invited to speak out – in medium close-ups – in *Tongues Untied* help create an unfixed understanding of black gay identity. By including the innumerable, the film manages (albeit indirectly) to question the often fixed notions of black and gay identity. And while presenting an (imaginary) correlated black gay history that serves to elucidate the need for historical identity, *Looking for Langston* presents a similar critique of fixed identity categorising by mixing past and present as well as different national cultures.

I would argue that the very ambivalence by which both films deal with essentialism points towards openness, rather than closure. This ambivalence is much informed by contradictory desires, and by giving voice to these desires, which are inter-racial, these texts choose to linger between two paths, as if not really wanting to make a choice. It is this contradictory movement – the desire of the same that simultaneously is a desire of the other – that gives them their vibrant and engaging political and poetic meanings. By giving voice and image to inter-racial (homosexual) desires, black essentialism is presented as a complex goal that is only partly desired.[37] Partly, because both films offer openings that stretch towards a future that makes inter-racial relations possible and equal. However, for that future to ever be, the films argue, black men must first turn to their own and find collective power among themselves. There are clear differences though: while *Tongues Untied* is strong and explicit in its advocating of black essentialism, *Looking for Langston* is more subtle and vacillating in its expression and politics. *Tongues Untied* is a much angrier film and this fury is most directly conveyed in its fast, aggressive and loud form. The voices and images portray vexation, but also sadness. The experiences given voice to, as the social actors tell their life stories to a static camera, put race and gayness at the centre of the straight, white and black eye. These experiences have often included oppressive and abusive attitudes and treatments. But, as these voices implicitly express, it is only by daring to be true to the self that one can start to accept and love that self. Self-love, then, in undermining practices of domination, is revolutionary.[38] Yet with a final intertitle like 'Black men loving black men is *the* revolutionary act', *Tongues Untied* speaks up and tries to reach out not only to all those closeted blacks, but also to other groupings.[39] At other times, a photo or a film extract is given the power to speak. Still, the black separatism advocated here differs from any fixed essentialism. The heteroglossia and the multiple representations of black gay men avoid every fixed stereotypification. While explicitly and effectively deconstructing racist stereotypes of black people in *Ethnic Notions*, this film more implicitly sets out to destruct similar images by showing other, very seldom seen, images of blackness, and more importantly, of black queerness.

Both films, I would argue, stress that moving through an essentialist phase may be a prerequisite for positioning oneself as an active, self-creative subject. For how else is one to break with an internalised racism or with the heterosexist suffocating demand to 'pass' as straight? It is only through the strength in the group – both as group and as many individuals – that one can start deconstructing the cultural forms and structures that try nailing one down. Perhaps an initial separatism can be useful. Is it not only by travelling through – and experiencing – the meaning(s) of essentialism that the individual and the grouping can reach beyond essentialist notions? Is it not only when realising that essentialist and biologist answers do not reach that far and fail to offer an absolute truth that one can start seeing essentialism for what it is? And from there, seeing further. For, as Hall asks, following bell hooks, 'where would we be, without a touch of essentialism? Or, what Gayatri Spivak calls strategic essentialism, a necessary moment?'[40] Though spotting some serious, unavoidable problems and weaknesses in this 'essentialising moment' (which he understands to be over by now),[41] Hall admits that black essentialism has been crucial for the civil rights movement and for the production of self-images.[42] Yet, Hall feels that we are now at 'the end of the innocence of the black subject' or, rather, at 'the end of the innocent notion of an essential black subject'. But, as he concludes, 'this end is also a beginning'.[43] This is where both films seem to take off: through a smooth montage technique, as in *Looking for Langston*, or through a more contrapuntal montage technique that emphasises the performative, as in *Tongues Untied*, the two films point towards an end and a beginning. By representing black queerness as diversity, juxtaposing different time periods and different places, and by stressing the variety of individual and collective experiences, the directness and the ambivalence of desires, the notion of an essential black queer subject can no longer be.

MONTAGE AESTHETICS: HYBRIDISATION AND SEAMLESS TEMPORALITY

Interestingly, Julien's and Riggs's films are composed and structured with the use of similar montage technique(s). Not only do they involve the more classical montage of attraction (often described as a juxtaposing of various shots and images to create 'new' meanings); they also include the juxtapositions of sound and lyrics that – in relation to the images – serve to create meanings on a much wider and holistic level. The montage of attraction, therefore, is one that must be understood to be primarily audio-visual. For example, *Looking for Langston* – as an oneiric meditation on the Harlem Renaissance and Langston Hughes – juxtaposes material that in many ways differs from more traditional montage cinema. The film mixes poems, experimental fiction (extracts from the work of Oscar Micheaux, the reconstructed spaces of Harlem and the Cotton Club), still photographs (e.g. by Carl van Vechten and Robert Mapplethorpe), vintage newsreels, blues songs and extracts from television and radio.[44] Various historical elements are thus mixed and strung together with the fictional reconstructions, forcing them effortlessly to share the same space and time, creating an imaginary past. Through a seductive aesthetic influenced by Mapplethorpe's titillating black-

and-white photography, the use of music, poetry and archival footage, all put together in a seamless montage, the film creates, in Mercer's words, 'a dreamlike space of poetic reverie, historically framed by images of the Harlem Renaissance of the 1920s'.[45] Hence, the aesthetics of *Looking for Langston* can be understood to constitute a smooth hybridisation as the clashes between different images, voices and discourses are sewn together seamlessly: there is a certain flow to the narration that seems to insist on melting paradigms and differences. Likewise, transnational, or transatlantic, pairings are created by the flow: on an imaginary level there is little difference between the queer Harlem Renaissance and today's British black queer scene. Consequently, *Looking for Langston* may be said to constitute an almost perfect example of the Deleuzian cinematic time crystal. Through this perspective, black queer experience is represented and enacted *over time*; by letting it take place in the same spatial context (whether on screen or in off screen space) silences may start to speak and histories can be told.[46]

Tongues Untied, on the other hand, shows no indication of being influenced by the seductive shimmer and titillating objectification offered by Mapplethorpe's lens. In colourful photography, long takes and close-ups of the narrating social actors, *Tongues Untied* offers an intimate presentation of men, their individual and more collective experiences and everyday issues. The film, in Mercer's words, 'foregrounds autobiographical voices that speak from the lived experiences of black gay men in the here and now', emphasising 'the immediacy, the direct address and the in-your-face realism'.[47] Poetic and didactic in its hybridisation, *Tongues Untied* combines autobiographical material, art, dance, singing and poetry to narrate the inextricability of being black and queer. By opening up for his private story, and inviting other black gay men to untie their tongues with him, Riggs manages to reach out to a more public experience, making the private collective. Still, Riggs's own life story gets to constitute the red line that connects the multiple components of the film. These components consist of other black men's stories, poems performed by Essex Hemphill, Steve Langley, and Alan Miller, songs by Nina Simone and Roberta Flack, to mention a few. Other components include the fictive sequences showing homophobic black voices ridiculing and rejecting love between black men (and between black women). There are also archival and private footages and still photos from Gay Pride marches, television, the Castro area, and family albums. While emphasising Riggs's own story, all these components stress a dialogic voicing in the film, the plurality in experiences, the 'diversity-in-unity'. Hence, the film elegantly avoids falling into the trap of 'the burden of representation', which Mercer has found to be characteristic of black cinema and representation.[48] It avoids this trap by speaking *from*, and not *for*, black gay experiences.

Tongues Untied resists any fixedness and any rest, stressing the hybridic and the performative, and hence constituting an almost perfect example of new queer cinema ('fresh, edgy, inventive, unapologetic, stylistically daring').

It is continually dissolving, overlapping, superimposing and inter-cutting visuals and words, creating a strange fluidity that moves with rhythm. This rhythm both upsets and comforts, offers both beauty and contrapuntal imagery. Just like the pain offered in the visuals is softened by the poetry, the lyrics and the various tones on the soundtrack, the discontinuity of the cut is softened by a dissolving technique, keeping the previous image lingering on. Also contributing to this strange yet remarkably smooth rhythm is the use of voices: sometimes Riggs's voice becomes indistinguishable because it melts together with many other voices, voices that rhythmically together make a collage, voices that speak the personal yet together make the collective. The blurring of voices, the smooth cacophony, therefore suggests shared experiences and shared memories.

As mentioned above, the spectator is directly addressed and invited to share the stories of queer experience told. This address is one that is performative to its form: for example, the Snap!-divas snap, the Lavender Love Light Quartet sings, and Riggs is dancing and reading, incessantly coming out to the spectator. The performance and the performative, it needs pointing out, are both the public presentation of self and the utterance 'that executes, enacts or performs the action that is uttered' (as for example 'I am coming out [to you]').[49] Consequently, there is no way to escape the invitation in *Tongues Untied*: with a steady look, which never ever tries to avoid the spectator's gaze, she is acknowledged. What Teshome H. Gabriel calls 'face-to-face tellings', as a central device in Third Cinemas, here becomes a most important tool.[50] Furthermore, this kind of oral and visual straight forwardness recalls what hooks labels 'the oppositional gaze'.[51] This gaze refuses to stop looking: the spectator is bound to listen and to be an object of this gaze. This reversing of the eye, which is a direct quest for recognition, echoes the Fanonian demand: 'I demand that notice be taken of my negating activity insofar as I pursue . . . a world of reciprocal recognitions. He who is reluctant to recognize me opposes me'.[52]

Also crucial to both texts is the traditional African-American oral trope called 'call-and-response'.[53] This trope does not necessarily equal dialogue: it includes recognising the other across time and space. In the films, the call is created by its placement in the montage and the answer is positioned as a response to that call. The films' archaeological inquiry excavates what has always been hidden from history: the fluidity of sexual identities within the black cultural expression as well as the intertwining of black culture and Euro-American modernism. However, a past that is connected to its present must also be connected to its future. In its historicising attempt to open up a transgenerational dialogue between black queer men, *Looking for Langston* becomes a most political film. Albeit on a different level and from a slightly different perspective, so is *Tongues Untied*. Here, it is the present situation for black gays that constitutes the centre of political discourse. However, the past is never far away. Referring to old stereotypes of black people within Western culture, the text claims that these images still help form the contemporary view of black people. Also, there are references to the civil rights movement, slavery and Martin Luther King. Black people's struggles within the USA are lined up chronologically as an African-American history, and within this history, the specific struggle of black homosexuality is situated. Moreover, as constantly acknowledged throughout the film, this is a struggle that more recently has come to be increasingly informed by AIDS and the silences surrounding it. Given that AIDS is such a crucial issue within the New Queer Cinema that was to develop during the 1990s, the two films focused upon here, in explicitly dealing with AIDS, must be seen as its forerunners.

The restrictions AIDS puts on gay men and the constant fear of catching it hold a central position in both texts, but more so in Riggs's. There is an understandable reason for that: Riggs, who was HIV-positive while filming *Tongues Untied*, had a close relationship to the disease and the dying process that, at that time, accompanied it. Already marked by it while filming *Tongues*, he died from AIDS in 1995. The heartbeat heard sporadically but loudly throughout *Tongues* can be interpreted as a bomb waiting to explode, or rather, as a time bomb waiting for time to stop. In one sequence, Riggs's voice fills the soundtrack, accompanying images of black gay men who have all died from AIDS over the past years, as he confesses that he has 'discovered a time bomb ticking in my blood'. Newspaper photos of black men who have died from AIDS fill the screen, one by one. On the soundtrack Riggs's voice says: 'I watch, I wait. I watch, I wait'. Then suddenly, when the photos of deceased men have passed by, the black-and-white photo of Riggs himself fills the screen, placing him among those who have already died. This is followed by a shift: old photos of black men and women are followed by footage of black people participating in a civil rights march, which then is followed by footage of Martin Luther King, and then more footage of black people demonstrating and marching, and finally, footage of black gays participating in a Gay Pride march. There is a connection between past and present, between different groups of black people fighting for rights and visibility. Moreover, a connection is made between the sufferings of black gay men with AIDS and African-American history, which to a large extent has been a history of suffering.[54] Again, the connection to the New Queer Cinema that would follow these two films is obvious: as one of its main characteristics is the conscious negotiation of the past and the present, bringing to light the difficult histories of queer being and experience (to which AIDS and homophobia are central) while also expressing hope and demand for social change.

While the two films have much in common with Third cinema – the deconstruction of Western mainstream conventions and meanings through an insistence upon spatial representation rather than temporal manipulation, through an emphasis on the spoken word but also on silence – their affinity is not only a fruitful line of enquiry but decidedly queer.[55] Silence, especially, resonates in its connection to AIDS and queer politics, and the compact silence surrounding AIDS within the black community. But the two films also have a clear and unavoidable connection to Western experimental cinema and to European art cinema at large (with a clear link with the 'ancestors' such as Jonas Mekas and Kenneth Anger).[56] Yet, both films clearly queer or subvert the traditional Western avant-garde genre: Diawara suggests that one ought to think of *Looking for Langston* as a text that serves to *defamiliarise* the avant-garde, and that it does so simply by placing black (and gay) subjects at the centre.[57]

Throughout this chapter, I have been stressing the crucial importance the two films have for the new queer cinema. While most critics have chosen to read them as black and/or gay films, I have tried to argue that they are queer, rather than gay. Their queerness lies not only in the subject matters presented and dealt with in the films, i.e. their political projects in a specific cultural moment, but also in their innovative subversion of film form and cinematic expression and narration. By relying on performativity and the characteristics this entails; by emphasising the hybridity of identity; by explicitly dealing with AIDS; and by fulfilling (if not informing) Rich's definition of queer cinema, both films unquestioningly deserve to be understood not only as forerunners to, but also as vigorous sources of inspiration for, the New Queer Cinema that would develop after 1989.

NOTES

1 Kobena Mercer, 'Introduction: The Cultural Politics of Diaspora', in *Welcome to the Jungle: New Positions in Black Cultural Studies* (New York and London: Routledge, 1994), p. 31.
2 Ibid., p. 6.
3 Valerie Smith, *Representing Blackness: Issues in Film and Video* (New Jersey: Rutgers University Press, 1997), p. 4.
4 Michelle Parkerson, 'Birth of a Notion: Towards Black Gay and Lesbian Imagery in Film and Video', in Martha Gever, John Greyson and Pratibha Parmar (eds), *Queer Looks: Perspectives on Lesbian and Gay Film and Video* (London: Routledge, 1993), p. 236. However, the lack of lesbian black film is a main issue for Parkerson.
5 Ron Simmons, 'Tongues Untied: An Interview with Marlon Riggs', in Essex Hemphill (ed.), *Brother to Brother: New Writings by Black Gay Men* (Boston: Alyson Publications, Inc., 1991), p. 190.
6 However, black lesbians have been more open about their lesbianism than have black men about their gayness. Mentioning the work of Audre Lorde, Michelle Parkerson, Barbara Smith, Cheryl Clarke and Jewelle Gomez, Simmons states that: 'For over a decade, black women have been vocal in affirming the strength of lesbianism in their lives. [They] have given black people and the world glimpses of women loving women through their words'. See Simmons, 'Tongues', p. 190.
7 These are Riggs's words in *Tongues Untied* when describing his first desire for white gay men and white gay culture.
8 B. Ruby Rich, 'Queer and Present Danger', *Sight and Sound*, 10:3 (March 2000): 23.
9 José Esteban Muñoz, *Disidentifications: Queers of Color and the Performance of Politics* (London and Minneapolis: University of Minnesota Press, 1999), p. 57.
10 Other collectives and workshops worth mentioning are Black Audio, Cardiff Film and Video Workshop, Ceddo, Retake, Macro, and Star.
11 Isaac Julien and Kobena Mercer, 'Introduction: De Margin and De Centre', *Screen*, 29:4 (Autumn 1988): 3.

12 Kobena Mercer, 'Recoding Narratives of Race and Nation', in Kobena Mercer (ed.), *ICA Documents*, no. 7, special issue 'Black Film/British Cinema' (London: BFI, Autumn 1988), p. 4.

13 With women filmmakers taking active part in the filmmaking, issues of gender within various black communities were focused upon. See for example Sankofa's *Territories* (Isaac Julien and Sankofa, 1985) and *The Passion of Remembrance* (Maureen Blackwood and Isaac Julien, 1986), both of which also examine the issue of homosexuality. See also Menelik Shabazz's *Burning an Illusion* (1981) which focuses on a black woman's awakening sense of black consciousness (though her growing consciousness seems to be related to her imprisoned boyfriend and his encounters with the white police).

14 Mercer, 'Recoding', p. 5.

15 Stuart Hall, 'Minimal Selves', in Lisa Appignanesi (ed.), *ICA Documents*, no. 6, special issue on 'Identity' (London: BFI, 1988), p. 44.

16 Stuart Hall, 'Cultural Identity and Diaspora', in Patrick Williams and Laura Chrisman (eds), *Colonial Discourse and Post-Colonial Theory* (London: Harvester Wheatsheaf, [1990] 1994), p. 394. This shifting of positionings can be seen in relation to Mercer and Julien's discussion on the de-marginalisation within black British film and its representations of ethnicity:

> Ethnicity has emerged as a key issue as various 'marginal' practices (black British film, for instance) are becoming de-marginalised at a time when 'centred' discourses of cultural authority and legitimation (such as notions of a transhistorical artistic 'canon') are becoming increasingly de-centred and destabilised, called into question from within.

See Julien and Mercer, 'Introduction: De Margin and De Centre', p. 2.

17 Having raised the necessary funding (like his earlier productions, it was funded by Channel 4 and the BFI), and having carried out the research – which took him almost three years – he started the shooting in 1988.

18 See Simmons, 'Tongues Untied', p. 189.

19 See Bill Nichols, *Representing Reality: Issues and Concepts in Documentary* (Bloomington, IN: Indiana University Press, 1991), p. 191.

20 Bill Nichols, 'Performing Documentary', in *Blurred Boundaries: Questions of Meaning in Contemporary Culture* (Bloomington, IN: Indiana University Press, 1994), p. 102. Almost turning poetic himself, Nichols continues: 'Such works offer figuration to alternative forms of social subjectivity and the human self . . . Location, body, self: these elements of a world we thought we knew turn strange and unfamiliar in the landscape of performative documentary'.

21 Ibid. p. 100. The expressive elements are, according to Nichols, the 'subjective camera movement, impressionistic montage, dramatic lighting, compelling music' (ibid.).

22 Thomas Waugh, 'Walking on Tippy Toes: Lesbian and Gay Liberation Documentary of the Post-Stonewall Period 1996–84', in Cynthia Fuchs and Chris Holmlund (eds), *Between the Sheets, In the Streets: Queer, Lesbian, Gay Documentary* (Minneapolis: Minnesota University Press, 1997), p. 109.

23 Mercer, *Welcome to the Jungle*, p. 13.

24 Mercer, 'Dark and Lovely Too: Black Gay Men in Independent Film', in Gever, *Queer Looks*, p. 240.

25 Richard Dyer's pioneering work on whiteness (*White* [London: Routledge, 1997], pp. 1–2) must be quoted here:

> As long as race is something only applied to non-white peoples, as long as white people are not racially seen and named, they/we function as a human norm . . . The point of seeing the racing of whites is to dislodge them/us from the position of power, with all the inequities, oppression, privileges and sufferings in its train, dislodging them/us by undercutting the authority with which they/we speak and act in the world.

26 See Tommy L. Lott, *The Invention of Race: Black Culture and the Politics of Representation* (Malden and Oxford: Blackwell Publishers Ltd., 1999). Du Bois defined race through cultural emphases (i.e. the common cultural and social, rather than physical, contexts that 'bind' people together): 'It is a vast family of human beings, generally of common blood and language, always of common history, traditions and impulses, who are both voluntarily and involuntarily striving together for the accomplishment of certain more or less vividly conceived ideals for life', 'The Conversation of Races', in Howard Brotz (ed.), *Negro Social and Political Thought: 1850–1920* (New York: Basic Books, 1966), p. 485.

27 Hall, 'Cultural Identity and Diaspora', p. 394.

28 Riggs interviewed by Simmons, 'Tongues Untied', p. 191.

29 Mercer, 'Dark and Lovely Too', p. 239.

30 Ibid., p. 239, emphasis in the original. Mercer continues: 'What follows from this is a recognition of the interdependence of different political communities, not completely closed off from each other or each hermetically sealed like a segregated bantustan but interlocking in contradictory relations over which we struggle'.

31 Hall, 'What Is This "Black" in Black Popular Culture?' [1992], in Smith, *Representing Blackness*, p. 128. By 'sides' I mean the interconnected and interrelated facets of one and the same, as if reading identity as a *crystal-like configuration*. To talk about identity as crystalline allows an opening for imagining how different aspects and facets of being take place *besides* one another whilst also constantly reflecting one another.

32 Ibid., p. 128 (my emphasis)

33 Ibid., p. 129 (my emphasis).

34 Mercer, 'Dark and Lovely Too', p. 239.

35 Ibid., p. 239.

36 According to Manthia Diawara, 'the film looks back at a discourse of Blackness that marked the second and third decades of the century in order to empower its own discourse in the present'. See Manthia Diawara, 'The Absent One: The Avant-Garde and the Black Imaginary in Looking for Langston', *Wide Angle*, 13.3 and 4 (July–October 1991): 97.

37 Both films present the black and white relation as the one and only inter-racial relation that matters. There is no reference to Asian gays, for example. On the power ascribed to the black and white relation and the overall cultural silencing or othering of the Asian within such a scenario, see Brian Locke, ' "Top Dog", "Black Treat", and Japanese Cats: The Impact of the White-Black Binary on Asian-American Identity', *Radical Philosophy Review*, 1:2 (February 1999): 98–125. For a critique of the non-existence of Latin-Americans in queer cinema, see Gabriel Gomez, 'Homocolonialism: Looking for Latinos in Apartment Zero and Paris is Burning', *Post Script: Essays in Film and the Humanities*, 14:1–2 (Fall 1994/Spring–Winter 1995): 117–24.

38 See bell hooks, *Black Looks: Race and Representation* (Boston: South End Press, 1992), p. 20.

39 For example, what such a bold and provocative statement has done is to invoke in black lesbians a desire to stand up and shout: 'No! Black women loving black women is *the* revolutionary act!' See Amy Taubin's critique of the film's supposed misogyny in that it leaves black lesbianism out in the cold, in 'Beyond the Sons of Scorsese', *Sight and Sound*, 2:5 (September 1992).

40 Hall, 'What is', p. 130. On 'strategic essentialism', see Gayatri Chakravorty Spivak, 'Subaltern Studies: Deconstructing Historiography', in *In Other Worlds: Essays in Cultural Politics* (New York: Routledge, 1988), p. 207.

41 As does Smith, writing that texts analysing black representations through a focus on the negative/positive binary (thereby imposing on readers a notion of a true racial essence to be (re)discovered) 'legitimated a binarism in the discourse around strategies of black representation that has outlived its usefulness'. See Smith, *Representing Blackness*, p. 3.

42 Hall, 'What is', p. 130.

43 Ibid., p. 132.

44 The film is not a documentary (claiming to present the truth), nor a fiction. Rather, it should be understood as a meditation on Langston Hughes, The Harlem Renaissance and early black gayness. And, as Hemphill emphasises, any meditation on the Harlem Renaissance would have been impossible without taking Langston Hughes into consideration, given that he was – and still is – its leading icon. See Essex Hemphill, 'Undressing Icons', in *Brother to Brother*, p. 181. The Harlem Renaissance is understood to be an important epoch for the entire black community as it provided the Western world with images and words previously kept invisible and silent. It was also a period – and an art community – very much formed by queerness. Not to acknowledge this is to deny the fact that the Renaissance was 'as gay as it was black', that 'many of its key figures – Claude McKay, Alain Locke, Countee Cullen, Wallace Thurman, and Bruce Nugent – were known to be queer, one way or another'. See Mercer, 'Dark and Lovely Too', p. 249.

45 Ibid., p. 241.

46 Gilles Deleuze, in his *Cinema 2, L'Image-temps* from 1985, describes 'les cristaux de temps', a crystalline time that in which past, present and future relate to one another as the facets of a crystal. Constituting one single block, they have to be seen and read from different perspectives. They are contemporary, yet separated. See Gilles Deleuze, *Cinema 2: L'Image-temps* (Paris: Minuit, 1985).

47 Mercer, 'Dark and Lovely too', p. 241.

48 See Kobena Mercer, 'Black Art and the Burden of Representation', *Third Text*, 10 (Spring 1990).

49 Waugh, 'Walking on Tippy Toes', p. 110.

50 Teshome H. Gabriel, 'Towards a Critical Theory of Third World Film', in Jim Pines and Paul Willeman (eds), *Questions of Third Cinema* (London: BFI, 1989), p. 349.

51 hooks, 'The Oppositional Gaze', in *Black Looks*, pp. 115–31.

52 Franz Fanon, *Black Skin, White Masks* [*Peau Noir, Masques Blancs*, 1952], trans. Charles Lam Markmann (New York: Grove Press, 1991), p. 218.

53 Muñoz, quoting Gayl Jones, writes that this call-and-response tradition is 'the antiphonal back-and-forth pattern which exists in many African American oral traditional forms, from sermon to interjective folk tale to blues, jazz and spirituals and so on' (*Disidentifications*, p. 61). The quotation is taken from Gayl Jones, *Liberating Voices: Oral Tradition in African American Literature* (Cambridge, MA: Harvard University Press, 1991), p. 197. On the tradition of call-and-response, see also John E. Callahan, *In the African American Grain: Call-and-Response in Twentieth-Century Black Fiction* (Middletown, CT: Wesleyan University Press, 1988).

54 See also Riggs's *Black Is . . . Black Ain't* (1994); *Non, Je Ne Regret Rien* (1992); and *I shall not be Removed: The Life of Marlon Riggs* (Riggs together with Karen Everett, 1996), of which all deal explicitly with AIDS.

55 There are several reasons for drawing this connection. One is the argument made by Reece Auguiste, who stresses that Third Cinema is also 'the cinema of diasporic subjects living and working in the metropolitan centres of London, Paris, New York etc' (Reece Auguiste/Black Audio Film Collective, 'Black Independents and Third Cinema: The British Context', in Pines and Willeman, *Questions*, p. 215). A second reason is the 'globalisation' of the concept of Third Cinema stressed by Gabriel, who recognises the 'importance of certain white European-American oppositional practices within this framework' (Pines and Willeman, 'Preface', in *Questions*, p. viii). Hence, Third Cinema is neither bound to a specific body nor to a specific place.

56 See Nichols, *Blurred Boundaries*, p. 103.

57 Diawara, 'Absent', p. 98. It should be pointed out that Julien has recently turned to the scene of 'pure' art cinema, producing films to be screened within the context of the art museum. See *The Attendant* (UK, 1993); *Three* (USA, 1996–99); and *The Long Road to Mazatlan* (USA, 1999).

11. NATIONALITY AND NEW QUEER CINEMA: AUSTRALIAN FILM

Ros Jennings and Loykie Lominé

The heady excitement in the early 1990s when an explosion of youthful and mostly American independent filmmaking, later to be labelled New Queer Cinema, swept the international festival circuit has been well documented. In terms of both production and criticism, New Queer Cinema has been conceptualised as a North American moment/movement. Consequently, what might be called the 'geography of New Queer Cinema' is a rather restricted one and one that is firmly centred in the northern hemisphere. In contrast, however, the following discussion sets out to dispute this American model/ monopoly by looking beyond the US-centricity of the phenomenon to locate and establish a key example of New Queer Cinema within another cinematic terrain, that of Australia.

Using the 1997 film *Head On* as a case study, we will argue not only that Ana Kokkinos' film provides a uniquely Australian example of New Queer Cinema, but (by contextualising this text in relation to a specifically anti-podean set of negotiations around overlapping and often contradictory expressions of culture, diversity and sexual identity) we will also contend that Australia provides an ideal site to reconsider 'the geography of New Queer Cinema'. In fact, because the socio-cultural conditions of constantly being 'down-under' are so complex, we extend a claim to the effect that Australian identities are constructed from such diverse and competing sets of co-ordinates that the notion 'queer' takes on a wider emphasis than usually considered in the North American and European context. As a result, throughout this discussion, we will tend to use the term queer more broadly than is perhaps usually the case.

Contemporary Australian cinema is located within a cultural and economic nexus of production that negotiates issues of national/international cinema and localism/internationalism or globalism. Hollywood films dominate Australian domestic mainstream exhibition and, as a medium-sized English language cinema located in the southern hemisphere Australian cinema has had to create itself mainly as a festival cinema in order to export itself and attract widespread distribution. As a result, a mixture of funding strategies consisting of both Australian (including state intervention) and overseas money has been required to support an Australian filmmaking culture and this, in turn, has played a part in the particular formation of Australian cinema as a national cinema. Consequently, as Tom O'Regan has so eloquently argued in his 1996 book, *Australian National Cinema,* no one single and unified Australian national cinema can be identified, but, rather, one that is constantly in the process of renegotiating its own identity and repositioning itself within its material conditions of film production.[1]

In some instances, to assert its distinctiveness, it has drawn on an unrelenting use of recognisable and iconic signifiers of Australian-ness (whether it be the kangaroo or the Sydney Opera House) in what Alan McKee has referred to as a kind of 'desperate Australian-ness'.[2] At other moments, it has transformed and reworked ('Australianised') classic genres, illustrating that: 'All national consumption and production is internationally derived but simultaneously localized'.[3] Increasingly, however, as McKee explains: 'The nation-building project in recent cinema has largely moved away from the insistent use of recognisable symbols of Australian-ness, either rejecting them in favour of more banal and everyday ways of representing parts of Australian culture, or returning to them in an openly parodic way'.[4] This new cinematic turn would seem to fall in line with the more far-reaching effects of Australian multiculturalism. A top-down government policy or officially sanctioned policy was instituted in the early 1970s bringing about what Jon Stratton and Ien Ang call the 'mainstreaming of multiculturalism in Australia'.[5] This policy was designed to recognise the 'real' diversity of being Australian and attempted to be more inclusive than previous 'national fictions' of identity.[6] The previous Anglo-Celtic fiction of Australian history and identity was shifted so that, theoretically at least, people of indigenous and 'other' diasporic settler background were embraced within the nation. This policy also led to a reconsideration of the dissonance between Australia's geographical position and its experience of cultural identity, for, despite being situated in the Asia-Pacific region, white Australia had aligned itself culturally with Europe and America. One way of explaining Australia's complex and often dissonant antipodean relationship to global culture is that Australia is looking awry at dominant Western culture. As such, Australia occupies a marginal space that could even be interpreted as resembling a 'queer' space. Though undoubtedly a pragmatic policy, institutional multiculturalism would still, in some measure, seem to acknowledge that a unified national identity is ultimately impossible, and that the formation of national identity is as much of a process as the formation of personal identity. Therefore, if as Ramesh Thakur has suggested: 'multiculturalism is a fluid set of identities for the individual as well as the nation',[7] then Australia's multicultural policy would seem to allow for a plurality of positions which might be claimed as Australian, including a recognition of 'the integrity of society's social margins'.[8]

So why did it take Australia a further six years before it was able to produce in *Head On* a film that might qualify as an example of 'New Queer Cinema'? In many ways, this delay in engaging with New Queer Cinema might seem quite surprising, especially since Australia's own version of multiculturalism would seem to predispose it to an extended examination of questions of identities and differences including the problematics of sexuality and sexual difference. Certainly in terms of academic scholarship, Australia had swiftly joined the queer bandwagon: queer theory and queer studies were there alive and vibrant.[9]

On another level, however, Australia's tardy engagement with New Queer Cinema is not really astonishing. As a land once described by one of its own Prime Ministers as being at 'the arse end of the world', it is perhaps understandable that a certain cultural anxiety is located around expressions of queer desire and issues of homosexuality.[10] The outback myth, until recently so foundational to notions of Anglo-Celtic Australian settler identity, was established on homosocial values of mateship and unsurprisingly, therefore, in order to ward off accusations of homosexuality it was also swaggeringly 'anti-poofter'.[11] As a result, it would be true to say that in Australia, the filmic representation of queer characters remained securely within the closet until the 1990s.[12]

The closet door was broken open with a camp cinematic flourish in 1994 with the popular international success of Stephan Elliott's *The Adventures of Priscilla Queen of the Desert*. In this Australian reworking of the road movie genre, the creation of three main protagonists who so clearly disrupted hegemonic notions of a stable trinity between sex, gender and sexuality, invited audiences to question their own perceptions of Australian sexual identities and lifestyles. Pre-conceived notions of the relationship of the mainstream to the margins became destabilised by putting these three characters at the centre of the narrative. In spite of this, however, the film's queer (non-mainstream) pleasures were offered safely: there was certainly no queer on-screen sexual activity. As Deb Verhoeven suggests, however, while Australian films in the 1990s were beginning to explore queer subjectivities, these queer pleasures still had to be read decidedly 'against the groin'.[13] *Muriel's Wedding* (P.J. Hogan, 1994), for instance, offers such pleasures in both its moments of high camp performance and in its interesting subversions of the cinematic gaze in order to underscore a lesbian reading of Muriel and Rhonda's friendship. Ultimately, however, it did not follow through and assigned Muriel (Toni Collette) and Rhonda's (Rachel Griffiths) choice to be together as one of carer and dependant. In the same way, Geoff Burton and Kevin Dowling's 1994 film, *The Sum of Us,* despite being explicitly polemic in its intent of promoting tolerance for gay identities, only presented a rather worthy and apologetic exploration of a father/son relationship where the resolution leaves the unambiguously gay son (played by Russell Crowe) to devote himself to the care of his stroke-victim father. The values of the family are presented, therefore, not only as dominant but also as redemptive for gay identity and gay acceptance in society. Despite experimentation with some formal cinematic expression to the contrary, the narrative resolutions of both *Muriel's Wedding* and *The Sum of Us* overwhelmingly confirm that 'the threat of same-sex eroticism is sublimated into the socially measurable and sexually benign activity of ministration'.[14] It is Emma Kate Croghan's (1996) feel-good film *Love & Other Catastrophes* that provides the first real co-ordinates for an unapologetic depiction of lesbian desire in Australian cinema. The presence of lesbian desire is not, however, at the centre of the narrative and although visibly a part of the narrative, it was kept deliberately peripheral in order to naturalise and represent this desire in a positive light.

Coming some six years after the American fanfare for New Queer Cinema, it is Ana Kokkinos' 1997 film *Head On* that marks a watershed in Australian queer representation. The film does not provide the kind of wholesome representations of lesbians and gays that Australia's multicultural context had just previously tried to nurture, but produced uncompromising representations of sexuality. Based on Christos Tsiolkas' 1995 semi-autobiographical novel *Loaded,* the film is centred around Ari (Alex Dimitriades), a 19-year-old Greek-Australian from Melbourne.[15] It follows him from a traditional community wedding through furtive backstreet homosexual encounters to an uncertain future, reflecting the multi-layered specificities inherent to the Australian multicultural context. A low budget independent film, *Head On* comprises the key features of New Queer Cinema in its formal inventiveness, its representations of sexualities and sexual desires, and its problematisation of identity politics.

In a fly-on-the-wall sort of fashion *Head On* follows Ari for 24 hours punctuated by sexual moments, sexual tensions and desires. Just as Jon (Craig Gilmore) at the beginning of Gregg Araki's 1992 American-made film *The Living End* sprays 'Fuck the world' on the wall, the opening voiceover narration in *Head On* begins: 'Fuck it, I'm no scholar, I'm no poet, I'm no worker'. Right from the start (a graphic sequence of Ari masturbating in bed), this film doesn't have to be read against the groin, the groin is explicit. *Head On* is about sex, about Ari's sexual life. Later, Ari will have rough sex with a Chinese man near a busy market street, with only a brick wall between them and the heteronormative world; Ari will try to have sex with a Greek woman, yet without getting aroused; he will jokingly pretend to have sex with his best friend Johnny/Toula (Paul Capsis), a Greek male ostracised transvestite who in a key scene of the film is beaten up by vicious homophobic police officers in an interrogation cell; Ari will also have sex with an old Greek man in a grimy backstreet behind a night club, exchanging few words but 'pull me'; Ari will have sex with Sean, a good-looking White young man he fancies but starts beating up. That last episode is highly significant: from his first encounter with Sean, a new flatmate of his brother's, Ari seemed predetermined to end up in bed with him, in a love-story sort of way. Most of the film is about Ari searching for Sean and were it a classical 'boy-gets-boy' narrative, the film would imply a 'happy-ever-after' resolution. However, after finding each other in a nightclub and after kissing ferociously they unexpectedly end up in a fight provoked by Ari himself. It is Ari who eventually finds himself alone, bruised, and naked on the doorstep, whispering 'sorry', but it is too late. This is the first sexual experience of the film linked to any feeling, but as soon as Sean declared his feelings, Ari reacted violently, unable to cope with sentiments and ideas of love. Ari is seen and defines himself solely through complex sexual desires and rapid physical gratifications, draining sex from any emotional involvement and thus separating him from any of the cosy associations with positive images that formed part of Australia's earlier attempts to portray non-hegemonic sexualities on screen.

Ari is not really gay in the socio-cultural sense of the term: following the commonly accepted meaning of gay as 'a positive assertion of a certain identity and lifestyle, which challenges both traditional sexual and social relationships between the sexes'.[16] The usual semiotics of gay culture and gay identity do not apply to Ari. If occasionally he goes dancing in gay clubs, it is because he enjoys the music there, and even then he does not mix with a gay crowd but stays with his straight Greek friends, males and females, who do not suspect that Ari, the virile, straight-looking and straight-acting bloke they grew up with, might be wrongly interested in men rather than women. This cultural refusal/impossibility of gayness is actually a recurrent theme in Tsiolkas's writings. For instance in his 1994 short story 'Bypassing Benalla' he invokes the following: 'How the fuck – jesus fucking Christ – how the fuck could you be gay when you don't mince . . . when you look and sound like a man . . . Your back is too broad, your voice too low'.[17] In the novel *Loaded* itself, he then further explores such signifiers:

> I do a good job of talking-like, walking-like, being a man. I've got the build, the swagger, the look. More, I've got the fuck-ya-I-don't-give-a-shit attitude perfected to an art form. Faggots love sleeping with me, they think they've scored a real man . . . I get a buzz off faggots thinking I'm straight.[18]

In terms of gayness, Ari is the exact opposite of Adam/Felicia (Guy Pearce) in *The Adventures of Priscilla Queen of the Desert*: Adam is camp and flamboyant to the extreme, yet does not seem to have a sex life; Ari is only presented through his sex life and homosexual desires, yet with no gay signifier. If Ari is not gay, he is not straight either, and his half-hearted performance of oral sex with Betty (Elena Mandalis) only results in failure and insults of 'poofter', which he half-laughingly accepts. Unlike his friends and cousins, and against all societal expectations, he is not attracted sexually to women. Being different, being other, queer is the best way to define him, and *Head On* as a whole then appears as a cinematographic attempt (for the first time in Australia) to define or rather illustrate what queer means in practice, not as a concept but as an embodied experience.

The representation of Ari's queerness is as complex and plural as Ari's queerness itself: it self-consciously contains typical and expected elements (such as key queer issues about the visual limits of traditional dichotomies such as gay/straight and masculine/feminine), yet it remains marked by an original refusal of identity politics. Unlike his counterpart Johnny/Toula, Ari is not a herald of gay/transgender rights or gay/transgender visibility. Toula challenges these dichotomies in a more obvious way (transgressive gendered behaviour) and her identity is more politicised. She adopts her late mother's name and even goes as far as wearing her outdated clothes. At one point in the film, she applies her lipstick as she must have seen her mother do countless times, and issues a challenge to the mirror in front of her: 'Toula's back, get used to it'. That line typifies her whole attitude in the film, where she asserts her right to an alternative identity both within the Greek community and the straight community. This is in complete contrast to Ari who avoids confront-ing his sexual identity. After the violent police interrogation, which left Toula bruised and battered, Ari tells her: 'You should have kept quiet'. He just cannot comprehend why she remained so openly defiant. Her resistance lies in her attempt to retain her dignity, under the hateful gazes of the White Anglo cop (who made her get undressed and become 'male' Johnny again) and his Greek subordinate (who reacts violently to this deviant and un-Greek beha-viour). That act of quiet defiance to the multiple humiliation of her assault makes the now quivering Ari look pathetic in comparison, and accentuates the contrast between them: the naked and muscular Ari is now self-pitying and helpless in front of the men in uniform, but the naked and frail Toula has her dignity reinforced in what must be read as a stronger performance of her queer identity.

If Toula's attitude can be summed up by 'Get used to it', Ari's refusal to engage with sexual politics is best summarised by his own words: 'Fuck politics, let's dance'. Indeed it is through dancing that he survives his disabling general disenchantment with the world. Through dancing Ari transcends hegemonic notions of sex, gender and sexualities: dancing gives him pride, power and respect, and – more importantly – an identity. Not a group identity (that of queer, acculturated Australian youth), not a burgeoning ideology worth fighting for (the kind that his friends explore by discussing politics till dawn in Melbourne's Greek taverns), but an identity born both out of Greek music and of the high energy techno music always blasting though his ever present headphones. Ari's queerness and Ari's dancing are similar: they are both sexual and individual, powerful and problematic, beautiful and ultimately frustrating.

A good example of this is indeed prefaced by his use of the phrase 'Fuck politics, let's dance': he leads Ariadne, an attractive Greek woman, to the dancefloor and they begin to dance in a very fluid and sensual way. Ari is then performing the role of the conventional Greek male in this dance, also signifying typical heterosexuality, but under Sean's disconcerted and jealous gaze this very act becomes queer. As the scene progresses further, Kokkinos' direction of the sequence of shots subverts dominant cinematic understanding of the male controlling heterosexual gaze. The music then changes into a slower bouzouki-led melody when all women leave the dancefloor to the men. The men then perform their traditional dance and Ari becomes the centre of attention, in his masterful and assured command of this aspect of his Greek cultural heritage. Kokkinos skilfully intercuts the admiring gaze of Ariadne and the desiring gaze of Sean in such a way as to offer the audience some specifically queer pleasures/readings. This is encapsulated in a sequence of exchanges/cuts where the audience become implicated in Ariadne's realisation that, for Sean too, Ari is the object of an erotic gaze. This moment is queer not only because it breaks the usual rules of cinematic looking, but also because it is an example of complex sexual and cultural significations: in the context of Greek dancing, the film has shown that it is acceptable for Greek men to look at other Greek men without destabilising their masculinity. Sean looking has a different signification: as a non-Greek, his gaze becomes problematic and shifts the meaning from a homosocial paradigm to one of homosexual/queer significations.

Ari's queerness can only be understood against the background of an Australian postcolonial and Greek diasporic legacy. Like thousands of others, Ari's parents left Greece after the 1967 military coup for Melbourne, where today the local Greek community is the second largest one in the world after Athens. As a whole, nearly a million Greeks left their homeland between 1950 and 1975, a fate collectively known as the *xerizoma* (uprooting). Ari's parents still live in a Greek environment, exclusively frequenting Greek immigrants like themselves with whom they speak Greek, eat Greek, drink Greek, dance Greek and live Greek. That Ari's younger sister Alex (Andrea Mandalis) goes out with a Lebanese must remain a secret, and even Ari himself feels ill at ease with that, which is symptomatic of his problematic acculturation as a whole. Ari is less Greek than his parents are, and less Greek than they wished him to be. Certain limits of the treatment of Greekness and Greek cultural heritage in *Head On* have been identified by critics such as Mousoulis, Tsaconas and Veresis on the basis of the genuineness of the representations of Greek Australian culture: it is true that *Head On* perpetuates some ethnic stereotypes such as the subservient Greek mother and the overbearing patriarchal Greek father (a type which Kokkinos also used in her 1994 award-winning short feature film *Only the Brave*), yet *Head On* does not pretend to primarily portray Greek lives: this is the background of the story and the background of Ari's life, not the main theme.[19] The film resolves around Ari, who is more than just one more cocky, young Greek Australian but a 'fallen-angel hero'.[20] His queerness, which Mousoulis, Tsaconas and Veresis fail to problematise, gives the film its internal dynamics and its cinematic edge. His acculturation operates at two levels: the sexual one (gay/straight/queer) and the ethnic one (Greek/Australian/Greek-Australian). The nexus of Greek/sexuality that Kokkinos introduces has little to do with classical paradigms of sexualities and Mediterranean homosexuality.[21]

The film's attempt to concomitantly problematise government-sanctioned multiculturalism and socially disapproved sexuality gives *Head On* its first Australian originality. The second originality of the film resides in the way that queerness is more fully realised. New Queer Cinema, as initially defined by the American experience, has been criticised for being 'only queer by half', in that the inherent diversity that queer embraces, at least conceptually, was not apparent at the start.[22] Its celebrated darlings (such as Haynes, Araki, van Sant and Kalin) were almost exclusively young white male filmmakers. An openly lesbian film-director of Greek origin, Kokkinos adds a further layer of queerness to the film. The result is a distinctive style, one that makes the 'normal' look dull, and the queer look 'normal'. Kokkinos uses super-16 film stock, blown up on the big screen to reinforce the evocation of grey, suburban and familial existence. The rich filmic texture and the visual vibrancy of scenes of Ari's drug-fucked predatory subjectivity are positioned in sharp contrast. In a similar binary exposition, Kokkinos stresses Ari's place in the symbolic discourse of *xerizoma*, by integrating both historical documentary footage of Greek migrants coming to Australia, and recreations of Ari's parents' earlier political activism. The aim of this strategy is to make the viewer see Ari as the painful product of these tensions between the Old World and the New World. It was precisely such tensions, between the past, the present and the future, that were isolated by Rich in her initial characterisation of New Queer Cinema.[23]

In her monograph *Queer-ing the Screen*, Samantha Searle argues that queer can be conceptualised as 'both identity-based and identity-critical'.[24] Queer in *Head On* is particularly identity critical. This is both deliberate and incidental in that, although the politics of identity (whether gender, sexuality, race and ethnicity and so forth) are not in Ari's repertoire: in the film, he embodies a terrain of contested identity, without realising it. His outsiderness gives him the critical distance necessary to challenge the Australian dream of harmonious multiculturalism. A good example of this would be his comment to Ariadne: 'That's what's wrong with this country; everyone hates everyone. The Skips hate the Wogs. The Wogs hate the Asians. And everyone hates the Blacks'. Ariadne, fully immersed in politically correct multiculturalism, can only reply: 'What are you? A wanker?' Ari does not even bother to answer: he is beyond the constraints of political definitions of identity. The only way to make his position intelligible is through recourse to an understanding of identity-critical queerness. In this cinematic adaptation of *Loaded*, Ana Kokkinos remains true to the spirit of Tsiolkas' book, where Ari's identity crisis is the crux of the narrative. This is well illustrated in the following lines where he states: 'I'm not Australian, I'm not Greek, I'm not anything', 'You're either Greek or Australian, you have to make a choice. Me, I am neither. It's not that I can't decide; I don't like definitions', 'Words such as faggot, wog, poofter, gay, Greek, Australian, Croat are just excuses. Just stories, they mean shit'.[25]

True to the style of New Queer Cinema, *Head On* offers no answer to Ari's existential ennui. The last shots of the film are of Ari slowly dancing to the music of his now trademark headphones. In the silvery light of a Melbourne dawn, the camera pulls back to offer one last image of him, dancing alone, forming the gestures of a Greek dance, an isolated figure in the post-industrial cityscape of Melbourne's docklands. This image can be read as one of relative liberation against Ari's accompanying voiceover which offers him no redemption:

> I am a whore, a dog, a cunt. My father's insults make me strong. I accept them all. I'm sliding towards the sewer, I'm not struggling. I can smell the shit, but I'm still breathing. I'm gonna live my life. I'm not going to make a difference. I'm not going to change a thing. No one's going to remember me when I'm dead. I'm a sailor and a whore, and I will be until the end of the world.

These bleak words, reminiscent of Jean Genet, reinscribe Ari in a European literary tradition of queer outsiders (such as in *Querelle* and *Notre Dame des Fleurs*) and in the cinematic tradition of New Queer Cinema (and films such as *The Living End*), suggesting an explicit re-working of these resonances within the Australian context.

In *Head On*, the 'in your face' aesthetics and politics of New Queer Cinema are remodulated and, for the very first time, 'Australianised'. Within the Australian socio-political context, the film operates as both an example of, and a reaction to, taken-for-granted notions of multiculturalism. On one level, it verifies Scott Murray's statement that 'Australians almost never make any effort to actually stop people being different', but on another level the film presents the real difficulties of the existential struggle to embrace and live non-hegemonic identities.[26] Moving away from the ideal of positive and clear-cut images (exemplified by *The Sum of Us*), *Head On* dares to engage with the graphic representations of diverse and complex human sexual identities. This is where *Head On* breaks new ground: for the very first time in the history of mainstream Australian cinema, queer is explicit on the screen, both as desire and as sexual gratification. Kokkinos' film is not just about queer characters (as in *The Adventures of Priscilla Queen of the Desert*) or queer subtexts (as in *Muriel's Wedding*), but it is about the uncompromising depiction of queer life. All this makes *Head On* a unique Australian response to New Queer Cinema.

NOTES

1 Tom O'Regan, *Australian National Cinema* (London: Routledge, 1996).
2 Alan McKee, 'Suck on That, Mate! Perverse Centres in Australia', in Deb Verhoeven (ed.), *Twin Peeks: Australian and New Zealand Feature Films* (Melbourne: Damned Publishing, 1999), p. 122.
3 O'Regan, *National*, p. 229.
4 McKee, 'Suck', p. 122.
5 Jon Stratton and Ien Ang, 'Multicultural Imagined Communities: Cultural Difference and National Identity in the USA and Australia', in David Bennett (ed.), *Multicultural States: Rethinking Difference and Identities* (London: Routledge, 1998), p. 156.
6 See Graeme Turner, *National Fictions: Literature, Film and the Construction of Australian Narrative* (Sydney: Allen & Unwin, 1996).
7 Ramesh Thakur quoted in Stratton and Ang, 'Multicultural', p. 157.
8 O'Regan, *National*, p. 324.
9 See Michael Hurley, 'Gay, Lesbian and Queer Studies in Australia', in Raymond Donovan and Leong K. Chan (eds), *Gay, Lesbian and Queer Studies in Australia* (Sydney: Australian Centre for Lesbian & Gay Research, 1999) and Annamarie Jagose, *Queer Theory* (Melbourne: Melbourne University Press, 1996).
10 Quoted in McKee, 'Suck', p. 119.
11 This notion of 'anti-poofter' masculine culture provides key arguments for the following two authors: Terry Colling, *Beyond Mateship: Understanding Australian Men* (Sydney: Simon & Schuster, 1992) and John Webb, *Junk Male: Reflections of Australian Masculinity* (Sydney: HarperCollins, 1998).
12 For a comprehensive discussion see Samantha Searle, *Queer-ing the Screen: Sexuality and Australian Film and Television, The Moving Image* (St Kilda: Australian Teachers of Media, Australian Film Institute, Deakin University, 1997) and also Deb Verhoeven, 'The Sexual Terrain of the Australian Feature Film: Putting the Out:back into the Ocker', in Claire Jackson (ed.), *The Bent Lens: A World Guide to Gay and Lesbian Film* (St Kilda: Australian Catalogue Company, 1997).
13 Verhoeven, 'Sexual Terrain', p. 25.
14 Ibid., p. 32.
15 Christos Tsiolkas, *Loaded* (Sydney: Random House, 1995).
16 John Hart and Diane Richardson (eds), *The Theory and Practice of Homosexuality* (London: Routledge & Kegan Paul, 1981), p. 2.
17 Tsiolkas, 'Bypassing Benalla', in Garry Dunne (ed.), *Fruit: A New Anthology of Contemporary Australian Gay Writing* (Sydney: Blackwattle Press, 1994), p. 2.
18 Tsiolkas, *Loaded*, p. 92.
19 See writings by Bill Mousoulis, 'Is your Film Language Greek? Some Thoughts on Greek-Australian Film-makers', *Senses of Cinema*, 1 (December 1999); Vicky Tsaconas, 'Are their Eyes Greek?', *Senses of Cinema*, 4 (March 2000) and Con Veresis, '*Head-On*: A (too) personal view', *Senses of Cinema*, 9 (September 2000).
20 See Dimitri Kakmi, 'Queer Cinema: A Reality Check', in *Senses of Cinema*, 8 (July 2000).
21 See Robert Aldrich, *The Seduction of the Mediterranean: Writing, Art and Homosexual Fantasy* (London: Routledge, 1993).
22 Amy Taubin, 'Queer Male Cinema and Feminism', in Pam Cook and Philip Dodd (eds), *Women and Film: A Sight and Sound Reader* (London: Scarlett Press, 1993), p. 179.

23 B. Ruby Rich, 'Homo Pomo: The New Queer Cinema', *Sight and Sound*, 2:5 (September 1992): 32, reprinted in this book.
24 Searle, *Queer-ing*, p. 9.
25 Tsiolkas, *Loaded*, pp. 149, 115, 141.
26 Scott Murray, cited in Verhoeven, 'Sexual Terrain', p. 29.

12. NEW QUEER CINEMA
AND THIRD CINEMA

Helen Hok-Sze Leung

Late Capitalism and a Tale of Two Cinemas

At first sight, New Queer Cinema and Third Cinema seem to have very little in common, except for the doubts concerned critics have recently expressed about their continued viability. New Queer Cinema owes its roots to the independent work of British and American filmmakers like Derek Jarman, Tom Kalin, Gus Van Sant, and Issac Julien, who pioneered in the making of an 'outsider cinema' of gay-themed films that broke with both the aesthetic conventions of realism and the philosophical sensibility of humanism during the early 1990s. In the ensuing decade, its themes and concerns – though arguably not its politics – have successfully found their way into mainstream Hollywood productions. While the original moment of New Queer Cinema was inseparable from the then emergent politics of AIDS activism and Queer Nation, the current incarnation of its legacy appears less associated with radical politics than with commercial trends and commodity culture. B. Ruby Rich, who first identified the phenomenon and coined the term 'New Queer Cinema' in 1992, expresses scepticism about the continual survival of the 'movement' which Rich, in retrospect, suggests should more rightly be thought of as a 'moment' when queer work, marginalised by Hollywood, was still driven by an independent spirit and radical impulse.[1] The successful integration of queer films into what Rich calls a 'niche market', accompanied by Hollywood stars' unprecedented interest in playing queer roles, has tamed the aesthetic experimentation, political edge, and community-driven production method characteristic of the formative films of New Queer Cinema. More recently, in an article written on the tenth anniversary of New Queer Cinema,

Rich draws attention to the diminishing quality and waning tide of queer cinema in Hollywood and calls for a renewal of radical queer expressions.[2]

Conceived as an intimate part of the anti-colonial independence struggles in the Third World in the late 1960s and early 1970s, Third Cinema was first and foremost an engaged and oppositional political cinema. It aimed to formulate both an aesthetic and a production method that would reflect the economic situation and the political aspirations of Third World peoples. The philosophy of Third Cinema, documented in the now famous manifestos of Latin American filmmakers Glauber Rocha, Julio Espinoza, Fernando Solanas and Octavio Getino, was inspired by the anti-colonial thought and activism of Third World intellectuals such as Franz Fanon, Amilcar Cabral, and Aimé Césaire. Opposed to both the commercial cinema of Hollywood and the auteurist tradition of the European avant-garde, Third Cinema envisioned an independent, anti-imperialist, and anti-capitalist cinema that would contribute to socialist political struggles.[3] By the 1980s, however, the euphoric period of decolonisation and revolution in the Third World had given way to an era of disillusionment. Political upheavals, economic devastation, and social contradictions continue to plague most Third World societies while the neo-colonial world order had become virtually a globalised empire where capital traverses across national borders with unprecedented impunity, threatening older paradigms of political organising and crushing the Third Worldist aspiration of economic de-linking from the First World. Teshome Gabriel's *Third Cinema in the Third World* emerged at this critical juncture.[4] This important study theorises the practice of Third Cinema while placing it in the landscape of academic film theory. Yet, despite the immense influence of Gabriel's work, many have voiced doubts about the continual relevance of Third Cinema under such an inauspicious economic and political context, especially when popular commercial genres, rather than the radical practice of Third Cinema, have begun to flourish in many of the most successful film industries in the Third World.[5] Mike Wayne notes that when a filmmaker declared Third Cinema to be dead at a BFI-sponsored conference on African cinema in 1996, the pronouncement was met without a single voice of dissent.[6] Wayne himself would later respond passionately against such a judgment in a book-length study arguing for a new understanding of Third Cinema's role in the current global order.[7]

Given the dystopian political climate and the seemingly inexhaustible capacity of late capitalism to remake any outlawed aesthetic into its own image, New Queer Cinema and Third Cinema actually have much to learn from each other. The mainstreaming of New Queer Cinema is in part a reflection of a more general trend within American independent filmmaking. As Maria Pramaggiore suggests in an article that situates New Queer Cinema within the independent tradition of the New American Cinema that emerged in the 1960s, the indie circuit has become a highly profitable sector on which Hollywood is only too keen to capitalise.[8] For Pramaggiore, New Queer

Cinema is now an inadequate rubric because it no longer identifies a body of work that is distinguishable from Hollywood productions, whether in terms of genre innovation, formal devices, production methods, or distribution channels.[9] Yet, aside from the commodification of American independent cinema, there are also specific reasons why the *queer* politics of New Queer Cinema is particularly vulnerable to mainstream recuperation. Urvashi Vaid argues in her 1995 study, *Virtual Equality*, that the 'mainstreaming strategy' of the gay and lesbian movement in North America has prioritised the attainment of civil rights at the expense of securing genuine equality in political, social, and economic terms. The apparent increase in tolerance for and visibility of queer communities merely reflects a 'virtual equality' that masks the absence of genuine and fundamental systemic changes.[10] It is precisely under this climate of 'virtual equality' that New Queer Cinema's once outlawed and marginalised representations of sexuality become transformed into palatable, even marketable, commodities.

In a more recent study *Profit and Pleasure*, Rosemary Hennessy provocatively argues that the queer movement's fervent concern with visibility has led to a commodification of queer culture and politics, to the extent that queer liberation has come to mean equal participation in late capitalist consumption.[11] Hennessy's reading of *The Crying Game*, which is perhaps one of the earliest examples of a profitable marketing of dissident sexuality, points to the film's mythical displacement of historical contradictions (the unequal political and economic relation between Northern Ireland and England) onto the bodies and desire of queer subjects (the relationship between the black transgender English hairdresser and the IRA insurgent).[12] For Hennessy, the visibility of queer love in this film serves to obscure the historical relations of racialised and colonised subjects, thus rendering *invisible* the structure of global power:

> Mythologizing a more flexible heterogender system in films like *The Crying Game* empties the ambivalent, desiring subject of its history, obscures the contradictory relation between ideology and labor, and forestalls inquiry into why more fluid pleasures and sexualities have become the signature claim of a postmodern common sense.[13]

The fundamental premise of Hennessy's critique is that neither postmodern aesthetic experimentation nor visible expressions of queer identities undermine the global structure of unequal power. In fact, the façade of queer liberation (understood as consumption) obscures the underlying relations of inequality that enable our 'liberation' in the first place. A *new* New Queer Cinema – that is, a more radical queer cinema that aspires towards more than creating a new niche market in Hollywood – would have to address the complex relation between late capitalism and sexuality, or in the terms of Hennessy's book title, between 'profit and pleasure'. Such a cinema necessarily intersects with the legacy of Third Cinema, which has not only pioneered the critique of colonial history and of capitalism, but also developed cinematic forms and production methods that mobilise the audience's critical awareness of the material circumstances of their own spectatorship. At the same time, such an intersection would create an important space of renewal for Third Cinema by attending to one of its major blind spots: the suppression of queer sexualities in the history of anti-colonial nationalist resistance and the future role of sexuality in socialist politics.

In 'The Changing Geography of Third Cinema', an article that tries to locate the contemporary terrain of Third Cinema, Michael Chanan suggests that the change in media technology and the intensification of global capitalist expansion have moved both the existence of, and the need for, Third Cinema outside of the Third World and 'into a new space akin to what Teshome Gabriel has recently called nomadic cinema'.[14] Such a cinema would tap into the potential of new video (and digital) technology, draw its resources from while serving communities that struggle against oppression and, most importantly, engage with and resist the decentred and dispersed forms of late capitalist domination that operate transnationally and across different identity formations. There are signs that a new wave of queer films, emerging from diverse locales, are moving in precisely such a direction. Not only do these films explore non-normative sexualities and gender practices from new perspectives, they do so by rendering strange - indeed queering - existent narratives of history and culture as well as the institution of filmmaking. They are thus 'queer' in the most radical sense of the term. It is too early to tell if they will form a coherent rubric of work (a Queer Third Cinema?) but they certainly offer important lessons for anyone concerned with the unfinished projects – both cinematic and political – started by Third Cinema and New Queer Cinema. In the rest of this chapter, I will outline two major directions – one thematic, the other aesthetic – in which recent queer films deploy (though not necessarily consciously) some of the fundamental tenets of Third Cinema. I hope that a reading that situates such films within the traditions of Third Cinema and New Queer Cinema will provoke more future efforts to theorise the intersections of these important cinematic legacies.

QUEER SEXUALITY, COMMUNITY, AND THE CRITIQUE OF COLONIALISM

In *Political Film: The Dialectics of Third Cinema*, Mike Wayne attempts to construct a 'dialectical relationship' between Third Cinema 'then and now' by recognising 'the threads of continuity that connect us with the past as well as the transformations in theory and practice provoked by new historical contexts'.[15] I would like to extend Wayne's analysis to construct alongside his account a dialectical relationship between his vision of contemporary Third Cinema and recent queer cinema. There are numerous threads of continuities between the thematics identified by Wayne in current practices of Third Cinema and the strategies of recent queer films. At the same time, the centrality of queer sexuality in these films sheds new light on and transforms the critique of colonialism and capitalism.

The question of sexuality has long been present in the politicised cinemas that emerged in the wake of the Third Cinema tradition. It is one of the most important allegorical vehicles for the representation of power and its abuses. Wayne argues that allegory became a crucial strategy in Third Cinema in the post-revolutionary era, when the major force of oppression was no longer readily discernible in the form of a foreign ruling power, but lurked behind the 'normality' or even 'inevitability' of the current social order.[16] In such a context, allegory gives a concrete face to the relatively invisible systemic reality. Senegalese director Ousmane Sembène's *Xala* (1974) is one of the most famous examples of the way in which sexuality – in this case, sexual impotence – is deployed as a metaphor for the predicament of the corrupt and dependent postcolonial state. In her study of post-Third Worldist cinemas, Ella Shohat shows how feminist heirs of Third Cinema critique both anti-colonial nationalism and First World feminism by reinterpreting the relation between the public domain of radical politics and the private domain of sexuality and desire.[17] These works show how female sexuality serves often as a figure for what has been suppressed, sacrificed, or side-stepped by nation-alist struggles and the subsequent formation of the national state. It is thus no surprise that when *queer* sexuality appears in films influenced by a politicised cinematic tradition, it also becomes linked to questions of colonialism and nationalism. Yet, these films also move sexuality beyond its allegorical function. At the same time that queer sexuality alludes to the larger question of the predicament of postcolonial nationalism, its *literal* place in the social and political order is clearly of central importance as well. One recurrent concern is the vexed relation between queer sexuality, nativist/nationalist traditions, and the revolutionary legacy. Cuban director Gutiérrez Alea's *Strawberry and Chocolate* (1993), for instance, discloses the history of homophobic persecution in the Cuban Revolution at the same time that it considers the possibility of change. The gay character Diego's eventual departure from Cuba vies with his friend's claim that a new revolutionary credo is possible and that there is a place for queer communities in Cuba. Similarly, the documentary by Lucinda Broadbent *Sex and the Sandinistas* (1991) illustrates the difficulty of being out as queer during the revolutionary struggle in Nicaragua. Yet, the film also emphasises the pre-colonial existence of queer love in indigenous mythologies. Both films suggest, if only implicitly, that despite the histories of homophobic repression in Third World revolutions, queer desire has a possible and legitimate place in the post-revolutionary order.

Guinean director Mohamed Camera's *Dakan* (1997), a film that is often hailed as the first queer feature from Sub-Saharan Africa, more pessimistically situates male homosexuality categorically outside of 'traditional society', at least as it is conceived by the various characters in positions of authority in the film. *Dakan* is most interesting when it draws a parallel between gay love and other relationships that have no place in the postcolonial social order. The film raises the anxious question of where these outsiders belong. By contrast, the documentary *Woubi Chéri* (1998), co-produced in France and the Ivory Coast and directed by Philip Brooks and Laurent Bocahut, shows exactly to where such outsiders may turn by locating queer and transgender communities that are already in existence in West Africa, though they may be known by other names. This strategy is an important response to the 'no way out' pessimism of *Dakan*. *Woubi Chéri* shows that there are culturally specific ways of conceiving of queer politics and communities: it is not a matter of either embracing the West or being abandoned by one's own culture and community. Such a strategy is also found in a recent wave of powerful documentaries by and for queer communities of colour in North America. These films confront the legacy of colonialism from the perspective of diaspora communities by linking experiences of racism to the history of colonial domination. At the same time, they explore culturally specific experiences of queerness that resist a universalist narrative of gay liberation. Moreover, these films are often produced with labour and resources from the sectors they set out to serve, thus creating and sustaining community in the very process of filmmaking. The video *Rewriting the Script: A Love Letter to Our Families* (2001), directed by the Friday Night Collective in Toronto, documents the coming out stories of queer South Asians and the responses of their families. *I Exist: Voices from the Lesbian and Gay Middle Eastern Community* (2001), directed by two Puerto Rican directors Peter Barbosa and Garret Lenoir who made the film as a result of their involvement in different queer communities of colour, explores the diversity of the Middle Eastern diaspora and the various ways in which queerness is lived, negotiated, and received in the community. Both video works can serve as a powerful educational tool and weapon against racism and homophobia. Thus, their very creation provides part of the solution to the problems they portray.

Ke Kulana He Mahu: Remembering a Sense of Place (2001), directed by Kathryn Xian and Brent Anbe, is a thoughtful anti-colonial critique that gives centrality to the issue of queer sexuality. One of the directors, Kathryn Xian, is an Asian-American filmmaker who made the film in solidarity with the native Hawaiians' struggle for self-determination.[18] Xian co-founded Zang Pictures, an all-volunteer-run production company that aims to promote the concerns and interests of Asian-Pacific Islander communities in Hawaii through the medium of film.[19] A high degree of community involvement is encouraged in all their projects, as is evident in *Ke Kulana*, which draws most of its resources – funding, crew members as well as the performers, activists, and scholars interviewed in the documentary – from the community the film aims to serve. In contrast to the earlier examples mentioned, where queer sexuality is perceived to be at least partly at odds with nativist or revolutionary

Ke Kulana He Mahu: Remembering a Sense of Place
(used with permission from Zang Pictures)

discourses, thus occupying an ambivalent role in the struggle against colonial and/or capitalist domination, *Ke Kulana* provocatively suggests that it is precisely the colonial displacement of, and capitalist incursions into, the native

Ke Kulana He Mahu: Remembering a Sense of Place
(used with permission from Zang Pictures)

communities in Hawaii that form the bedrock of discrimination against queer
and transgender people. The film looks backwards to native historical records
to find evidence of a diverse range of queer practices at the same time that it
explores contemporary expressions, such as that of choreographer Sami
Akuna (a.k.a. Cocoa Chandelier) who merges movements from indigenous
dance forms with the queer aesthetics of drag. The film also alludes to the

1998 referendum on the legislature's right to outlaw same-sex marriages, suggesting that the mainstream gay and lesbian movement lost support from native communities because their understanding of queer relationships was uncritically homogeneous and Eurocentric. The film's own interrogation of native Hawaiian notions of queerness and community is thus in part an effort to redress that failed campaign.

These films are but the tip of the iceberg of an emergent cinema that is capable of resisting the commercialisation of New Queer Cinema and re-vitalising the vision of Third Cinema. By intersecting the expressions of queer sexuality and queer gender practices with the concerns of Third Cinema, these films have radicalised both cinematic traditions. Difficult and timely questions are raised: What is the role of colonialism in the dissemination of homophobic and transphobic ideologies? What is the place of queer people in revolutionary history? How to envision queer liberation and queer community outside of capitalist relations? Creative answers to such questions can potentially trans-form not only filmmaking practices but also the future of queer and socialist politics.

An Imperfect Cinema: the Queer Underground

Aside from thematic concerns, there is another aspect of Third Cinema that is relevant to our understanding of the new directions in queer cinema. One of the central tenets of Third Cinema is that the production method of a film should resist the hierarchical and technocentric process typical of First Cinema. The Cuban filmmaker Julio García Espinosa's (1969) manifesto 'For an Imperfect Cinema' directs specific criticism against the credo of technical perfection.[20] For García Espinosa, the 'perfect' cinema offers a beautiful façade that tames viewers into passive consumers of idealised images. The ideology of 'perfection' also privileges commercial filmmaking while marginalising filmmakers who have to work in poor economic condi-tions. The notion of an 'imperfect cinema' democratises the filmmaking process by replacing hierarchy and technical expertise with collectivity and amateur participation. Such a production method also forges a particular kind of aesthetic expression, which the Brazilian director Glauber Rocha calls 'the esthetic of hunger'.[21] For Rocha, the conditions of scarcity foster, rather than hinder, aesthetic expressions. Shohat and Stam characterise this synthesis of idealism and necessity succinctly: 'the lack of technical resources was meta-phorically transmogrified into an expressive force'.[22]

As the dynamics of global power and resistance movements change, the strategy of imperfection also takes on different significance. In an article that tries to map out the future directions of Third Cinema, Michael Chanan calls our attention to two crucial factors affecting the continual survival of Third Cinema practices. First, Chanan points out that the philosophy of imperfec-tion was itself enabled by the development of cheaper and more accessible filmmaking technology.[23] Without the development of the 16mm film at the beginning of the 1960s, Third Cinema would not even have been possible. Chanan himself credits the advances in video technology and the expansion of reception through cable and satellite transmission in the 1980s as the breeding ground of a new kind of media activism. By the same token, the rapid development of digital technology since the 1990s has opened unprecedented avenues for the democratic filmmaking methods once championed by Third Cinema.[24] Second, as the mass revolutionary movements envisioned by radicals in the 1960s did not materialise and as more and more of the world become thoroughly absorbed or bypassed by the pathways of global capital, the forms of resistance exemplified by the original Third Cinema also need to adapt to the changing locus of power. For Chanan, Third Cinema can no longer depend on a fixed geography of resistance (the Third World). It must locate itself in the margins and interstices of global power:

> The original Third Cinema was premised on militant mass political movements of a kind which in many places no longer exist, and upon ideologies which have taken a decisive historical beating . . . The survival of Third Cinema depends on its origins within the margins and the interstices.[25]

These twin factors – the development of accessible technology and the turn from mass political movements to localised resistance – have nurtured a new cinema that uses imperfection as a weapon of subversion: what film critic and programmer Tony Rayns recently calls 'a new queer cinema in China'.[26]

This new wave in Chinese filmmaking has produced a queer cinema with an aesthetic style and production credo that are fostered by oppressive conditions. Ironically, these oppressive conditions are not the result of under-development but are caused by homophobic and transphobic repression within a society increasingly integrated into the global economy. While alienation from the global economy left China uniformly destitute during the Maoist era, the country's insertion into global capitalism has created a wealthy elite alongside a disenfranchised and disaffected majority that is persistently baited into desiring more. The post-1989 milieu, which boasts of economic openness at the same time that it cultivates stringent ideological control and censorship, has created ample opportunities for marketable filmmaking. A film that fits into domestically approved ideological parameters while remaining attractive to foreign investment is a profitable commodity. In defiance of this doubly domesticated cinema, a wayward underground cinema has emerged. Unlike the previous generation of filmmakers who made abstract, philosophical masterpieces meditating on the plight of the peasant, the nation's cultural roots, and the revolutionary heritage, this new wave of Chinese filmmakers turn to a radically different source of inspiration: what director Zhang Yuan calls the 'controversial minorities'.[27] Zhang Yuan, a filmmaker who has been blacklisted by the Film Bureau numerous times, was famous for making films about those living on the edge of legitimate society. It was no coincidence that it was this filmmaker who made one of the earliest attempts to film queer lives in Beijing in the 1996 film, *East Palace, West Palace*.[28] For underground filmmakers, queer spaces – as yet unassimilated by mainstream cinema – are affiliated with other outlawed and marginalised pockets of a society that has left its revolutionary history behind. As China veers away from the political path of Third Worldist radicalism, thus eclipsing the climate once favourable to Third Cinema practices, queer cinema arrives on the scene to become the new icon of rebellion.

While the stylised and performative visuality of *East Palace, West Palace* portrays gay desire as an allegory of power, the queer films that follow in its wake favour a more down-to-earth documentary realism that combines unpretentious humour with astute social commentary. Virtually all of such films were shot without the official approval of the National Film Bureau, which means that both the filming and the post-production process would have to stay more or less underground. The finished film could not be shown in legitimate channels and would often encounter obstacles when travelling to film festivals abroad.[29] As a result, the filmmakers usually film on smaller and less expensive formats such as 16mm, BetaSP and, increasingly more popular now, DigiBeta. Because of the lack of legal distribution channels, underground circulation of VCD and DVD copies becomes the films' main line of dissemination within China. The films often make use of interesting guerrilla tactics such as undercover location shooting and improvisation. The participation of members of the local queer communities is evident in different stages of the production process, from directing to screenwriting to acting, as they are often the only ones willing to risk harassment or legal trouble to be included in the films. Liu Bingjian's *Men and Women* (1999) tells the story of ordinary people in Beijing who find themselves exploring their queer sexuality.[30] The film's untheatrical pace (reviewer Shelly Kraucer has observed that the film 'lopes along, at virtually one shot per scene')[31] and detached perspective reflect queer passion as an everyday reality on screen, in ironic contrast to its 'unnatural' repression in real life. The film also takes a whimsical look at an imagined queer public space, comically featuring a magazine that publishes 'found art' from public toilets and a queer-themed radio show broadcast from the gay host's home. Most of the characters are played by non-professional actors while Gui Gui, the radio show host, is played by out gay writer, activist, and filmmaker Cui Zi'en, who is also responsible for the screenplay. Cui himself has directed two recent features filmed on DVD: *Enter The Clowns* (2001), which is one of the first Chinese films to feature characters from the transgender community; and *The Old Testament* (2002), which looks at the contemporary reality of homosexuality in China and the experience of people living with HIV/AIDS. Similarly, Li Yu's *Fish and Elephant* (2001), a film about a zoo keeper and the women in her life (girlfriend, ex-girlfriend and mother), also relies heavily on the participation of members from the queer community. The lead actresses are in fact ex-lovers, both active in the Beijing lesbian scene and have never acted before. The film capitalises on the actresses' real-life connection to create an understated, documentary-like style, marked by long takes and straightforward editing. In a scene where the zoo keeper is pressured by her mother to meet prospective suitors, the director recruits actors through placing fake marriage ads in the newspapers and then filming respondents' improvised reactions to the actress' revelation that she is a lesbian. Such 'guerrilla' realism is pushed to a further extreme in *The Box* (2001), an experimental documentary by Echo Y. Windy. Windy met a lesbian couple on the Internet and was invited to plant her mini-DV camcorder in their house, recording the intimate and self-contained box-like world of their passion. Devoid of market-driven tendencies to produce slick and seamless productions, these recent queer films from China strive instead for a spontaneous and participatory cinema that is honest and daring in its very imperfection. Such films resist assimilation into the mainstream film industry precisely because they do not appeal to the consumption taste of the average viewer. Their survival depends on innovative filming and distribution strategies and, above all, on the support of the outlawed communities they set out to represent.

Towards a Queer Third Cinema

Whether or not we can talk meaningfully of a 'Queer Third Cinema' in the near future still remains to be seen. However, it is clear that many new queer cinemas are emerging, from the 'margins and interstices' of global power. These films are 'queer' not only in the sense that they explore sexual and gender practices outside of normative heterosexuality and the dichotomous gender system. They are queer – indeed more than a little strange – because they unsettle current notions of history and politics while going against conventional paradigms of filmmaking. Most of all, they answer to the legacies of Third Cinema by remaining on the side of the disaffected and disenfranchised. Whether these films are rewriting the grand narratives of progressive causes from queer perspectives or creating innovative production and distribution methods to beat a hostile system, they will warrant our critical attention for a long time to come.

Notes

1 See B. Ruby Rich, 'Queer and Present Danger', *Sight and Sound*, 10:3 (March 2000).
2 See B. Ruby Rich, 'Searching for the Diamond in the Rough: Vision Quest', *Village Voice*, 20–26 March 2002.
3 For a concise analysis of the historical conditions that produced Third Cinema, see Ella Shohat and Robert Stam, *Unthinking Eurocentrism: Multiculturalism and the Media* (New York: Routledge, 1994), pp. 248–91.

4 Teshome Gabriel, *Third Cinema in the Third World* (Ann Arbor, MI: UMI Research Press, 1982).

5 See Roy Armes, *Third World Filmmaking and the West* (Berkeley, CA: University of California Press, 1987).

6 Mike Wayne, *Political Film: The Dialectics of Third Cinema* (London: Pluto Press, 2001), p. 2.

7 Ibid., p. 2.

8 Maria Pramaggiore, 'Fishing for Girls: Romancing Lesbians in New Queer Cinema', *College Literature*, 24.1 (February, 1997): 3.

9 Ibid.

10 Urvashi Vaid, *Virtual Equality: The Mainstreaming of Gay and Lesbian Liberation* (New York: Doubleday, 1995).

11 Rosemary Hennessy, *Profit and Pleasure: Sexual Identities in Late Capitalism* (New York: Routledge, 2000), pp. 111–42.

12 Ibid., pp. 143–74.

13 Ibid., p. 158.

14 Michael Chanan, 'The Changing Geography of Third Cinema', *Screen*, 38:4 (Winter 1997): 388.

15 Wayne, *Political*, p. 108.

16 Ibid., pp. 129–30.

17 Ella Shohat, 'Post-Third-Worldist Culture: Gender, Nation, and the Cinema', in M. Jacqui Alexander and Chandra Talpade Mohanty (eds), *Feminist Genealogies, Colonial Legacies, Democratic Futures* (New York: Routledge, 1997), pp. 183–209.

18 For information on the background of the movement and the debates on the Native Hawaiian federal recognition bill, see the articles on http://www.nativehawaiians.com/

19 For the history and philosophy of the company, see http://www.zangpictures.net

20 Julio García Espinosa, 'For an Imperfect Cinema', (trans.) Julianne Burton, in Michael T. Martin (ed.), *New Latin American Cinema* Volume One: *Theory, Practices, and Transcontinental Articulations* (Detroit: Wayne State University Press, 1997), pp. 71–82.

21 Glauber Rocha, 'An Esthetic of Hunger', (trans.) Randall Johnson and Burnes Hollyman, in Martin, *New Latin American Cinema*, pp. 59–61.

22 Shohat, *Unthinking Eurocentrism*, p. 256.

23 Chanan, 'The Changing Geography', p. 383.

24 See the documentary *Seeing Is Believing: Handicams, Human Rights and the News* (2002) by Peter Wintonick and Katerina Cizek for an exploration of this 'new visual revolution' and its significance for social and political activism.

25 Chanan, 'The Changing Geography', p. 288.

26 Quoted in Alexandra Gill, 'The Good, the Bad, and the Indie', *Globe and Mail*, 27 September 2002: R10.

27 Zhang Yuan, interview with Tony Rayns, *Sight and Sound*, 6:7 (1996): 26.

28 For an account of the difficulty surrounding the production of Zhang Yuan's film, see Chris Berry, '*East Palace, West Palace*: Staging Gay Life in China', *Jump Cut*, 42 (December 1998): 84–9.

29 For instance, *Men and Women* was withdrawn from the Hong Kong International Film Festival due to pressure from the National Film Bureau in China and the print of *Fish and Elephant* 'disappeared' for a while when it was dispatched from one festival to another through Chinese customs.

30 The title of the film is also sometimes translated as *Man Man Woman Woman*.

31 Shelly Kraucer, 'Man, Woman and Everything in Between', *Virtual China*, available on: http://www.virtualchina.com/archive/leisure/film/060200–dengye-sk-alo.html

PART IV

WATCHING NEW QUEER CINEMA

OVERVIEW

What does the popularisation of queer images and themes signal about contemporary culture, and, more importantly, its consumers? Do queer texts encourage or even guarantee a queer spectatorial experience? Is queer emptied of meaningfulness as it becomes attached to mainstream cinema? The following two chapters consider NQC's impact upon the audience.

Harry Benshoff in Chapter 13, through a survey and analysis of online reviews of *The Talented Mr. Ripley* (Anthony Minghella, 1999), exposes the gap between the queered text and viewers' reception of it. He finds that most of his sample group miss the director's queer project and remain unaffected by advances in queer theory and representation. For Michele Aaron in Chapter 14, the disavowal of queerness, which characterises mainstream cinema *and* the spectator's relationship to it, is strikingly absent from films emerging in the wake of NQC. Through consideration of a spectrum of contemporary North American films, she suggests that the spectator appears more queer-friendly but warns that this might not be as reassuring as it seems.

13. RECEPTION OF A QUEER
MAINSTREAM FILM

Harry M. Benshoff

The Talented Mr. Ripley is 'queer' cinema for a straight audience.[1]

This chapter examines the reception and cultural meanings of *The Talented Mr. Ripley* (1999), Anthony Minghella's film adaptation of Patricia Highsmith's 1955 novel. While few critics would probably describe the film as New Queer Cinema *per se* – it was an expensive, star-studded film widely distributed in American multiplexes – the film does partake of concepts either drawn from or consistent with queer theory and the New Queer Cinema. In some ways, *The Talented Mr. Ripley* might be understood as a by-product of New Queer Cinema's economic success and subsequent influence upon mainstream film practice. Yet how did actual viewers receive and decode the film's queerness? Did the film articulate for its viewers new queer ideas about human sexuality, or did it reinforce preexisting notions about sexual deviance and criminality? Ultimately, while *The Talented Mr. Ripley* may have been an attempt to mainstream the politics and poetics of New Queer Cinema, this study indicates that many basic concepts about human sexuality – let alone complexly queer ones – remain as mysterious to most moviegoers as was Mr. Ripley himself.

The Talented Mr. Ripley is a film about a queer murderer. The killer queer is a character type frequently found in mainstream Hollywood films, as well as in many New Queer Cinema films, including *Swoon* (1991), *The Living End* (1992), *Sister My Sister* (1994), and *Heavenly Creatures* (1994). Critics and filmgoers have debated the broader social effects of this character type for many years. Some have decried Hollywood's killer queers as negative and dangerous stereotypes, while others have argued that New Queer Cinema's killer queers represent sophisticated attempts to deconstruct the Hollywood stereotype, and/or show how social and cultural forces can shape murderous identities. *The Talented Mr. Ripley* falls squarely within the parameters of those debates: does it reinscribe or deconstruct the killer queer stereotype? Does it merely link together queer desire and criminality, or does it attempt to explain how violence can and does arise from conflicted social and sexual identities? The following analysis explores how actual moviegoers negotiated those questions. It draws upon a random sampling of approximately 150 film reviews and/or user commentaries collected via several searches on the World Wide Web, and from clipping files housed at the AMPAS library in Los Angeles.

The Talented Mr. Ripley thematises murder, secrecy, queer sexuality, and the ways in which 'the closet' works to construct social and personal identity. As Eve Sedgwick has noted, the 'closet is the defining structure for gay oppression in this century', as it seeks to uphold the binary constructions of Western patriarchal and heterocentrist discourse.[2] However, in attempting to police a strict gay–straight dichotomy, 'the closet' actually creates a myriad of queer subject positions, due to its being a complex constellation of interrelated social and psychological phenomena. As such, interrogating 'the closet' – as *Mr. Ripley* and many New Queer films attempt to do – can be a difficult task, giving rise to multiple readings dependent upon the viewer's subject positioning, his or her own 'homosexual/homophobic knowing'.[3] Homophobia is a term frequently used to describe and explain the more flagrant examples of anti-queer sentiment that create and enforce 'the closet', yet homophobia is itself a contested and misunderstood term, because like 'the closet', it too is inadequate to describe the variety of social and psychological processes that it seeks to define.[4] Psychologist Gregory Herek argues that there are at least three types of homophobia. *Experiential homophobia* is based on actual negative experiences with homosexual people. *Symbolic homophobia*, 'abstract ideological concepts that are closely tied to one's notion of self and to one's social network and reference groups', is more usually spoken of as *heterosexism,* and can be both conscious and unconscious.[5] Finally, Herek identifies *defensive homophobia* as a clinical condition that arises from ego-dystonic homosexual desires – a condition of psychic conflict that arises when an individual has same-sex feelings but also a great deal of internalised heterosexism, or *symbolic homophobia*.[6]

Sigmund Freud first proposed a model of *defensive homophobia* and it was expanded upon by Sandor Ferenczi in 1914 when he suggested that 'men's feelings of aversion, hostility, and disgust toward male homosexuality really are reaction formations and symptomatic of defense against affection for the same sex'.[7] While the dynamics of defensive homophobia have long been observed anecdotally by both researchers and lay people, in 1996 a scientific study was published which purported to find scientific proof of it. In 'Is Homophobia Associated with Homosexual Arousal?' published in the *Jour-*

nal of Abnormal Psychology, researchers recounted how they separated male subjects into two groups based upon Hudson and Ricketts's *Index of Homophobia* and then measured their sexual response (via penile plethysmography) to various forms of erotic stimuli – straight, gay male, and lesbian.[8] Men who had been rated as non-homophobic showed no measurable response to the gay male erotica, whereas men who had been rated as highly homophobic did exhibit a significant sexual response to gay male sexual images. The researchers concluded that Freud was right: 'Homophobia is apparently associated with homosexual arousal that the homophobic individual is either unaware of or denies'.[9]

In light of these findings, one could map out at least four possible and overlapping constructions of queer male identity in relation to the functioning of social and psychological closets.[10] (1) Individuals may be both psychologically and socially out of the closet. However, being out still means negotiating various closets on a daily basis, and thus type (1) queer male identity blurs into type (2), the state of being self-consciously queer but socially closeted. Still other queer individuals might be (3) psychologically in the closet but socially out, a seemingly rare situation in which friends and family recognise queerness in an individual before he does.[11] Finally, there are individuals who are (4) both unconsciously queer and, as a result of that, socially closeted as well. These individuals might exhibit *defensive homophobia* depending upon the degree to which their unconscious same-sex desires conflict with their conscious ego functioning and social self-image. Arguably, the conflict between same-sex desire and the need to maintain a straight social identity is what leads some young men to first approach and then harass, beat, or murder more openly gay men. ('Over-kill' – the brutalisation of the gay victim's body long after life his life has been taken – is an aspect common to many of these murders, and is thought to be indicative of the attacker's highly volatile and repressed psychosexual dynamic.) Thus, type (4) queer identity, wherein (social) heterosexism combines with (psychological) *defensive homophobia*, is a highly volatile recipe for anti-queer violence.

These complex and interrelated concepts of 'the closet', homophobia, and the performative nature of queer identities (as opposed to essentialist straight or gay ones) have been important topics for many New Queer films. These ideas have also been sounded in recent documentaries such as Arthur Dong's *Licensed to Kill* (1997) and PBS's *Frontline: Assault on Gay America* (2000), films that focus on how defensive homophobia can and does lead to gay bashing. Within more mainstream media, the idea has been satirised on the television show *South Park*, via the character of Mr. Garrison, a virulently homophobic repressed homosexual. And at the multiplex, a subplot of the Oscar-winning *American Beauty* dramatised (via its violent ex-Marine character) how murderous effects arise from the *repression* of homosexual desire and not from homosexuality *per se*. Arguably, *The Talented Mr. Ripley* also explores multiple queer identities and how (homo)sexual repression can and does lead to murder. However, as this study suggests, the film was unable to make most of its points about queer identity politics understood to a mass audience, partly because of its own textual ambiguity, but also because the audience itself lacked a sufficient understanding of those ideas in the first place.

ADAPTING MR. RIPLEY

The Talented Mr. Ripley (1955) was the fourth published novel by Texas-born mystery writer Patricia Highsmith.[12] In her most famous works, including Strangers on a Train (1950), Highsmith created homoerotic relations between male characters, often associating deviance and guilt over criminality with a diffuse connotative queerness.[13] A similar homoeroticism runs through The Talented Mr. Ripley, the first of five books Highsmith wrote about the character of Tom Ripley.[14] Ripley is frequently described by literary critics as an amoral criminal, often involved with murder, espionage, forgery, and other forms of theft. While Ripley is never written as explicitly homosexual, and he does gain a wife in one of the books, his exact sexual nature is a point that critics of the novels have debated at length. Some see no queerness in the text at all. Even for those who do, the meaning of homosexuality is itself contested. For example, Russell Harrison argues that 'Tom Ripley is not, in point of fact, a homosexual. There is never any indication in the novel that he has had sex with a man (or a woman, for that matter), though there are a number of indications that he is interested in men'.[15] According to Harrison, Tom may have *homosexual desires*, but since he does not act upon them, he should not be labelled as a *homosexual*. Conversely, Chauncey Mabe argues that in 'the book, Ripley is clearly gay, but so repressed as to be asexual'.[16]

Although they differ over the labels they use to define him, both critics suggest that Tom Ripley should be understood as a queer man whose sexuality is so repressed that even he doesn't realise what it is. True to the type (4) queer identity outlined in the previous section, Ripley is both socially and psychologically in the closet, and it is from this precarious position that his homoerotic violence can and does erupt. As Harrison puts it, 'Ripley's violence results from his feelings of rejection and acts as a kind of substitute for sex'.[17] Harrison also sees Tom's acquisitive criminality as a key to understanding his psyche. Tom seeks to control his uncontrollable life by acquiring possessions. As such:

> Repressed drives are deflected into possessions the characters can control. Commodities are the perfect focus for this cathexis because it is in their essence to be possessed. The power that such objects possess . . . derives from their role as the repository of emotions whose 'correct' object lies elsewhere. It is the power of suppression and displacement.[18]

This formula holds true for both novel and film of *The Talented Mr. Ripley*, in which Tom Ripley's sexual fascination with Dickie Greenleaf is connoted through various homoerotic touches, while that same fascination is manifestly explained by his desire to acquire Dickie's possessions and position in life. This conflation of the desire *to have* Dickie and the desire *to be* Dickie are at the core of *The Talented Mr. Ripley*. That conflation allows the text to be understood as either a story of queer desire or of asexual acquisitiveness, depending upon the reader's subject positioning.

The Talented Mr. Ripley was first filmed in France by René Clément as *Pleine Soleil/Purple Noon* (1960), and that version maintained the novel's ambiguous queerness through its use of mirrors, intense homosociality, and copious amounts of beefcake.[19] Minghella's adaptation also makes use of deliberate ambiguity, figuring Tom Ripley's sexual identity as part of his mysterious nature. In some interviews, Minghella stated that it was his intention to make Tom Ripley barely cognisant of his own repressed homo-sexual desires: Tom 'has no idea who he is'[20] even as he 'falls in love with Dickie Greenleaf'.[21] Yet how can a film text encode *repressed* desire, as opposed to encoding no sexual desire whatsoever? In attempting to dramatise Tom's closeted desires, Minghella's film employs various connotative motifs. Chet Baker's smoothly androgynous rendition of 'My Funny Valentine' is used as a signature of the Tom–Dickie relationship, and the two share everything from clothes to hugs and kisses. The film's 'chess in the bathtub' scene (wherein Tom asks if he might join Dickie in the tub) strongly suggests that Tom's friendship for Dickie includes an erotic component. Tom even refers to life in Italy with Dickie as 'one big love affair'.[22] Yet, as obvious as these signifiers might be, neither Tom nor the film text forthrightly speaks his homosexual desire. While this affords Tom (and the text) a certain queer 'undefine-ablility', it also muddles the issue for audiences unable (or un-willing) to follow the film's ambiguities.

From its start, Minghella's film suggests that Tom Ripley should be understood as a protean and queer continuum of subject positions and not as a fixed, essentialist identity. As the title of the film appears onscreen, the word 'talented' is quickly transformed into a plethora of other adjectives including 'confused', 'lonely', and 'troubled', while the very first word that speeds by appears to be 'innocent'. During this opening sequence, the spectator's view of Tom is blocked by shifting black masks that slowly reveal his face, and then as the credits continue, the screen is blocked with coloured gels. These visual touches suggest that Tom is hiding something and/or possesses an unfixed identity, that he must be seen through variously-coloured lenses. Perhaps most significantly, the opening and closing shots of the film are pointedly framed from within a closet whose door swings slowly open and closed, intermittently revealing for the spectator a melancholy Tom. In order to maintain his secret (presumably straight) identity as Dickie Greenleaf, Tom has just murdered Peter Kingsley-Smith, a comparatively happy and healthy gay man who has offered him love and affection. In using this scene to 'book end' the film, Minghella underlines the thematic importance of the closet, a point furthered by a sad, extra-diegetic voice singing 'the heart of you not whole for love . . . cast into the dark, branded with the mark of shame'.

Minghella's elaboration of the Peter Kingsley-Smith character (who was barely mentioned in the novel) was of great importance to his project of both humanising Tom as well as shifting the focus of his pathology away from homosexuality *per se* and onto the *repression* of homosexuality instead. As Minghella put it, 'Peter, the most centered character in the film, also serves as a reminder that Ripley's pathology is not explained by his sexuality'.[23] Rather, Ripley's murder of Peter (as his earlier murder of Freddie) is instead explained by Tom's need to suppress public knowledge of his true (possibly homosexual) identity. However, rather than making those ideas explicit, Minghella again turns to formal and generic allusion. Much of the film's appeal as a 'mystery' centres on Tom's attempt to 'be' Dickie after he has murdered him. Who is the 'real' Tom Ripley and exactly what is his relationship to Dickie Greenleaf? The mystery of Tom and Dickie baffles everyone and mimics the conditions of the social closet in barely metaphorised terms. For example, there is a great deal of confusion among the film's characters over whether or not Tom is now secretly living with Dickie, and if so, why might that be? Freddie's loaded suggestion to Tom that 'something's going on' is as suggestive of an illicit homosexual affair as it is of murder. And while the final third of the film revolves around the question of why Tom has Dickie's rings, no one dares to speak the obvious (romantic) reason.[24] Ripley's sexual identity becomes the real mystery of the film – a mystery most moviegoers were not interested in solving.

RECEIVING MR. RIPLEY

A survey of comments about *The Talented Mr. Ripley* suggest that very few American moviegoers understood the film to be about the concerns, dynamics, and tragic consequences of the closet, let alone queer concepts of sexual identity. Furthermore, many reviews themselves demonstrate various discourses of the closet, from total silence about or ignorance of the film's homosexual dynamics, to a curious 'performative heterosexuality' embedded within many of them. Typical of most lay and journalistic film commentary, the overwhelming purpose for the majority of these writings was evaluative: according to various subjective criteria, reviewers judged whether or not the film succeeded as 'entertainment'. In this case, a majority of reviews were concerned with the film's perceived failure as a mystery thriller, and not whether it was a film that extended Minghella's auteurist impulses towards literary adaptation and/or identity politics. And as a failed mystery thriller, comments such as 'Horrible', and 'Just Awful' were common among Internet reviewers.[25]

Viewers' inability to approach the sexual politics of the film is demonstrated by the fact that approximately one half of the reviews surveyed never acknowledged any gay, queer, or homoerotic dimension to the film whatsoever. This is itself a testament to the power of the closet as a widespread phenomenon, that even in a film so ripe with homoerotic dynamics, many viewers are unable to see them and/or speak them aloud. In other reviews, the film's homosexual dynamics are cited as irrelevant and unnecessary to the mystery plot: 'the homosexual under/overtones of the film were too obvious and distracting on the whole, without proper resolution to justify all of its ambiguous references. Did it really matter what his sexuality was?'[26] Given that this reviewer found the gay themes too 'distracting', homosexuality obviously did matter to him, if not in an understandable or pleasurable manner. Still others cite the film's homoerotic dimension in order to condemn the film outright. 'On the sour side, *Mr. Ripley*'s homosexual themes are awkward at best'.[27] Or: 'The key complaint I found from people who saw Ripley was it was long and gay. And they're right'.[28]

Tom's unfixed sexual identity caused a great deal of confusion and consternation for most reviewers: 'The question of Tom's sexual preferences occasionally hangs over the proceedings like a dour cloud of smog'.[29] While the film refuses to explicitly state his sexuality, most reviewers tried to fix Tom's identity as best they could with the language available to them. Those who avoided discussing his sexuality altogether assigned to Tom (by default and/or heterosexist presumption) a heterosexual orientation, calling him an 'unstable but highly intelligent sociopath',[30] a 'geeky, insubstantial sycophant',[31] or simply 'evil'.[32] Other reviews named him 'a homosexual sociopath'[33] while still others called him a 'bisexual charlatan'.[34] One review noted, perhaps more accurately, that 'Ripley's confused nature leads him to have occasional homosexual thoughts'.[35] 'Queer as the result of repressed homosexual desire' is a phrase that comes close to 'fixing' Tom's identity (even as the phrase itself problematises the very concept of a fixed identity). However, as this research reveals, 'queer' and 'homosexual repression' are themselves terms that are not readily understood by most of the public. Furthermore, they may be concepts alien to the narcissistic identificatory pleasures of Hollywood cinema. How does one identify with an onscreen character whose characteristics – especially the highly volatile one of sexuality – keep changing? While some proponents of the novel have suggested that 'it is Tom Ripley's very indeterminacy, including his sexual indeterminacy, that attracts the reader to him',[36] the same cannot be said of American filmgoers, of whom many seemed almost panicked at the idea of such indeterminacy. 'I was never quite sure . . . was he gay or not?'[37] Or: 'Is Tom Ripley the protagonist or the antagonist? I'm still not sure'.[38]

While cinematic spectatorship (temporarily identifying with and objectifying various onscreen characters) may be a prototypically queer phenomenon,[39] it nonetheless appears that American moviegoers are more comfortable identifying with amoral sociopaths than they are with queer characters (repressed or otherwise). Many reviewers took Minghella to task for making Tom more overtly sympathetic than in the novel: 'In attempting to humanize Tom, director Anthony Minghella ironically robs the character of much of his charisma'.[40] Again missing the point that Tom's murders arise from his entrapment in the closet, one review concluded that '[b]y burdening Tom Ripley with a conscience, the movie not only makes his multiple murders harder to understand, it also transmutes a uniquely fascinating character into something more familiar and less disturbing: a mere con man'.[41] For many reviewers, a film about a murderous repressed queer was not as much 'fun' as one about a charming (straight) sociopath.[42] Indeed, for some viewers, Tom's homosexual desire was understood as more disturbing than his murderous behavior.[43]

An occasional commentary did grasp to some degree the dynamics of the closet that were being dramatised by the film. One such review came agonisingly close to understanding the film as a parable about sexual repression, but ultimately still missed the point: 'I've been reading reviews about this movie for hours now . . . and I still can't figure out why Tom Ripley killed Peter . . . I really liked Peter . . . even though he was gay . . . he was a likeable guy and he was telling Tom all the good things about him when Tom decided to kill him, what was up with that? Oh well, I guess I'll never know'.[44] This review attests to its author's liberal tolerance, but she is unable to move beyond that stance to comprehend how the social and psychological effects of the closet itself are what compels Tom to murder Peter. In another example of such confusion, *Rolling Stone* praised the film for explicitly 'not making Tom's psychotic tendencies appear to be the product of his repressed homosexuality'.[45]

Viewer comments also reveal aspects of heterosexism and homophobia at work within the arena of reception itself. For example, several reviews reveal how the film's more overtly homosexual scenes were received by some audiences. Sixteen-year-old Rebecca (in an Internet chat room) wrote of her movie going experience that 'whenever Matt Damon stared at Jude Law, I heard people say "Oh God" and when I looked back, I saw some men rolling their eyes'.[46] When homosexuality is made manifest onscreen and cannot be denied, audience members frequently 'act out' in some way (groans, moans, homophobic comments) to announce to those around them that they are indeed straight. This 'performative heterosexuality' as a defence against possible homosexual identification can also be found in many written reviews. Amanda affirmed her own heterosexuality in writing that 'the only thing I liked seeing was Jude Law's ass'.[47] Or: 'This was one of the most boring movies I have ever seen, I was ready to leave within 20 minutes. Both my wife and I hated this movie as did most people around us'.[48] Note how the author of these comments communicates his heterosexual status (via his wife and his utter disinterest in the film), as well as how he projects his negative evaluation onto the rest of the audience, an attempt to bolster both his own opinion and consolidate his (and the audience's) heterosexual status.

Internet commentator Rebecca also noted how heterosexism and homophobia were factors in how other people spoke about the film: 'I think the people who said it was a horrible movie without explaining themselves are just repelled by Matt Damon being gay'. Another positive review of the film raises a similar point: 'Whoever hated this movie probably hated the gay angle'.[49] Thus, while some Internet reviews homophobically referenced the movie's gay themes as a warning to others to stay away from it, other Internet commentators exposed that very ploy within their own writings. Interestingly, the very language of some of the more homophobic reviews frequently uses words and phrases associated with (homo)sexual behavior. 'All in all, [the movie] pretty much sucked', wrote Amanda.[50] It 'BLOWS!' and 'The movie sucked ass', said two others.[51] One viewer named 'teenage emotional problem' went on at length with sadomasochistic homosexual metaphors: 'it sucked! . . . this is the fake crap that gets shoved down our throats. The new marimax [sic] slogan must be: "shut up and like it!" yea, well they can shove this!'[52] Pervasive heterosexism has made most words, ideas, and acts associated with male homosexual behaviour into popular epithets. Still, in this context, the use of such phrases seems to suggest a fascinated approach to and avoidance of homosexuality, a pattern of denial and displacement seemingly activated by the film's reception.

For example, sometimes a review, because of its excessive fixation on the film's homosexual themes, seems to reveal the dynamics of an individual writer's psychological closet. One such reviewer labels the film (repeatedly and with emphasis) 'totally gay!' He continues: 'A terrifying thriller? Not by a long shot. It's way more benign. Not to mention way more gay'. This review jokingly asserts that watching the film will make viewers act in a stereotypically gay manner: 'I left the theater fighting the urge to sing along to Cher videos and creatively redecorate the house . . . If I had clippers I'd style hair like nobody's business!'[53] It is difficult if not impossible to tell the author's sexual identity from these comments. Clearly on some level they indicate a phobic response to homosexuality, yet the author seems unusually well-versed in gay culture for a heterosexual, breathlessly referencing Cher, Prada fashions, Andrew Cunanan, and even simulating in print an act of metaphoric fellatio: 'If someone had dangled a boom mike over my head I would have tongued it for sure'.[54] (The review begins and ends by complaining that the boom microphone was visible in the film's opening scenes.) Furthermore, the style of writing employed by the author suggests nothing so much as the campy post-Wildean frippery that often passes for journalistic style within the gay press. When the author starts to obsess about the size of Matt Damon's penis within his 'atrocious day-glo yellow swimsuit', one again begins to wonder what is motivating these comments. Even a closing turn of phrase – 'I liked *The Talented Mr. Ripley* more and more the farther I got from it' – seems to speak of a confused attraction/repulsion towards the text and its homosexual thematics.

Ultimately, only a few commentators appeared to understand that Minghella was humanising Tom so that viewers might empathise with his conflicted state. For example: Tom 'is not the cool calculating and remorseless sociopath of Highsmith's novels, but a man doomed to kill in order to preserve the lie he has made of his own life. Ripley kills because he can't face up to who he is'.[55] And for another: 'The emotionally devastating ending [in which Tom murders Peter] is only possible because the cinematic Ripley is capable of open gay love'.[56] However, the vast majority of reviews surveyed thought the ending to be absurd, silly, or simply incomprehensible. As one review put it, the film grows 'increasingly preposterous and convoluted during its resolution . . . I guess these concluding scenes are thematically related, but the story goes out on an extraneous tangent which, as effective as it is, is just a nonsensical way of prolonging the ending'.[57] Another commentator asked 'Did I miss something about the ending?' – and in so asking answered her own question in the affirmative.[58]

Self-identified queer commentators were also divided over the meaning(s) of the film. It seems that even they had a hard time reconciling the differing meanings of queerness, homosexuality, heterosexism, and homophobia, not to mention sexual repression. Michael Bronski expressed seemingly contradictory approaches to these issues in his tripartite review of *The Talented Mr. Ripley*, *American Beauty*, and *Fight Club*. Bronski praised *Ripley* because it explored 'the intricacies of homosexual identity in repressive society', but then lambasted *American Beauty* for its 'ultimate horror of the repressed violent-ex-Marine-homo-next-door'.[59] (If anything, *American Beauty* makes the connection between sexual repression and violence much more clearly than does *Mr. Ripley*.) *Village Voice* columnist Michael Musto acknowledged – but then rejected – the idea that the film was a 'deft comment on panic, oppression, and self-loathing', noting that

> Ten years ago, *The Talented Mr. Ripley* might have had queers in the street, screaming 'not another gay sociopath!' Today, the gay press has validated the movie as a penetrating study in intimacy problems – and really hot to boot . . . So we should *thank* Minghella for giving us a gay killer?[60]

Queer theorist Cynthia Fuchs also understood what the film was attempting to dramatise, although she too downplayed the film's exploration of the closet in favour of a reading (one of the very few) about class.[61]

Reaction to the film among more 'everyday' gay moviegoers was often hostile. 'I found the movie *The Talented Mr. Ripley* to be offensive and homophobic . . . The character of Ripley is a traditional Hollywood stereotype'.[62] Even those commentators who were more sympathetic to the film still faulted it for its reliance on commercial formulas and its failure to make its points about sexual repression more clearly understood:

> [T]his film is not a subversive, controversial gay rights tale documenting the overall effects of toxic homophobia, nor is it meant to be. It is a suspense film, released by Miramax over the holiday season for maximum financial and Oscar-related benefits. It is a film that takes its apparent premise – Tom is gay and he kills – and contorts it to such a degree that another very different reading – Tom kills because he is gay – rears its ugly head.[63]

Far from challenging homophobia and heterosexism by exploring the dynamics of the closet, for many viewers *The Talented Mr. Ripley* failed to transcend the usual Hollywood conflation of homosexual and homicidal maniac. The film may have been a cinematic attempt to explore the dynamics of queer identity – to mainstream some of the concerns and issues of New Queer Cinema – but, as the comments sampled throughout this section have attested to, that attempt generally failed to make itself understood to a mass audience.

Partly that may be the film's fault – its presentation of complex queer issues is perhaps muddled and connotative rather than forthright – but its failure to be understood also reflects the fact that knowledge about sexuality in America at the turn of the millennium remains appallingly low. While some sex-education books now address homosexual desire as part of a queer spectrum of 'normal' human sexual functioning, the overtly homophobic best-selling sex 'education' manual *Everything You Always Wanted to Know About Sex But Were Afraid to Ask* was recently republished without bothering to update its scandalous section on homosexuality. And arguably the most vocal 'medical expert' on homosexuality in America, Dr Laura Schlesinger, has used her radio advice show to call gay people 'biological errors' and revive old child molestation myths for eager listeners.[64] Equally disturbing is the fact that basic tenets of queer theory have failed to penetrate into many large secular universities, not to mention smaller, religiously-affiliated institutions. Recently, some of queer theory's founding proponents have even denounced the term 'queer' within the pages of *The Advocate*, without bothering to address the theoretical meanings or implications of the concept.[65] Despite the recent mainstreaming of gay ideas and imagery within popular culture (*Will and Grace, Queer as Folk*, etc.), this chapter attests to the fact that many Americans, both straight and gay, have yet to consider what queer theory might have to contribute to their understanding of human sexuality. The theoretical and formal challenges posed by works of New Queer Cinema remain, like the movement itself, relatively marginalised.

NOTES

1 Cosmo Landesman, 'Closet but no Cigar', *The Sunday Times*, 27 February 2000: 7.

2 Eve Kosofsky Sedgwick, *Epistemology of the Closet* (Los Angeles: University of California Press, 1990), p. 71.

3 Ibid., p. 97. Sedgwick uses the term 'homosexual/homophobic knowing' to describe a 'form of knowledge that represents at the same time "knowledge itself" and a diagnosable pathology of cognition . . . In a more succinct formula, paranoia'. I find it highly descriptive of the ways that most Americans' understanding of homosexuality is always constructed within the phobic space of the closet. See also Eve Sedgwick, *Tendencies* (Durham, NC: Duke University Press, 1993) and Eve Sedgwick, *Between Men: English Literature and Male Homosocial Desire* (New York: Columbia University Press, 1985).

4 Overviews of homophobia can be found in Byrne Fone, *Homophobia: A History* (New York: Metropolitan Books, 2000) and David Plummer, *One of the Boys: Masculinity, Homophobia, and Modern Manhood* (New York: Harrington Park Press, 1999).

5 Gregory M. Herek, 'Beyond "Homophobia": A Social Psychological Perspective on Attitudes Towards Lesbians and Gay Men', in John P. DeCecco (ed.), *Bashers, Baiters, and Bigots: Homophobia in American Society* (New York: Harrington Park Press, 1985), p. 1.

6 Herek's three types of homophobia are themselves multiple, complex, and queerly intertwined. For example, a subject may generalise *experiential homophobia* onto all queers if the very act of meeting one open homosexual is understood via *symbolic homophobia* to be unpleasant. And, while many researchers and social critics continue to caution against seeing all anti-homosexual attitudes as the result of defensive homophobia, it is nonetheless probable that such defence mechanisms play a large part in fueling the social expression of anti-queer rhetoric. For example, high degrees of *symbolic homophobia* are often correlated with male homosocial groups, wherein the possibility of homoerotic desire is continually present and must therefore be constantly denied in a variety of performative ways. Likewise, a religious culture that professes to celebrate love between men must be highly prone to the dynamics of defensive homophobia. Consider the fundamentalist Christian bumper sticker that reads 'Real Men Love Jesus'. The slogan simultaneously raises and quells homoerotic implications by defensively pointing out that Christian men are still 'real men', that is to say, not homosexuals, despite their love for one another and for the blood and body of Jesus Christ.

7 Summarised by Herek, 'Beyond "Homophobia" ', p. 5. Herek also surveyed twenty years of empirical research on anti-homosexual attitudes. According to his conclusions, many of those dynamics

> make sense if we assume that negative attitudes are based in part on a defensive function: the finding that people are more negative towards homosexuals of their own sex than toward those of the opposite sex (since same-sex homosexuals presumably are more threatening); the positive correlations between hostile attitudes towards homosexuality and variables such as authoritarianism, cognitive rigidity, intolerance of ambiguity, and dogmatism (all of these personality traits presumably indicate higher levels of defensiveness); and the positive correlations between hostility and sex-guilt, sexual conservatism, and non-permissiveness (all of which might indicate conflicts about sexuality) (ibid., p. 11).

8 Henry E. Adams, Lester W. Wright, Jr. and Bethany A. Lohr, 'Is Homophobia Associated with Homosexual Arousal?', *Journal of Abnormal Psychology*, 105:3 (1996): 440–45.

9 Adams et al., 'Arousal', p. 440. This theorisation of defensive homophobia does seem to be born out by the evidence collected from many cases of actual gay bashings

and murder, in which the attackers themselves are often revealed to have repressed or denied homosexual inclinations. (See C. L. Anderson, 'Males as Sexual Assault Victims: Multiple Levels of Trauma', in John Gonsiorek (ed.), *Homosexuality and Psychotherapy* [New York: The Haworth Press, 1982], pp. 145–62.) Unfortunately, this model of defensive homophobia has also been used perversely to 'justify' gay bashings US criminal courts. (For a mass cultural introduction to this topic, see Joshua Hammer, 'The "Gay Panic" Defense', *Newsweek*, 8 Nov. 1999: 40–1.)

10 For an introduction to the processes of homosexual identity formation, see V.C. Cass, 'Homosexual Identity Formation: A Theoretical Model', *Journal of Homosexuality*, 4 (1979): 219–35; J.S. Nevid, 'Exposure to Homoerotic Stimuli: Effects on Attitudes of Heterosexual Viewers', *Journal of Social Psychology*, 119 (1983): 249–55; E. Coleman, 'Developmental Stages of the Coming Out Process', in Gonsoriek, *Homosexuality*, pp. 31–44; A.K. Malyon, 'Psychotherapeutic Implications of Internalized Homophobia in Gay Men', also in John Gonsiorek, *Homosexuality*; and Gonsiorek (ed.), *Homosexuality: The End of an Illness*, special issue of *American Behavioral Scientist*, 25:4 (March–April 1982).

11 This version of the closet was the subject the Hollywood comedy *In & Out* (1997), in which an entire town seems to accept unproblematically a teacher's homosexuality before he himself does.

12 While Highsmith never publicly came out as a lesbian to her critics or readers, her biographic profile is highly suggestive of a closeted queerness common to public figures of the pre-Stonewall generation. In the late 1940s, with the help of Truman Capote, she was accepted at the Yaddo artists' colony. (Russell Harrison, *Patricia Highsmith* [New York: Twayne Publishers, 1997], p. xv.) In the 1960s she became a reclusive American expatriate who lived alone (save a cat) in various European locales, while 'deftly reflecting recurring inquiries about her sexual orientation'. (Laura Dempsey, 'The Talented – and Disturbing – Ms. Highsmith', *San Jose Mercury News*, Feb. 2000 [Exact date and page number lost].) What was perhaps less well known was that Highsmith had also authored (as Claire Morgan) a best-selling 1952 lesbian love story entitled *The Price of Salt*.

13 As products of the early 1950s, both *Strangers* and *Ripley* are steeped in Cold War paranoia and the claustrophobic atmosphere of its closets. Highsmith's prose exemplifies a linguistic closet wherein language itself bespeaks repression by way of euphemism and evasion, luridly hinting at queerness while not forthrightly naming the thing itself. This 'language of the closet' can often be discerned in interviews with closeted or semi-out individuals. The use of gender non-specific pronouns, ellipsis, and silence can also mark this mode of discourse. For several good examples, see some of the interviews conducted by Boze Hadleigh with queer Hollywood stars, in Boze Hadleigh, *Hollywood Lesbians* (New York: Barricade Books, 1994) and Boze Hadleigh, *Hollywood Gays* (New York: Barricade Books, 1996).

14 The five novels are: *The Talented Mr. Ripley* (1955), *Ripley Under Ground* (1970), *Ripley's Game* (1974), *The Boy Who Followed Ripley* (1980), and *Ripley Under Water* (1992).

15 Harrison, *Highsmith*, p. 24.

16 Chauncey Mabe, 'Believe it or Not, Ripley's Better in Print', *South Florida Sun-Sentinel*, 2 January 2000: F5.

17 Harrison *Highsmith*, p. 24.

18 Ibid., p. x.

19 The queer politics activated by that film have been explored by Chris Straayer, in 'The Talented Poststructuralist: Heteromasculinity, Gay Artifice, and Class Passing', in Peter Lehman (ed.), *Masculinity: Bodies, Movies, Culture* (New York: Routledge, 2001), pp. 115–32.

20 Comments by Minghella on the director's commentary audio track of the DVD release of the film.

21 Minghella, quoted in Garth Pearce, 'The Talented Mr. Ripley', The Sunday Times, 9 January 2000: (page number lost). Although this chapter explores Minghella's comments as well as various viewer comments regarding the film, it is not meant to privilege the idea of authorial intent or to claim that there is some sort of 'correct' reading of The Talented Mr. Ripley that Minghella's comments somehow 'prove'. Rather, Minghella's words about the film are used to contextualise further what the author of the film consciously understood he was encoding into the text. His comments are just as likely to be shaped and shaded by various closets (personal, industrial, commercial, cultural) as are those made by the film's viewers.

22 Interestingly, Minghella works to actively heterosexualise Dickie, making him the cause of a young Italian woman's suicide after she discovers she is carrying his child. If anything, in the film, Dickie comes across as an omnisexual libertine, although one who is still unwilling to admit to homosexual desires.

23 Anthony Minghella, 'Introduction', The Talented Mr. Ripley: A Screenplay (New York: Hyperion Books, 1999), p. xiii.

24 These scenes allowed Minghella to critique patriarchal disavowal of the feminine as well as the homosexual. As he put it: 'No one in this story sees truth in front of them because of the distortions of their own particular prejudices and preconceptions. Only Marge Sherwood . . . has a sufficiently uncluttered spirit to both welcome Ripley and then suspect him. But the collusion of men, which is such a feature of this story and of the times, undermines her' (Minghella, 'Introduction', p. xiv).

25 For example, see the 'Review Summary' at Yahoo!Movies newsgroup, available on: http://messages.yahoo.com/bbs

26 JoBlo, 'Review of The Talented Mr. Ripley', online posting, newsgroup JoBlos Movie Emporium, http://www.jobl.com/talentedmrripley.htm

27 Christopher Null, 'Review of The Talented Mr. Ripley', online posting, newsgroup http://www.filmcritic.com/misc/emp

28 U2 Pulp Radiohead, online posting, newsgroup Yahoo!Movies, http://messages.yahoo.com/bbs

29 Jamey Hughton, online posting, newsgroup http://www.atnzone.com/moviezone/reviews/talentedripley.shtml

30 Jamey Hughton, online posting, newsgroup http://www.atnzone.com/moviezone/reviews/talentedripley.shtml

31 Hazel Ellis, 'The Talented Mr. Minghella', Reel Magazine, Mar.–Apr. 2000: 24.

32 Maddy Van Hertbruggen, 'Review of The Talented Mr. Ripley', online posting, newsgroup Ed's Internet Book Review, http://www.edsbookreview.com/mystery/highsmithtalentedripley.html

33 Jon Popick, online posting, newsgroup Nzone Magaz, http://www.atnzone.com/moviezone/reviews/talentedripley.shtml

34 Anthony Leong, online posting, newsgroup http://www.atnzone.com/moviezone/reviews/talentedripley.shtml

35 craig roush, online posting, newsgroup http://www.atnzone.com/moviezone/reviews/talentedripley.shtml

36 Harrison, Highsmith, p. 25.

37 Catherine, online posting, newsgroup http://www.jobl.com/talentedmrripley.htm.

38 tanya marsh, online posting, newsgroup http:/messages.yahoo.com/bbs

39 For an overview of these phenomena, see Caroline Evans and Lorraine Gamman, 'The Gaze Revisited, or Reviewing Queer Viewing', in Paul Burston and Colin Richardson (eds), A Queer Romance: Lesbians, Gay Men and Popular Culture (New York: Routledge, 1995), pp. 13–56.

40 James Berardinelli, online posting, newsgroup http://www.moview-reviews.collossus.net/movies/t/talented.html

41 Mabe, 'Believe', F5.

42 'Bringing the secret of Tom's sexual longings to the surface, [Minghella] risks losing the profound chill that made Ripley so disturbing in the first place. The character is several

shades less loathsome and more conscience-stricken than he was to begin with, and his homosexuality is more openly expressed'. Janet Maslin, 'The Talented Mr. Ripley: Carnal, Glamorous and Worth the Price', The New York Times, 24 December 1999. Online at http://www.nytimes.com/library/film/122499ripley-film-review/html

43 When Matt Damon appeared on Oprah, he said that there were aspects of the character with which he had difficulty relating. One young male audience member immediately assumed that Damon was speaking of his character's queerness, and yelled out a comment about the film's bathtub scene. Damon corrected the fan, saying he had trouble relating to the character's murderous behavior, not his sexuality. Reported in Brent Simon, 'Believe it or Not . . .' Entertainment Today, 24–30 Dec. 1999: 6.

44 Beth, online posting, newsgroup http://www.joblo.com/talentedmrripley.htm. Ellipses in the original.

45 Peter Travers [film review of The Talented Mr. Ripley], Rolling Stone, 30 Dec. 1999: 151.

46 Rebecca, online posting, newsgroup http://www.jobl.com/talentedmrripley.htm

47 Amanda, online posting, newsgroup http://www.jobl.com/talentedmrripley.htm

48 Marty, online posting, newsgroup http://www.jobl.com/talentedmrripley.htm

49 Mary, online posting, newsgroup http://www.jobl.com/talentedmrripley.htm

50 Amanda, online posting, newsgroup http://www.jobl.com/talentedmrripley.htm

51 r u livin la vida loca and mackenzieroberts, online posting, newsgroup Yahoo!Movies, http://messages.yahoo.com/bbs

52 teenage emotional problem, online posting, newsgroup Yahoo!Movies, http://messages.yahoo.com/bbs

53 Mark Ramsey, 'The Talented Mr. Ripley – La Dolce Vita Loco', online posting, newsgroup www.moviejuice.com/1999/talentedmrripley.html

54 Ibid.

55 Jim Emerson, 'Reeling: Nowhere Men', Reel Magazine, March–April 2000: 15.

56 Mabe, 'Believe', F5.

57 Bret Polish, online posting, newsgroup http://www.atnzone.com/moviezone/reviews/talentedripley.shtml

58 Becky, online posting, newsgroup http://www.jobl.com/talentedmrripley.htm

59 Michael Bronksi, 'The State of Queer Film', Z Magazine, February 2000: 56. Bronksi seems most offended that in American Beauty the ex-Marine collects Nazi dinner plates rather than 'butch grenades or machine guns', which he sees (however correctly) as stereotypical associations from bygone eras.

60 Michael Musto, 'La Dolce Musto: My Mirror', Village Voice, 11 January 2000: (page number lost).

61 Cynthia Fuchs, online posting, newsgroup www.popmatters.com/film/reviews/t/talented-mr-ripley.html

62 Steve Glickman, letter, The Advocate, 29 Febuary 2000: 6.

63 The review continues: 'The two moments in the film where the serial killer Ripley's gayness is affirmed through a physical connection with the desired occur specifically just before, during, or after he has murdered someone. The confirmation and consummation of his sexuality is thus conjoined with his murderous sociopathology. This presentation inextricably merges the homicidal Ripley with the queer Ripley. There can be no effective separation between the two when they are placed together as layers embedded within each other'. jserpico, 'Review of The Talented Mr. Ripley', online posting, newsgroup Pop Matters Film, www.popmatters.com/film/reviews/t/talented-mr-ripley.html

64 See David R. Reuben, Everything You Always Wanted to Know About Sex ** But Were Afraid to Ask, All New Edition (New York: HarperCollins, 1999). For an overview on Dr Laura and her relationship with queer communities, see Jon Barrett, 'Diss Jockey', The Advocate, 15 February 2000: 28–35.

65 Gabriel Rotello, 'The Word that Failed', The Advocate, 15 August 2000: 112.

14. THE NEW QUEER SPECTATOR

Michele Aaron

Hasn't there always been something fundamentally, if obliquely, 'queer' about spectatorship? From the female spectator's virtual 'transvestism' (as Laura Mulvey put in the 1970s) to the general spectator's ability to 'cross-identify', psychoanalytic film theory (and not only psychoanalytic film theory) has attributed a fluid, and often transgressive position to the otherwise conventional (and conventionally gendered) viewer.[1] But, of course, this position was always only temporary, housed and sanitised not just in the reassurances of say closure but in the ever-popular palliative of disavowal. What is queer about spectatorship, then, has always been contained . . . and, therefore, perhaps, not queer at all. The aim of this chapter is to suggest that the most striking effect of New Queer Cinema has been its intervention into this process of disavowal so intrinsic to mainstream spectatorship. Through an analysis of a selection of contemporary films I will demonstrate how queerness is not contained in these texts but, instead, rather knowingly indulged. Inevitably, this discussion will be accompanied, if not haunted, by the ongoing concern with what queerness, as a description of contemporary culture, is actually worth.

New Queer Cinema's impact upon mainstream cinema can be measured not only in terms of the influx of lesbian and gay directors, or of 'defiant' characters or queer themes, but in terms of the audience's consensual flirtation with gender and sexual ambiguity within some of the most popular texts. It is not simply that NQC can be seen to have opened up a space for avowing, for affirming, homosexuality, but that this space has been worked to divulge the knowingness or complicity at the heart of spectatorship. In other words, this New Queer Spectator becomes an important coordinate in our continuing understanding of the machinations of cinema, but we must not forget that he or she is a product of the old queer haunts, and these haunts the very stuff of classical film. Indeed, as Patricia White says of those 'uninvited' inferences and coded figures of Classical Hollywood: '[they] are uninvited not because they are forbidden entry but because they are already at home'.[2]

There is a great moment, one of many, in Rob Epstein and Jeffrey Freidman's documentary of Vito Russo's *The Celluloid Closet* (1995).[3] In it, to a clip from Hitchcock's *Rebecca* (1940) 'illustrating' Mrs Danvers' lesbian obsession, Susie Bright exclaims dramatically that 'she opens the underwear drawer'. In her shocked delight, her feigned horror, lies the undoing of that disavowal of homosexuality so integral to Hollywood cinema. In a way Bright appears here as the archetypal New Queer Spectator, positioned precisely through the debates of the 1990s to call both innocently and conspiratorially upon the clearly queered common sense of her unknown audience. Whether because of the production code, or the normative thrust of popular narratives, screen homosexuality frequently existed in the twilight between secrecy and reprimand. Mainstream cinema, whether in the form of *Rebecca*, *Rope* (Hitchcock, 1948), *Top Gun* (Tony Scott) or *Thelma and Louise* (Ridley Scott, 1991), has always depended upon a whole range of disavowing techniques to implicate yet contain any homosexual possibility, demanding its denial yet exploiting its appeal. What I am doing in this chapter is suggesting how contemporary cinema, and the contemporary spectator, can be seen to willingly avow homosexuality rather than disavow it.

I will be focusing on two main areas as a means of identifying what I see as an altered stake within contemporary cinema, two distinctly cinematic strategies for avowing homosexuality and exploiting this new queer spectatorship. The first is the revision of the crossdressing film post-NQC. Through a discussion of *Boys Don't Cry* (Kimberley Peirce, 1999) and, to a lesser extent, *Being John Malkovich* (Spike Jonze, 1996), I'll demonstrate how the genre which has most disavowed queerness can now do quite the opposite. The second instance of this New Queer Spectatorship will be located in the undoing of the heteronormativity of the gaze, a project also distinctly queer but differently expressed. I will discuss this with reference to *Mansfield Park* (Patricia Rozema, 1999) but, primarily, through Rob Marshall's 2000 adaptation of Bob Fosse's stage-hit *Chicago*.

PASSING/FAILING

It is in response to its generic and mainstream appeal (and, please note, *not* to Brandon's transgendered status) that one can consider *Boys Don't Cry* (*Boys*) as, ostensibly, a cross-dressing film. Such films feature a central character disguising him- or herself as the opposite sex, and fulfil a set of similar characteristics with regard to narrative structure and thematic concerns.[4] Like them, *Boys* builds from the initial assumption of disguise to its grand disclosure, it prioritises a love story, and has as its key concern (and more inclusively than most) 'the fixity or otherwise of gender identity'.[5] But, as will be shown, this film reinvents the basic formula, and does so most significantly in terms of the disavowal of spectatorial implication which is central to the genre.

Primarily comedies, cross-dressing films, like *I Was a Male War Bride* (Howard Hawks, 1949), *Some Like It Hot* (Billy Wilder, 1959), *Victor/Victoria* (Blake Edwards, 1982) and *Mrs Doubtfire* (Chris Columbus, 1993), derive their effect from the slapstick, sexually suggestive or supposedly absurd scenarios resulting from the central character's 'mistaken identity', that is, from the gap between the character's passing within the diegesis and the spectators' privileged position of knowledge (their being in on the disguise). Fuelled by heterosexual imperatives, the narratives progress towards the climactic disclosure of the protagonists' 'true' identity. Simultaneously, the narrations repeatedly remind the spectator of this real identity, either through the transparency of their disguise (e.g. Henri/Cary Grant in *I Was a Male War Bride*); or the dropping of the disguise afforded by co-conspirators (e.g. Curtis/Josephine and Lemmon/Daphne in *Some Like it Hot*); or by the involuntary intrusion of an 'innate' gender (e.g. Anshel unable to resist admiring the china in *Yentl* [Barbra Streisand, 1982]). But why does the spectator need reminding? On the one hand, such reminders reinforce the essentialism of gender even if the protagonists' (relatively) easy disguise confirmed its performativity. On the other hand, they make safe the gender play and, especially, the homoerotic implications arising from it. For some, therefore, the genre is insidiously conservative. It exploits transgression only to heighten the return to order, or, as Annette Kuhn notes, it 'problematise[s] gender identity and sexual difference . . . only to confirm the absoluteness of both'.[6] For others, it offers a rare and radical space for gender and sexual ambiguity – that is, for queerness – within the most mainstream of products. These reminders, then, these disruptions to passing represent the spectator's disavowal of queerness: they both deny and acknowledge, contain and permit, the queer by-products of crossdressing. They halt the illusion, but in so doing they guarantee its full affect (and if this sounds awfully like the machinations of spectatorship in general, it does so deliberately.) In this way, passing is shown to be intimately linked with failing to pass within the spectatorial experience of the cross-dressing film. While *Boys* exploits a similar dynamic between passing and failing, their relationship is at once more pervasive, more explicit, and more fraught with liability.

Like these predecessors, *Boys* is, inevitably, about the spectacle of transvestism: despite its NQC sensibility and elegiac thoughtfulness, it is Hilary Swank's cross-dressed success, her 'stellar stunt performance' as Brandon, which made the film an international hit, and garnered her an Oscar among numerous other awards.[7] Indeed, it was not so much Brandon's as Swank's passing as a man that was at stake in the reception of *Boys*, and she more than merely passed, she got gold. If her apparitional femininity at the Academy Award ceremony sniffed of mainstream recuperation (here finally was that 'original' identity: the pre-disguise girl missing from the film's start,) it did, nevertheless, consolidate the breadth and ease of gender performativity.[8] It also served to reiterate the absence of those essentialist details and disclaimers from the film itself. While *Boys* is suffused with reminders of Brandon's disguise, these work to *avow* queerness and, despite the film's sensationalist appeal, they extend spectatorial implication within the sexual (and social) workings of the diegesis rather than seal it off.

Brandon's true identity, that is, his transgendered identity, is ever-present to the spectator. Brandon is not so much trying to pass as someone else as trying to be 'him'self. Passing is not, therefore, a means to an end, as in the comedies, but the end itself. In general terms, in the spectator's constant awareness of Brandon's ambiguous identity – in the simultaneity of he and she – passing *is* failing: the reassuring distance between these 'events' (and the spectator's experience of them) dissolves. In addition, in the film, passing is tinged with the threat of punishment, symbolised by the speeding ticket and court summons stalking Teena, and reverberating on from Cousin Lonny's warning about Falls City: 'you know they shoot faggots down there'. It is always, then, haunted by failure as well. On a more local level, however, that there is no before-Brandon for the spectator to 'forget', no essential singular gender to intervene into the narrative illusion, the narrative reminders of disguise serve other purposes. There are two key moments where Brandon's biology disrupts his passing: when Brandon's period starts, and when Lana views his cleavage. Both of these are reminders of the physical: Brandon's breasts and bleeding index sex characteristics and not gender. Thus, the film suggests, the body joins with the Law as the (contested) arbiters of identity. *Boys* will later offer the ultimate statement on the separation of gender from anatomy in the climactic scene of public disclosure where John and Tom force down Brandon's underwear. Rather than reifying Brandon's essential identity as John intends, Lana responds to John's taunts of 'look at your little boyfriend' with 'leave *him* alone'. The significance of this response is stressed as the frame seems to freeze, and a fantasy sequence begins which reifies instead the distinction between gender and sex, as the divested Brandon splits from and stares at a clothed Brandon standing watching behind the other witnesses. The tableau has an eerie but obvious resemblance to the crucifixion of Christ: a semi-clad, brightly lit Brandon has an arm over the shoulders of Tom and John on either side of him; Lana kneels below him looking up; a small audience gazes on. The composition's purpose is to invoke not the simple martyrdom of Christ/Brandon but the complicity of the spectators (both inside and outside the frame).

The two earlier reminders of disguise are used to underline rather than undermine the queerness of the encounters between the central couple, as well as Lana's and the spectator's consciousness of it. The shot of Brandon grappling with a box of tampons at a store is held just too long for the approaching Lana not to see what he's doing, or, at least, for us not to think this. She may have been, as she confesses, 'so wasted', but Lana knows that store well – she's on first name terms with the teller, and she directs another customer to the beer at the back. Escorted home by Brandon, as their interaction gets more flirtatious she turns to look at him and says: 'wait a minute, what's your name again?' When Lana views Brandon's cleavage during sex, she does seem confused: she stares at the impression of his penis in his jeans, touches it gingerly, scrutinises his hairless chin . . . and then forgets the whole thing and resumes their love-making. That she subsequently lies to her friends, saying that following sex she and Brandon took off their clothes and went swimming, testifies to her wittingness. Lana definitely knows. And she knows to keep it quiet.

In *Boys* these reminders also serve to unsettle the spectators' fixed position of superior knowledge about Brandon's identity; their supposedly sharp contrast to the duped characters. As a shift in privileged perspective, this occurs most emphatically when we share Lana's point of view in spying Brandon's breasts. In being made aware of characters' suppressed knowledge about Brandon, the spectator joins them as a community of witnesses to Brandon's passing/failing. What is more, the concurrence of the heterosexual and homosexual implications arising from the cross-dressed figure, is explicitly conveyed here through Lana, who comes to represent the spectator's own inevitably unfixed or queer response to the cross-dressed figure in general and to Brandon in particular.[9] The queer implication of 'knowing' about Brandon is not only declared in every rejection of homosexuality in *Boys* (from Teena's 'I'm not a dyke' to Lana's 'I'm not a lesbian') but is also inscribed on the surface of the film. Candace, having discovered Brandon's disguise, comes to confront Lana, who is high on drugs and lying on her back on a spinning roundabout in a park. In a composition reminiscent of a certain sexual configuration (and one that occurred earlier when, similarly, Lana, as she declared to Brandon, was 'in a trance'), Candace is framed centrally between Lana's open legs. It is not just that Lana is exposed as having a woman in that position, but that Candace, Brandon's earlier admirer, is also exposed, also queerly configured.

The awareness of Brandon's identity is not set up solely through Lana. In an early scene, Lana's mother beckons him over, peers at his face, and feels his smooth skin. As she does so, John looks on, squinting with similar suspicions. The scene is reminiscent of one found in *Yentl* where an old woman caresses the cross-dresser's cheeks. Where her response, 'so young', is a convincing answer to the lack of hair growth, Lana's mother's exclamations at Brandon's handsomeness is not. That the old woman in *Yentl* has trouble seeing, emphasises Mom's voluntary sightlessness. In a similar vein, Brandon is not the only character straying from the idealisation of gender (at the same time, however, only Brandon is 'so handsome' – although this is, as Pidduck suggests, as much to do with class as with gender.[10]) Chloe Sevigny as Lana is far from the 'gangly' youth of J. Hoberman's description,[11] but, instead, her downy fleshiness is in sharp contrast to the lithe hairlessness of Brandon, or as Xan Brooks suggests: 'her heavy-jawed beauty contrasts nicely with Swank's more refined, aquiline looks and further blurs the tale's gender roles'.[12] Meanwhile Tom with his pubescent flourish of facial hair, and John, doe-eyed and long-lashed, cuddly yet sociopathic, further promote the film's deliberate inscription of a spectrum of gender expression.

Nor is Brandon singled out in his irregularity. John and Tom's excited embraces immediately after raping Brandon confirm their homosociality and an alternative network of implicated queerness. Brandon might, as he puts it, 'have this weirdness', but he is not alone. Tom is a self-mutilating ex-con with a pyromaniac past and John, Tom tells us, has 'no impulse control . . . that's what the doctors say'. It could also be argued that there is a sense of an otherworldlinesss to Falls City which is conjured as general, as shared; grounded in the inclusivity of objects rather than the fleetingness of John's good moods, or Brandon's life. This sense is created by a sci-fi quality which permeates *Boys*, from the cinematographic distortion of light, and time – periods of day and night are shown passing at warp speed – to the film's images of factories with the smoke and metallic splendour of space-stations, and of parked cars with the luminance of flying saucers. These are not just the stoned aesthetics of a 'surreal dreamscape' but, in their allusions to the iconography of popular sci-fi, they mean to invoke a community of aliens and dreamers, and to invoke it specifically for the spectator who oversees these extra-diegetic connections.[13] (Just in case these allusions aren't clear: not only is the drunken Mom discovered in front of a black and white sci-fi television programme, upon which the camera lingers, but Lana, in her last moment of hopefulness, wants that she and Brandon just 'beam' themselves out into the beautiful blue yonder.)

Boys avoids rigid categories, ready answers or the supposition of singular responsibility. As Brooks argues, 'the perpetrators are never demonised as brutish monsters' and neither is Brandon 'a simple martyr',[14] but the film's anti-exclusivity goes much further than muddying the distinction between good and bad. Indeed, it is precisely around the apportioning of responsibility or, rather, the opening up of implication that *Boys* seems so interesting and so important a film. Where in the cross-dressing comedies the relationship between passing and failing to pass reeked of reassurances for the no-less titillated spectator, in *Boys* their interaction constructs and confirms the knowingness, the implication, of *all* those witnessing Brandon's activities. Epitomising the mainstream appropriation and (arguable) success of NQC, *Boys* rescripts the classic cross-dressing narrative to avow the queerness not just of the characters in the film but of the firmly implicated spectator.

Being John Malkovich can be seen as another incarnation of the cross-dressing narrative: the bastard child but indisputable high point of another trajectory of the genre: the body-swapping comedy. Films like *Switch* (Blake Edwards) and *Dr Jekyll and Ms Hyde* (David Price) of the early 1990s are, again, all about the irrepressibility of essential identity, and their humour depends on it. In *Switch* for example, Ellen Barkin plays a man in a woman's body, all swagger and crotch adjustment. In *Dr Jekyll and Ms Hyde* the comedy resides in the actual and anticipated moments of transition, when painted nails protrude from manly hands, say, or hairy chest from chiffon shirt. The independent film *Being John Malkovich* affords many body-swapping scenes with its lead characters, Craig (John Cusack) and Lotte (Cameron Diaz), jumping in and out of John Malkovich (John Malkovich) through the portal Craig discovers in a wall at work. In this film, the overlapping or doubling-up of identity, intrinsic to the genre and its comedic intent, is neither unavoidable nor discomforting. Rather than disabling heterosexuality, as is the norm, body-swapping here actually enables homo-sexuality: Lotte conducts her affair with Maxine (Catherine Keener) by entering Malkovich's body at the appointed times, those when Maxine has arranged to visit. Where traditionally the genre is all about policing the boundaries between identities, this film is clearly about dissolving them. Indeed, it possesses an almost excessively self-conscious in-between-ness epitomised by the location of the portal, and workplace, on floor seven and a half.

RAZZLE DAZZLE

In Patricia Rozema's *Mansfield Park* the sexuality of looking is unhooked from its normative roots, and what could be more normative or better-bred than a costume drama. Despite its achingly straight heritage, in Rozema's hands *Mansfield Park* is a queer film indeed.[15] But it is not the quasi-lesbian encounters between Fanny Price (Frances O'Connor) and Mary Crawford (Embeth Davidtz) that mark it so – despite the fact that this is what was latched onto by critics.[16] Indeed, these encounters are misleading, too easy a target for those guarding the chastity of English literature or, even, for those celebrating the film's waywardness. Instead, it is the film's creation of a polyvalency of desire, a general air of erotic objectification available to both the characters and spectators and unhinged from the conventional love-story trajectory. The scene that epitomises this for me, is the entry of the Crawford brother and sister into the conservative and constrained world of Mansfield Park. The transformation of the starched collars and lowered eyes of gentility incarnate into a swell of deliciously conspicuous lust, is rendered the simple product of a multitude of shot-reverse shots released from heterosexual imperatives. The director creates a world in which an idealised heterosexu-ality, despite being the dominant force of the narrative, ceases to 'own' desire.

Something similar, but far less subtle, happens in the Hollywood blockbus-ter, *Chicago*. This is a fabulous example for several reasons. First, of course, because I am locating queerness at the very heart and heights of Hollywood production. Second, because, as a musical the film comes from a genre entrenched in the process of disavowal (most talked about as the negotiation of the spectacle-real dynamic). Third, and more specifically, the film's 'show-girl' focus heightens the heteronormativity of the gaze (and of the genre), but is clearly and persistently accompanied by a queerer context.

The film's sexualised self-consciousness is immediately apparent. Opening with an intense close-up of an eye, the screen then fills with an image of stilettoed feet leaving a car, and shapely, stockinged, legs walking towards the door of what is revealed to be a nightclub. The fragmentation of Velma Kelly's (Catherine Zeta Jones') body continues as she gets dressed for her musical act. Reminiscent of Gilda's (Rita Heyworth's) similar preparations, these scenes firmly construct the female spectacle: the female as spectacle for the male spectator.[17] Indeed, it is not until Velma is centre stage, in front of the, most noticeably, male audience, that we see her in her entirety. And, just in case her fetishisation wasn't absolutely clear, it is in the context of lack (and a threatening lack at that) that she is exposed: the emcee announces the fabulous Kelly Sisters, the lights hit the stage but Veronica, who Velma has just murdered, is missing.

Although it might seem that the predilections and psychological needs of the male spectator are being catered to, it soon becomes apparent that his is not the only, or even the most privileged, erotic site of the film. Indeed, it's worth noting that that opening image of the eye is a woman's, and the most desiring gaze in that first audience belongs to Roxy (Renee Zellweger). It is the film's third number, 'When you're good to Mama', which, while still alluding to, and enjoying, the governing heteronormativity of the spectacle, firmly instates the alternative lesbian economy. Having been introduced to the warden 'Mama', who runs the women's jail where Velma and Roxy now find themselves, a fellow inmate advices 'be good to Mama and she'll be good to you'. Being nice to Mama is immediately set up in that good old fashioned, sleep-with-the-boss, kind of way. The sexual connotation of the statement should not be lost on anyone, but, nevertheless, is reinforced both overtly and covertly. Mama is played by Queen Latifah who started to carve out an acting career for herself in Hollywood with her lesbian role in Set it Off (F. Gary Gray, 1996). The inmate offering the advice is none other than Chita Rivera, who, as well as starring in Fosse's stage production of Chicago, played one of the main dance-hall girls/prostitute figures in the film Sweet Charity, an obvious predecessor of this film. That it is sexual favours that are being spoken of is therefore indisputable. On a more general level we are in a women's prison which in the realm of representation rarely escapes a lesbian fold.

As so frequently happens, the musical number makes the implied connections (here between Mama, sexual favours and lesbianism) more explicit. Mama, shimmying away in gold lamé, tantalises a theatre's male audience with her raunchy number on, of all things, reciprocity:

There's a lot of favours I'm prepared to do,
you do one for mama she'll do one for you.

. . .

If you want my gravy, pepper my ragu
Spice it up for mama
She'll get hot for you[18]

Cross-cutting to and from the women's prison, Mama's placement of cigarettes in a garter belt and slapping of an inmate's thigh (as well as her description of women as 'cute' or 'hot') clearly establishes a lesbian rather than merely homosocial environment. The obviousness of this for the general spectator cannot be guaranteed. While the scene and, as I argue below, the film seem especially explicit, the spectator is still required to make these connections, or rather to deal with the discomfort that such connections might trigger. The number deliberately toys with the spectator's participation and, in so doing, innuendo becomes more than mere titillation, it marks the sexual/ queer reading as active rather than assumed (a crucial distinction in weighing up its productiveness). A perfect example comes in the lyrics: 'They say that life is tit for tat, and that's the way I live. So I deserve a lot of tat . . .'. And the line that should follow, of course, in keeping with the metre and clause content/pattern, is 'for all the tit I give'. However, the line that does follow is 'for what I've got to give'.

While it becomes clear that many women, especially Velma and Roxy, are indeed 'nice to mama' – we see Velma rubbing her shoulders at one point, and she and Mama sitting with their shirts open, camisoles displayed, at another (without any of the usual disclaimers, such as the excessive heat of the day) – the relationship between Velma and Roxy is queered too. It is quite clear that Roxy both wants to be Velma and wants her. Her rapturous gaze at Velma singing in that opening number could just be taken for a narcissistic envy framing her 'desire to be' – Roxy's musical ambitions are repeatedly expressed, and at one point we share in her fantasy of her performing Velma's number – but the film insists on more. Indeed, remembering Susie Bright, it all rests in the underwear again. Early in the film Velma will tell the star-struck Roxy to 'keep your hands off my underwear'. Later, in a scene of reconciliation between Velma and Roxy, a high angle shot sees Velma crouching to pick up some dropped papers. The camera lingers on her cleavage and her stocking-ed thighs. The gaze is clearly marked as sexual, and then clearly owned by Roxy, when it becomes her point-of-view shot. When Velma catches Roxy looking and self-consciously covers herself up, the dynamic is duly acknowledged.

Not only does the film avow queerness, but it favours 'spilling the beans' over anxious repression in other ways. Despite charting the triumph of murderesses over the judicial system, the truth is not so much masked as manipulated, the women's actions recovered as wrong but 'so defensible' (as

Billy the lawyer sings to the Press until they are quite in harmony). Rather than disavow castration, the film ignores or recycles those key Hollywoodian manifestations of the threat that woman represents: the undoing of the female character by way of removing her mystery, or, in fact, by punishing her; the undermining of her threat or potency by way of fragmenting and fetishising her body.[19] *Chicago* is all about getting the women off despite their guilt. There is little mystery to any of the characters. Their agendas are clear, from the mercenary dramatics of Velma, Roxy, Mama or Billy to the foolish devotion of Amos, Roxy's husband, as evidenced in his implicitly revealing song 'Mister Cellophane'. Indeed, the film makes a song and dance of the see-through-ness of all their intentions.

While the female form is, as I suggested earlier, clearly fetishised – and 'fetishizing techniques . . . are Fosse's signature' and Marshall's inheritance – at no point is this strategy merely at the service of some final reassurance.[20] Instead, it remains integral to the women's determination, if not packaging, of their own desirability. When Roxy and Velma perform their double-act to an adoring audience at the film's conclusion wielding huge Tommy guns, closure is far from the noirish reinstatement of moral order that one would associate with such femme fatales. Where 'classical Hollywood film and musical comedy in general . . . [operate] to proclaim, then contain, female sexuality', *Chicago* both celebrates and rewards its dangerous-and-oh-so-desirable wo-men from start to finish.[21] Instead, the final union of the two main characters has much more in common with the conventional sealing off of the romance narrative which underpins both the musical genre in general and Roxy and Velma's relationship in particular. Not only have the two women moved from a distanced to an intimate relationship, overcome obstacles and acrimony – as the genre dictates – but this final song symbolises their reconciliation in the best way a musical can, with their double-act as 'metaphor for the perfection of their relationship'.[22] The profoundly, and surprisingly, sex-less and duet-less role of Billy, the male lead (played by Richard Gere), further accentuates the women's pairing.

That said, the liberties that the women represent – of unbridled aggression, of uncontained, queer, sexuality – are, ultimately, limited in a very obvious way: through the confines of the grand musical spectacle, through the lavish fantasy and high entertainment that *Chicago*, the blockbuster, offers. Despite broaching new ground, we are forced to return to the ideological mechanisms of the self-conscious musical, and in particular Jane Feuer's seminal formula-tion of them.[23] According to Feuer, the genre used its self-consciousness or self-reflexivity to strengthen rather than undermine the spectacular-ness of the spectacle. It drew attention to its own artifice or contrived-ness in order to perpetuate its conservative, myth-making, functions rather than subvert them. The devices of the medium would be exposed in order that the devices of the character appeared that much more powerful, honest and natural in their singularity. In, for example, *Singin' in the Rain* (Gene Kelly and Stanley

Donen, 1952) Gene Kelly's character sings a love song to Kathy on an unused stage set. His exuberance in this scene outshines the camera lights he manipulates. In this way, the laying bare of the tools of fantasy-construction works to exacerbate the fantastic-ness of the character rather than critique it. This provides a useful rubric for understanding the final conservatism of *Chicago* in which it is not so much the physical but the sexual tools of fantasy construction that are laid bare. The explicitness surrounding the fetishisation and eroticised danger of Roxy and Velma similarly serves to underscore how sensational rather than how subversive the film is. The celebrity of the aggressive woman, and the allure of queerness, ultimately reinforce the fantasy rather than disrupt the status quo either inside or outside the film. They are all part of its packaging. The spectacle is more than the sum of its parts: the performances are more than the content. The star overwhelms the story, consigning it and all that rides within it, to the level of confection, to the self-serving needs of the blockbuster. What then is the value of queerness as it comes, however convincingly, to describe popular culture?

EVERYWHERE AND NOWHERE

The film examples discussed here are a highly selective group of films for sure, but, at the same time, they represent a broad spectrum: extremely popular independent cinema, middling heritage fare and blockbuster, but also queer/ ed films by both straight and gay directors.[24] Mainstream culture, I have no doubt, is queerer by far, but what does this statement mean? The character-istics I associated with New Queer Cinema in the first chapter of this book, have little to do with *Being John Malkovich*, *Mansfield Park* and *Chicago*, even if *Boys Don't Cry* sits fairly comfortably within their remit. At the same time, however, these films do not represent the 'gaysploitation' associated with Hollywood in the 1990s.[25] There is nothing remarkably defiant or titillating about *Being*, *Mansfield* or *Chicago*, their queerness is neither about radical ideas nor ready laughter.

Such a statement on our queerer western culture, then, reflects two things concerning the new queer spectator. First, that there is clear evidence for the cinematic construction of a queerer spectatorial experience. This has proven fairly easy to trace within the films' textual strategies but in terms of spectators' 'real' responses substantiation is far more complex. As Harry Benshoff has illustrated, through his audience study in the previous chapter, there exists a significant and troubling gap between a film's queer intent and the mainstream reading of it. It must be remembered, however, that reading queerly often involves reading against the grain, not just against the grain of the text but, more aptly for our times, against the grain of one's own preferences. While the films analysed in this chapter avow queerness, thereby directing the spectator to avow it too, this is not a given, but nor should the spectator's disavowal of queerness be deemed convincing. Second, my statement suggests that there has been certain progress (although no revolution) in the reception of lesbian and gay lives. It acknowledges that the western world appears a more liberal, more tolerant place. This is a good thing . . . but not unequivocally. For it is only certain forms of queerness that are flirted with, embraced or even championed by the mainstream. The queers who are accepted – those professionals who hold positions of power (in Hollywood, say); those who pass best (the 'akin-to-married' middle-class couple, for example) – mask the queers who aren't. The intolerance still exists, still grows, but elsewhere. As Michael Warner put it so well: 'More disturbing is the possibility that media visibility has brought a certain image of gays into the imagined mainstream of American culture only to banish the more challenging versions of queer life all the more effectively'.[26]

The films that I have explored here are queer in the sense that the sexual or identity categories that they offer are detached from the binary bound logic of normativity. None of them provides gay images (even more unusually, none of them focus on gay men). None of them disavows queerness. But nor do they provide provocation. *Chicago*, as the most startling example, is fairly meaningless stuff. What we must not forget, then, is that the critical power of queerness, its sheer force, is not to do with its content so much as its stance, its very oppositionality to conservative culture. Queer demands a rethink. *Chicago*'s pleasures are purely immediate, epitomising the instant-gratification ethos of Hollywood (and its franchises). As queerness moves into the centre of mainstream production, it inevitably loses its edge. As long as this edge – this critical questioning, this anti-conservatism, this antagonistic impulse – exists and thrives elsewhere, then all manifestations of (new) queer culture can be welcomed unhesitatingly. The problem, and it's a biggy, is that although the mainstream and the margin will necessarily continue to co-exist, the mainstream is becoming ever more firmly and broadly validated and validating, and those who don't or won't fit within it are ever more harshly judged and constrained as a result.

As I bring this chapter and indeed this book to a close, the question that resounds is the status of, and meaning of, queer as it comes to describe a whole range of textual images and creative practices. There is little doubt that there have been hugely significant developments in the production, content and reading of this (new) queer cinema. But optimism, especially when attached to 'fags' or fads, must not go unchecked.

ACKNOWLEDGEMENTS

I would like to thank the following forum and folk for their practical and intellectual input into my writing of this piece: University of Warwick's Film Studies Research Seminar, Anat Pick, Jules Pidduck and, especially, Monica Pearl.

NOTES

1 See Laura Mulvey, 'Afterthoughts on "Visual Pleasure and Narrative Cinema" inspired by *Duel in the Sun*', *Visual and Other Pleasures* (Basingstoke: Macmillan, 1988), pp. 29–38.

2 Patricia White, *Uninvited: Classical Hollywood Cinema and Lesbian Representability* (Bloomington, IN: Indiana University Press, 1999), p. xxiv.

3 See also Vito Russo, *The Celluloid Closet: Homosexuality in the Movies* 1981 (New York: Harper & Row, 1987).

4 For discussions of generic characteristics, see Annette Kuhn, *The Power of the Image: Essays on Representation and Sexuality* (London: Routledge and Kegan Paul, 1985), pp. 48–73; and Chris Straayer, 'Redressing the "Natural": The Temporary Transvestite Film', in Barry Keith Grant (ed.), *Film Genre Reader II* (Austin: University of Texas Press, 1995), pp. 402–27.

5 Kuhn, *Power of the Image*, p. 55.

6 Ibid., p. 57.

7 J. Hoberman, 'Use Your Illusion', *The Village Voice* (Sept. 29–Oct. 5 1999): http://www.villagevoice.com/issues/9939/hoberman.shtml. Swank received her Oscar on 26 March 2000. She also won the following, for best actress: BSFC award, BFCA award, CFCA award, Silver Hugo award, DFWFCA award, FFCC, Golden Globe, Golden Satellite award, Independent Spirit award, Sierra Award, NBR, FIPRESCI, LAFCA. See the International Movie Database for details of these awards: http://www.us.imdb.com/Pawards?Swank,+Hilary, p. 4.

8 This breadth, and its queerness, are even more apparent in Chloe Sevigny's role as a stone butch in *If These Walls Could Talk 2: 1972* (Martha Coolidge, 2000).

9 See Straayer 'Redressing', for a useful discussion of how these opposing desires interact within the mainstream transvestite film by way of the 'paradoxical kiss'.

10 Julianne Pidduck, 'Risk and Queer Spectatorship', *Screen* Debate on *Boys Don't Cry*, *Screen*, 42.1 (Spring 2001): 97–102.

11 Hoberman, 'Use Your Illusion'.

12 Xan Brooks, Review of *Boys Don't Cry*, *Sight and Sound* (April 2000): 44.

13 Pidduck, 'Risk', p. 99.

14 Brooks, *Boys*, p. 44.

15 The genre, however, has been distinguished as a forum for 'playing out contemporary anxieties and fantasies of national identity, sexuality, class, and power. Temporal displacement and cultural respectability license the exploration of difficult or taboo subjects such as the homoerotic passions'. See Andrew Higson, *English Heritage, English Cinema* (Oxford: Oxford University Press, 2003), p. 28.

16 See, for example, John Mullan, 'Fanny's Novel Predicament', *The Guardian*, 28 March 2000: accessed *Guardian* website www.guardian.co.uk.

17 See *Gilda* (Charles Vidor, 1946).

18 'When You're Good To Mama', *Chicago: Music from the Miramax Motion Picture Epic/Sony Music Soundtrack*, 2002.

19 See Mulvey, 'Visual Pleasure and Narrative Cinema', in *Visual and Other Pleasures*, pp. 14–28.

20 Linda Mizejewski, *Divine Decadence: Fascism, Female Spectacle and the Makings of Sally Bowles* (Princeton, NJ: Princeton University Press, 1992), p. 210.

21 Patricia Mellencamp, 'Sexual Economics: *Gold Diggers of 1933*', in Steven Cohan (ed.), *Hollywood Musicals: The Film Reader* (London: Routledge, 2002), p. 67. The film contains much evidence of this contra-disavowal agenda. For example, one of the songs 'inspired by the film' clearly loosens the fetish's association with masking lack. Rather than compensating for something missing 'high heels leave holes'. Queen Latifah and L'il Kim, featuring Macy Gray, 'Cell Block Tango (He Had It

Comin')', *Chicago: Music from the Miramax Motion Picture* Epic/Sony Music Soundtrack, 2002.

22 Lucie Arbuthnot and Gail Seneca, 'Pre-Text and Text in *Gentleman Prefer Blondes*', in Cohan, *Hollywood Musicals*, p. 83. For a discussion of the genre's 'dual focus narrative', of its link to conciliation, marriage etc., see Rick Altman 'The American Film Musical as Dual-Focus Narrative' and 'The Structure of the American Film Musical', in *The American Film Musical* (London: BFI, 1989), pp. 16–27, 28–58.

23 See Jane Feuer, 'The Self-reflective Musical and the Myth of Entertainment', in Rick Altman (ed.), *Genre: The Musical* (London: BFI, 1986), pp. 159–74.

24 *Chicago*'s 'creative team . . . was almost entirely gay' (Jeffrey Epstein, 'All that Jazz', *Out*, February 2003: 46).

25 Dennis Lim, 'The Reckless Moment: Two Pioneers of the New Queer Cinema Look Back on a Short-Lived Sensation', *Village Voice*, 26 March 2002: 39.

26 Michael Warner, 'Dangerous Liaisons: The Insidious Embrace of Gay Culture by the Media', *Village Voice*, Literary Supplement (Fall 2001): 102. Warner continues: 'Queers no longer set the gay agenda: The corporate managers of the mass media do' (ibid.).

INDEX

CPSIA information can be obtained at www.ICGtesting.com
Printed in the USA
BVOW010109280613

324559BV00003B/13/P

9 780813 534862